# THE BOOK OF JOIE

D1600818

# THE BOOK OF JOIE

## Or *A* Thousand Singing Hamsters
### *A Micro-Business Memoir*

BY LINDA GIVEN

JOIE DE LIVRE PRESS

First Edition

Copyright © 2023 by Linda Given

All rights reserved. No part of this book may be reproduced or transmitted in any form without the express permission of the author except in the case of brief quotations in articles and reviews.

Published in the United States of America by
Joie de Livre Press
23 Winslow Avenue, Somerville, MA 02144

ISBN 979-8-218-19006-4

Cover Art and Book Design by Nancy Given
Illustrations by Danielle Nekimkin

For Lore


And for everyone whose love and support
helped Joie de Vivre both begin and flourish.

"Small retail is the glue that holds our neighborhoods and our communities together, a place we go to where we feel at home."

—*Ken Reeves, Mayor of Cambridge*
*1992-85 and 2006-07*

# Contents

# Preface

For thirty-six and a half years, I ran a "lifestyle business," a gift store called Joie de Vivre. I didn't know that's what it was though, not until I read an article about small businesses in the *New York Times*. The author questioned why some small business owners "disavowed economic theory" and were "not trying to maximize their profits," then continued: "There are more than 27 million businesses in the United States. About a thousand are huge conglomerates seeking to increase profits. Another several thousand are small or medium-size companies seeking their big score. A vast majority, however, are what economists call lifestyle businesses. They are owned by people whose goal is to do what they like and to cover their nut. These surviving proprietors hadn't merely been lucky. They loved their businesses so much that they found a way to hold on to them, even if it meant making bad business decisions. It's a remarkable accomplishment in its own right."

I was one of that vast majority, a person who wanted to make a living doing something I liked and felt good about. This eventually led to a few bad business decisions, but I survived for a long time, through dramatic changes in the retail landscape. My business gave me much more than just a living. This is my story.

CHAPTER I

# Am I Really Doing This?

All I had to do was press send. Open on my desktop was a letter to my mailing list, announcing I would be closing my business after thirty-six and a half years, a decision I had been agonizing about for at least the last five. I knew it made sense, but who would I be without it? And how could I upset my extremely loyal customers this way? They would be both disappointed and sad; in recent years they'd begun asking me to promise I would stay in business "forever." Now I was about to send them unwelcome news. Close a cherished part of their community, a store that had fans in many parts of the country and even the world. In the midst of a life-altering pandemic.

Opening a gift store had not been a cherished dream. After years of doing odd jobs, I almost stumbled into it, a career that both truly suited me and miraculously, for most of my years in business, supported me. Joie de Vivre opened in 1984. Its beginning was crazy and fun. I dated customers, I married one. Some of my early staff remain my closest friends. Children that were a gleam in their parents' eyes grew up and graduated from college, even brought in kids of their own, while I saw the store through the yearly cycles of winter, spring, summer, fall and the new fifth season in my life, the holidays. And while many things about running a small business changed dramatically over the years, there was also an unvarying quality to the nature of the work, each day with its retail rituals, and each year with its mileposts: Valentine's, Easter, Mother's Day, graduations, Father's Day, and Halloween, ending in the all-important financially critical six week stretch between Thanksgiving and New Year's Day.

I never ran the business from afar and I still straightened the wind-up toy shelf, climbed up ladders to change lightbulbs, broke down cardboard boxes for recycling, thought up window displays, and handmade lots of little signs, "Plastic Goldfish 50 Cents," or "Ask Us To Show You This Amazing Toy." I'd loved running the store from the start and mostly still did. But it had gotten harder. And I found it hard to imagine closing, but there was a real problem, increasingly difficult to ignore.

The store was just breaking even. I had propped it up with my meager personal savings at times and now I was older, spending when I should have been saving. It was harder maintaining a small business in the internet age, and many of the things I enjoyed about it were changing in ways I found unappealing. I wanted to close it without being forced to, to make it my decision, so how and when to close was never far from my mind when suddenly, we were in a pandemic, which devastated already tenuous finances and worse, threatened our health. It gave me the push I needed to make the decision and now I needed to make it public. The staff, current and former, all knew, and I had warned some of our best customers. It was time to tell the world. Time to change a life I'd loved. I pushed the key.

# CHAPTER 2

# What Do You Want To Be When You Grow Up?

"What do you want to be when you grow up?" Adults always asked that question and I had no idea. There were lots of things I liked to do; swimming, pretending to be a princess, reading, making cakes, riding horses, looking for wild strawberries, playing with my pet rabbits. I'm just old enough that as a child I saw few female professional role models; careers for women still skewed heavily toward nurse or teacher. Or housewife and mother. Having read a few harrowing accounts of giving birth (thank you Pearl S. Buck and Margaret Mitchell) I was pretty sure I didn't want to be a mother, and housewife wasn't appealing either. When I reached my teens, my dreams ran more toward losing twenty pounds, meeting Prince Charming, maybe discovering the meaning of life. I certainly never said "I'd like to run a small retail store," and yet that is exactly what I wound up doing for almost thirty-seven years.

I was always intrigued with objects and decor. My father had built our family a simple 1950s ranch house in the Hudson River Valley, a stark contrast to the Victorian homes he and my mother grew up in. We bewildered our friends by calling our one-step-up second floor "upstairs," but my grandmothers' houses had double staircases, one for servants, one for family. Their houses had window seats, laundry chutes, nooks and crannies, and were filled with things I found fascinating, including a simple toy kaleidoscope I spent hours with. I can still hear the click of its glass pieces falling into place.

Shopping was not the major activity in the 1950s it later became. We went to MacGregors to buy school supplies and plastic horses, ordered clothes from Sears Roebuck, and bought sundries at Woolworths and Grants, the two five and ten cent stores. I loved Woolworths and enjoyed wandering its cluttered aisles looking at costume jewelry, toys, lipstick, Christmas ornaments and the pet section, with its big cage of colorful parakeets. Our first parakeets, Chirpy and Princess, were Woolworths birds.

When one grandmother moved to Vermont, we visited every summer, and my real interest in shopping began. I spent all the money I had in a shop we could walk to called Griffiths, ignoring its boring furniture and household items in favor of peppermint sticks, maple sugar leaves, china animals and Kodachrome postcards of horses. My grandmother took us to the Vermont Country Store to buy penny candy and to the Enchanted Doll House to marvel at the dolls, stuffed animals and toys. When our family began to spend two weeks at the Jersey Shore every summer, I saved up to buy shell jewelry and china rabbits at the Lucy Evelyn, a gift shop housed in a bona fide old schooner. These stores seemed much more exciting than the stores back home. But when I was about sixteen, a shopping experience changed my life, and it happened very close to home.

The Village Gallery was a wonderfully quirky small store, located next to a commuter rail station on the Hudson River line, run by Vernon and Lore Stromberg, and to me, a revelation, full of artwork and beautiful objects to be appreciated more for their aesthetic qualities than sheer practicality. My parents were practical. The idea of paying more for a glass or anything because of its design was not part of my experience and I began to haunt this alluring place. Happily, along with the more expensive arts, crafts, and design goods, they offered things even I could afford: cards, paper mâché boxes and "Argus" posters, quintessential 1960s artwork with quotes like "Hang in There" and "War Is Not Healthy for Children And Other Living Things," among them. The space felt enchanted to me, a treasure trove of unexpected wonders. There were other interesting stores in the building too: the "Niddy Noddy," selling exotic yarns and related supplies, a small bookstore, a toyshop and a Marimekko/Design Research shop with clogs, dresses, and vividly printed fabrics. It all felt excitingly non-suburban.

When my crowded high school had to go on double shifts my senior year, I was free at noon and decided to look for a job. The Village Gallery was the first place I asked and they were hiring; Christmas was coming and they needed "duster-wrappers," a position typically filled by local students. They agreed to give me a go and I was thrilled. The first day of work would be a Sunday afternoon in September, a workshop where we would learn their gift-wrapping techniques and get an orientation tour of the store.

I spent the night before with an adventurous girlfriend. We snuck out of her house around midnight to meet some boys and stayed out for hours. Sunday was hot and muggy and I was tired when I sat down to learn about poofs, firecrackers and other wrapping styles. Later we were brought to the stuffy back room where the gift boxes were stored and I started to feel woozy, standing up suddenly requiring a lot of concentration. Then things went dark. When I came to, I was being carried out of the store over Vern's shoulders. I was mortified but Lore just said "See you on Monday," and sent me on my way. She confessed years later that she was actually thinking "What have I got myself into?"

After a few weeks of dusting and wrapping, I felt dissatisfied. I didn't mind doing either; dusting gave me a chance to handle and get to know the stock and I liked gift wrapping, but I wanted to write sales slips and talk to customers like the salespeople did. I screwed up my courage and asked Lore if I could talk to her. With pounding heart, I told her that I was having a problem with the job. She looked at me, surprised. I explained that I wanted to learn how to do everything. She didn't immediately respond, leaving me to imagine her next words, "That's not possible." They turned out to be "We will still need you to dust and wrap, but okay, you can try working the front counter." I felt a jolt of relief and happiness. I was a quick study, and by the next summer, I was trusted enough to be left at the "main" desk for several hours on my own.

I loved my job, and loved having a life independent of my family. Employees got a store discount and I also loved the delight and praise I earned by giving the right thing to the right person. And there was more. Besides the lessons of retail, I learned valuable grown-up skills such as drinking black coffee, reading the *New Yorker*, and the fine art of gossip, all from the older staff who were a diverse and sophisticated group of people. None of them were anything like my parents and their friends; Inger was from Denmark, Lynn's father was a filmmaker, Charlotte wore Marimekko and had giant round glasses, and Richard was involved with another man. They talked about art and music and I found them exotic and sophisticated. The gallery became my second home and I would happily have worked every day all day if I could have.

A year later, I left for college after unsuccessfully trying to convince my parents that I didn't need to go. It was partly fear of the unknown, but I really loved what I was doing and didn't want to stop. Sadly, what we now call "gap years" were unheard of. As the oldest of four. I was told I had to "Set a good example for your sisters!" I satisfied myself with working as much as I could on my breaks and in the summers, often staying late talking with Lore about the store and life. School did not go well. Too many tragic love affairs, too many drugs. Feeling guilty about wasting my parents' money, I eventually dropped out and waitressed, modeled for art classes, worked as a secretary/administrative assistant, ironed and house cleaned, and even made a little money playing the violin, but I was not really finding my way in the world.

I kept visiting Lore and Vern and eventually returned to work for them full time. The store had grown larger, been divided into distinct departments, and renamed Gallimaufry, though it was always "The Gallery" to me. I began to manage their American Craft section, organizing exhibits, doing the buying, and paying the artists, all invaluable experiences. They sent me to the New York Gift Show, to wholesale craft shows, and gave me my own key. On my days off, I often went to New York and checked out the retail scene there. I learned a lot from all this, and felt appreciated and valued but after four years, had to admit I was ready to move on. I had been working there on and off for ten years and felt it was time to try something else — although true to my childhood response to "What do you want to be?" — I had no idea what I wanted to do next. I certainly wasn't thinking about opening a store when I bought a one-way ticket to London. I was off to see the world!

CHAPTER 3

# Woodworker's Girlfriend

Before leaving for my trip, I was promised I could take my brother-in-law's tiny but affordable apartment in New York on my return, when he and my sister Debra moved uptown. I had no idea what my new exciting city life would entail, but a place to live was a good start. My plan was little more than "something will happen," and something did. A month before my departure, I started to date Bill. I hadn't had a real boyfriend in years and he was charismatic and ardent. His photo was tucked into my passport wallet, and I pulled it out every night. We wrote each other letters as I traveled and I found my thoughts turning more to thinking of him than to plotting my new urban life. Then I heard that "my" apartment had gone to a relative of the landlord. When I flew home, I let Bill whisk me up to his home in Vermont. Three months later, he convinced me to move in.

Home became a big modern house my new boyfriend had designed and built on one hundred acres of land where although he was a published poet, he was of necessity making his living as a woodworker. I soon learned how to sand a rolling pin and use a bandsaw, how to cut plugs of maple and glue them in holes I drilled in cutting boards, how to sand, oil, and finish these pieces, and pack them up to send to stores and galleries around the country. After my initial pride at mastering new skills, I found the work boring but I did enjoy our travels to the wholesale and retail craft fairs where we sold our wares as part of the newly flourishing American Craft Movement. A hundred or more craftspeople would converge on a town, set up our displays, sell as much as we could, party at night, have a communal experience for a few days, then disappear back to our isolated homes. We did this maybe six times a year.

From the time I moved in, the plan was to move to Boston so Bill could share joint custody of his son, but first he had to sell the highly idiosyncratic house. That would take a while. It turned out that most would-be buyers with enough money to purchase the land were thinking quaint farmhouse, not quirky multilevel house with built-in furniture and over a hundred windows. I sympathized. I liked quaint farmhouses myself.

In my two years in Vermont, I learned a lot about running a whole-sale business, knowledge that helped me when I opened my store. I made friends with a lot of talented craftspeople, some of whose work ended up on the shelves of Joie de Vivre when we opened. And I walked to our mailbox every day with a mental list of the checks that were due to arrive. Lore had taught me to be honest with suppliers if you couldn't pay on time as a matter of respect, and I now saw just how important that honesty was. It was hard when you were expecting a check, needed the money, and the check didn't come.

The woodworking business didn't take all my time and there was a wonderful bookstore about a half hour away in Manchester, VT. They were looking for sales help and the competition was fierce — for a job that paid $3.50 an hour! There were a lot of ex-New Yorkers in town and everyone wanted to work there. It was a rigorous interview — what do you read, what novels, what periodicals; they wanted serious book people. When we got to references and previous work experience, I mentioned the Gallery and to my surprise, the bookstore owners knew it well. They loved it, had lived nearby and shopped there themselves before moving to Vermont. I got the job. In a few months, they were letting me order the greeting cards so I learned both the card and the book business up close.

Eventually, the magical "right people" appeared and we sold the house, found a small apartment close to Boston in Somerville, rented studio space and began a new life as urban woodworkers. After a year, things weren't going so well. While working, Bill lost himself in his writing ideas and art projects. I filled my work days mentally composing jaunty yet searing magazine articles along the theme of "Never Work with the Man You Love," and "I Was a Woodworker's Girlfriend." We were both bored and it was increasingly apparent that we were not a match made in heaven though neither of us was quite ready to admit it.

I was in my early thirties now. The new friends I was making in Boston were teachers, artists, professionals with careers, and I felt embarrassed when people asked me what I did. I found myself saying "Well, I make rolling pins and cutting boards, we just moved here from Vermont," with a notable lack of enthusiasm, wishing I could add, "It pays the bills, I'm really a poet, painter, musician, performance artist, but it's hard to make money at that." My questioners were actually usually quite interested in our business and would ask more about it, leaving me to explain that I'd just drifted into it by chance and it wasn't my thing.

I needed to find something that was important to me, and I wanted that important something to be able to support me. As it was, any unforeseen major expense would necessitate a call to my parents. At age thirty-three, this felt wrong. An idea began to form in the back of my mind. Our first winter in Boston, we had taken part in a local seasonal craft coop called The Christmas Store, open for six weeks during the holidays. I saw how well they did in those six weeks and began to think their customers might like a place to shop the rest of the year. I'd always liked my jobs working in stores. Maybe I could open one. A month or so later I got a call from a jeweler friend with a shop in the area. I had recently discussed my new idea with him over drinks. He told me that a space next to his was opening up. Soon. Was I interested? Was now the time? I quickly began to feel that it was. I would have to make a plan fast. But I was more excited than apprehensive. This might be my something important. I was ready to try.

CHAPTER 4

# And So It Began

If I was going to start my own business, I had more than a few things going in my favor. Retail experience, as both a salesperson and a buyer, wholesale experience, which had given me a different but equally valuable perspective, familiarity with trade shows, personal contacts, and a good sense of the neighborhood and community I would open up in. I had a vision of what kind of store it would be, and knew there was nothing like it around. I also had a (soon to be) ex-boyfriend and friends who could help me build out the space. What I didn't have was a credit rating. Or any money. Today's "crowd funding" did not exist.

Luckily, I did have two potential bankrollers on tap, my mother and father. I knew they were worried about my future, but I also knew them well enough not to expect an instant "What a great idea!" and I was right, they were more skeptical than enthusiastic. After a twenty-minute conversation, "What about going back to school?" and "Do you really think this will work?" were their main questions. Why don't you and Bill just get married was probably another but they were careful not to ask that. After this somewhat deflating but unsurprising conversation, I called my retail mentor, Lore. "I think it's a wonderful idea and you absolutely can do it!" she assured me. "If anyone can, it's you." We talked for quite a while. Her opinion meant a lot to me and my wavering confidence was renewed.

And ultimately, my parents did agree to lend me the money I needed to begin. I paid them back with interest one year later.

My space was presently a fancy food store/cafe that was relocating to larger quarters up the street. I met the landlords and signed on the dotted line, a three-year lease beginning on May 1st. It was early January. I had just enough time to go to the winter Gift and Toy shows, order inventory, and design the inside. I would have four weeks to build it out and display my wares to be up and running by June 1st.

Now I had a location, a lease and a vision — a gift shop selling everything from postcards to wind-up toys to books and American Crafts. Things that would give pleasure in some way and make my future customers smile, or laugh, or wonder. I would buy things I thought were great and see how it went. And no one would walk out feeling like they couldn't afford a thing. I had been in too many stores, gazing at beautiful objects that were completely out of my price range. I didn't like feeling shut out and I didn't want my customers to feel that way either. In this I was influenced by both the Gallery and a store I frequented in New York called Mythology, both run by true curators, people able to combine the small and the large, the high and the low.

While preparing for my first buying trip I suddenly realized I needed two more things: a name and a business card to put that name on. My friends in the craft world would understand if I hadn't picked a name yet but I didn't want to look unprofessional at the big-league New York Gift Show or the International Toy Fair. A night spent at the kitchen table with a few friends and a bottle or two of wine and I had my name: Joie de Vivre. In the end it was that or The Graham Cracker Club which was finally rejected as being a bit too esoteric. It also would have been outright theft — it was the title of a *New Yorker* cartoon drawn by my cartooning idol, Roz Chast.

"Joie de Vivre" seemed to sum up the feeling I wanted — a store where everything sold would be something that would bring a little joy to my customers, be it a twenty-five cent plastic goldfish or a hundred-dollar kaleidoscope. Did it cross my mind that people might find Joie de

Vivre difficult to spell or pronounce? Not for a second, though I have now spelled it out for people an untold number of times. Many of my vendors were afraid to even try to say it, but they did remember our name.

Several months after I opened the store, a French customer brought in a photograph of a playground called Joie de Vivre she had visited on a recent trip to France. She thought there was even a postcard of it, and later I actually came across and ordered the black and white card from a French distributor. Sitting on a swing in the middle of the playground was a young blond girl with two ponytails — a girl who looked a lot like I had once upon a time. There were large letters spelling out Joie de Vivre high up on scaffolding clearly visible behind her. Choosing a name for the store hadn't been easy. I really wanted it to be right, and discovering this playground and postcard made me feel Joie de Vivre had been the perfect choice.

I borrowed $25,000, a fairly limited budget. Bill agreed to donate some of the displays from the woodworking business. We had used them for shows, but they could easily be turned into permanent fixtures. He agreed to install them, and also make shelving for the stockroom, and I hired another friend to build the main desk, wall shelving for the front, and card racks. He knew an electrician, JoeD, who would do the wiring, and I found someone to lay down a rug. I could paint the walls myself. A stained-glass lamp from our house in Vermont would hang in the front window and I commissioned a local sign painter to paint our first sign. It would be simple, just the name.

Someone on the next block down was closing their antique shop and I bought their cash register for $50. It was a bona fide antique itself and quite the old workhorse. The register tape didn't work and it must have weighed at least 100 pounds but it was sturdy and simple, and I figured I would replace it someday. It was still there when I rang up the last sale thirty-six and a half years later. I also "knew" I would replace those old woodworking displays. They were still there too.

After the build out cost, I set aside a little money for initial advertising, and figured out how much I would need to survive for the first few months, assuming sales would be slow as people gradually discovered us. I then had about $10,000 left to spend on inventory. That sounded like a lot to me at the time, but looking back at photos of the store in the first months, it looks more like a minimalist art gallery, one thing here, one object there, though in a few years the shelves would be crammed with merchandise. I planned to sell rubber-stamps and had collected fifteen or twenty wholesale catalogs. $1500 was my budget for stamps, ink pads and related supplies. "I know how I'll do it," I thought as I sat down to write my first orders. "I'll just write up mock orders, getting what I want, then I'll add it all up and see how much I've spent."

Writing the orders was fun, there were so many wonderful images. Total spent after first round — $5000. Whoops! Half my total merchandise budget. It was surprisingly difficult to whittle down: take out that angel, we can do without the cat on the garbage can, maybe we don't really need that mountain range but the dancing bears and the upside-down rabbit in pajamas? Both musts! It was a painful process, but finally the rubber-stamp orders totaled $1500. Next up, cards, postcards and wind-up toys. Luckily, I had artist friends who were happy to consign larger work to me, and the spare look was offset by customer excitement over what we did have.

Some time went into figuring out what would go where in the store — where to put card racks, the shelving and the all-important front desk. It needed to be where I could see the whole store and assume command of my retail ship. I would be working alone and wanted to be able to keep an eye on the entire space. I was also short, so we "boosted my presence" by putting the desk on a raised platform (and confusing people who met me down on the floor where I suddenly shrank a few inches.)

By the end of April, merchandise orders were starting to arrive at my Somerville apartment. I remember sitting at the kitchen table, opening a box from Chesnik-Koch Kaleidoscopes and carefully removing the brass two-wheeled wonders. Looking through them, I marveled at the colorful images, they were breathtakingly beautiful. It was exciting to think that soon they would be on display at Joie de Vivre. Other packages arrived as well, jigsaw puzzles, porcelain rabbits, wooden flamingos, bubble bears, candles in the shape of cupcakes, and of course, rubber stamps. Soon they too would all be for sale at Joie de Vivre. My store. Soon I'd have some new boxes to check under "occupation." Small Business. Retail. Owner. I thought my three-year lease was perfect, I'd do it that long and see if it worked. See if I liked it. My new career was about to begin for real.

CHAPTER 5

# A Little Bump in the Road Named Frank Fox

The space I had rented was currently "Marcella's," a shop selling imported coffee and specialty foods along with a selection of elegant modern Italian kitchenware. It was crowded and hectic and most customers took their sandwiches and coffee to go, though there were a handful of tables crammed into the very back. Coincidentally, it was one of the first places I had eaten in Cambridge when Bill and I had come down from Vermont to look for a place to live; it was right next door to our friend Danny's jewelry shop.

Marcella's was famous for its food but also for its owner, one Mr. Frank Mazzarelli, a short, pugnacious grey-haired little dictator with a wonderful eye for design and an unerring sense of how to both select and prepare delicious dishes. Everyone called him Mr. Fox. He was a true neighborhood character, and truly unpredictable, described by his customers as crazy, irascible, misogynistic and more.

As my move-in date approached, I started haunting the neighborhood, keeping an eye on the new larger Marcella's a block away. It looked surprisingly unfinished and I started to worry. One day I continued down the street to the smaller store, "my" store. It certainly didn't look like anyone was about to move out. They must have a plan, I reasoned. After all, my lease started on May 1st. We were ready to get right in there and start building and painting.

A few days later I returned and approached Mr. Fox. "Hi, I'm the person who has rented this space," I began, then hesitated. "You'll... be out on May 1st, won't you?" He looked at me coldly. "This is a terrible neighborhood," he stated with evident enjoyment. "You're never going to do any business here." "Well, you're staying here, in fact you're moving to a larger space," I pointed out. "Food is different," he said dispassionately. We stared at each other for a moment. "When are you moving out?" I asked again. He looked at me. "I don't really know, things aren't ready at the new place yet." My face flushed red. "But I have a lease that begins on May 1st, you have to be out by then." He shrugged. "I doubt I will," he said, and turned back to the coffee machine. As soon as I got home, I called my landlord. "Oh, he'll probably be out," he told me.

I was beside myself. I had planned my opening carefully. June was a busy month and I wanted to open before people left town for the summer. I had also taken out an ad in the local Public Radio listener's guide announcing the opening as June 1st. My landlord promised to pressure Mr. Fox but I started checking on both the new space and "my" space every day and it was clear to me as the days ticked down that "Foxy" had no intention of leaving by May 1st or working overtime to make things move faster.

There seemed to be little I could do besides hastily change my ad copy from "Opening June 1st" to "Coming Soon." May 1st came and went and the boxes of inventory piled up in our apartment. I considered just showing up with some boxes and trying to move in, but I knew it would only be a dramatic gesture. I couldn't move his refrigerators and kitchen equipment out. I didn't even have a key yet. I spent my time fuming, calling my landlords, consulting a lawyer, and coming to the conclusion that I was basically at his mercy. He had agreed to move out on May 1st, it wasn't convenient, and he wasn't going to do it. That was that. Three weeks later he began the move, and the last day of May, my landlords called me to come and get the key.

I opened the door by myself for the first time on June 1st. Okay, we could finally get going. What did I expect? An empty space, broom clean and ready for painting. What did I get? A space that looked like

— someone had vacated the premises under cover of darkness, without looking back. The floor and walls were covered in cooking grease and grime, random pieces of abandoned equipment were scattered throughout, and the floor to ceiling mirrors in the very back had not been removed. I ran to the store to buy more cleaning materials.

Starting in on the floor, I quickly realized that simple washing was not going to do the job. After several days of scraping and scouring on my hands and knees, I learned the true meaning of elbow grease and cursed my predecessor with every breath. He had caused me to delay the opening of my store, and then added insult to injury. Encouraged by friends, I decided to sue him for damages. I wasn't looking for much, just enough to cover the costs of advertising and estimated loss of income for that first month I should have been open. A few months and a few hundred dollars later, this had gone nowhere but I resolved that I would never set foot in his establishment again.

Despite this bumpier than expected beginning, I was ready to open the doors by June 28th. It was a Thursday and we would open for a three-hour party at 5 pm, then have our first full day of business on Friday. I was proud and excited, but exhausted from the month's work, and there was another big event immediately following. Bill and I were splitting up and I was moving out of our apartment that Sunday. This had been planned for awhile, it was mutual and we intended to remain friends but the stress of actually splitting up was taking its toll. Still, it was thrilling to open the door and see neighborhood people and my friends come in. And many of them bought something — a card, a windup toy, a book. I had my first paying customers!

I also had a lot to drink. The libations on the backroom desk flowed freely and we continued celebrating well into the night, moving on to a bar and then to a friend's apartment. It was more than fun, it was a release from the last several months of tension. It was at least three in the morning when I finally went to bed.

When I woke up, my head was throbbing and I was a groggy mess. Hoping it would pass, I showered and had coffee but the official first morning of business for Joie de Vivre found me practically hanging on to the front desk. Again, we had customers, pleased and excited to see the store open. They bought a few things. I was mad at myself. My first day and I was having trouble acting like a normal human being — what was I thinking? But as the hours passed and I started to feel better, I gave myself a break. Okay, I'd been working every single day for over a month, morning to late at night, preparing to open. And I was moving in two days. Yes, I definitely had more than a few too many but — we were open! A month later than planned, but up and running.

As for Marcella's and Mr. Fox, I boycotted the place for over nine months. I had dropped my lawsuit when it became clear there was no hope of success. Besides, Joie de Vivre was open now and things were going all right. I had more important things to think about and there was another good coffee shop right across the street so I didn't lack caffeine. Then, one bitterly cold winter morning I arrived very early to work on some project and my usual place was not yet open. I started walking to a convenience store a few blocks away and passed Marcella's, which opened at seven. I inhaled the scent of their strong brew. It smelled heavenly but I kept walking, ears freezing and face smarting in the cold. There was a howling wind and my eyes teared up. I thought of the convenience store coffee I was about to buy. It would be awful, burned and weak. "Who am I really punishing here?" I suddenly thought. "No one but me." I stopped, turned back, walked into Marcella's and approached the counter. My former nemesis approached from the other side. "Can I help you miss?" he inquired, as though he'd never seen me before in his life. "Medium coffee with milk," I answered. It was the first of thousands of cups.

CHAPTER 6

# The Early Years

Our doors were open. Almost everything inside was new, new, new. No one had seen the King Kong bank, the little gorilla laboriously climbing the Empire State Building, penny in mouth, to make his deposit and slide down again. No one had seen the box on the wall with the rainbow trout who bobbed in place to the tune "As Time Goes By." No one had ever tried to float all the black spots onto the dalmatian, the bubbles into the bottle of champagne, or seen the other "Aquabatic" puzzles. And our rubber stamps were different — not the standard "Priority," "Void" or "Urgent" of the office supply store. We had dancing bears, leaping ballerinas, coffee cups, a pleading woman and a spray of stars. Few people knew what a kaleidoscope was then, or had seen one other than the blurry cardboard versions that passed as the real thing prior to the American Craft renaissance of the 1970s. Introducing customers to the joys of floating seashell mandalas or kaleidoscopic images of flowers or their friend's faces was like taking them on a trip without drugs, or so they often told us. No one had ever pressed their face into the thousands of straight pins that made up a Pin Screen (2744 as counted by Ian Gibson one slow afternoon) to create an eerily realistic self-portrait. Many had forgotten just how much fun a little plastic jumping mouse or swimming frog could be.

The things that people did know but hadn't seen for years produced equal fascination. An Etch-a-Sketch! A fortune telling fish! An alligator clicker! A wooden Jacob's ladder! A Magic Eight Ball! A Lava Light! The magnetic ballerina who danced, twirling away from her small rectangular mirror! We heard lots of "I didn't know they still made this!" and "I had one of those when I was a kid!" accompanied by smiles and wondering expressions. (By the end of our run, we heard the same comments from customers in their twenties and thirties about things we'd first sold years earlier: Space Tubes, Koosh Balls, and the Penguin Race to name just a few that made the leap from new sensation to time tested classic.) Soon bringing in new merchandise became a game of "What can we move? Where can we put this?" Our eternal conundrum: how can we keep selling everything we love while adding all the wonderful new things we keep finding?

I worked completely alone at first, and kept the store closed on Sundays and Mondays. This changed as our first Christmas approached, and I got through the holiday season with one employee — a friend of a friend, and the help of my sister Nancy. They both wanted to keep on part time afterwards, so we were now officially open every day. Things were quite casual. We didn't even have sales slips for the first year and a half, and very few people ever asked for one though we kept a blank receipt book at the desk just in case. When we finally got our own sales books, I had to remind people to use them. They did come in handy — I could look back through them and see what had sold each day.

Not much technical equipment was needed to run a business in the 1980s. Everything important came through the mail, happened over the phone or actually happened in the store. If customers had questions or needed directions, the phone rang. No email, no computer, no printer, no fax machine, just our telephone, a radio/cassette player and a manual charge machine. If we got a charge for over $25, we had to use the phone to call for authorization, reading the card number and information out loud in the front of the store. We didn't think anything of it and neither did the customers, that's just the way it was done. We didn't get that many charge cards in the beginning anyway, most people paid with a check or cash.

Our neighborhood was lively, with lots of shops and people on the street. The area was rent controlled, a nice mix of students, artists, and just starting out professionals, along with long time Cambridge residents, some of whose homes were big and beautiful indeed. Our business and retail neighbors along Massachusetts Avenue included an office supply store, a bakery, several hairdressers, a fabric store, a sporting goods store, a children's clothing store, and a few antique shops, including the one we called the witch store, with its charms, amulets, mysterious potions, and spooky proprietress. There was an Irish import store, a craft shop, a music emporium selling guitars and banjos, two old fashioned pharmacies, many restaurants, a local bank, vintage clothing stores, two health food stores, a small grocery, and lots of women's clothing stores.

Mr. Fox was certainly not the only eccentric shopkeeper in the neighborhood. One asked her customers to get down on all fours and bark like a dog if they wanted a discount. There was a family-run clothing and jewelry store where everyone who entered was treated like a thief and watched with the deepest suspicion the moment they entered. We had a gypsy-style clothing store on our block for awhile which also sold medieval-style velvets and chain mail. One of their customers asked me if Joie would like to participate in an S & M themed sale at a local night club. I politely declined but had to laugh at the idea of our rubber ducks and puppets at said event. Another shopkeeper asked one of my employees if she would mind picking up her little dog for her. "I can't do it myself," she said, pointing to her very short skirt. "I'm not wearing any underwear." This immediately went in the too much information file.

We even had a beat cop who walked the streets and often stopped in to say hello, and an assortment of neighborhood eccentrics like the tipsy fake priest with a tambourine who collected for "charity." He looked worse every time he came in and we quickly figured out that he was his own charitable organization. Another regular was a diminutive older woman with a basket full of cookies she sold for "Dr. Ann." Dr. Ann was a spiritual leader of some uncertain type; we read the literature, but never quite figured her out. Her cookies were good though. And then there was John, who roamed the streets in large fancy hats, or a Viking style helmet, sometimes wrapping himself in a blanket or a flag.

Anytime I had a business question, I just went down the block and asked Barbara how she would handle it. She owned Susanna, a women's clothing store, the first store in the neighborhood I had gone into back when I was still a woodworker's girlfriend. I had immediately loved it. The staff was friendly and welcoming and although I would find out they had opened only two years before me, it felt like it had been there forever — in the best way. My first January, I thought I should "do inventory" so when we closed on New Year's Day, my sister and I went in to count up the merchandise. We started with the postcard racks. An hour later, we were still counting postcards and I thought — this is insane. I called Barbara. "Do you do inventories?" I asked. She laughed. As it turned out there was a much simpler way to do it and for tax purposes, it was equally legal. Take the amount you paid for goods, subtract your sales and voila — your leftover inventory. The only actual inventories I did after that were for reordering purposes.

Over the next few years my business friendship with Barbara became a real one, with the bonus that we could share our various business complaints and dilemmas. Back in those early days, both of our stores were doing well, but later on, when things got tougher, it was wonderful to have a friend I could be completely honest with, one who really understood business woes. Not everyone was as open about their businesses as she was with me, though a lot of friendships developed in the neighborhood and on the block. It didn't matter if you were a store owner, or an employee, we certainly paid no attention to the "never become friends with those who work for you" advice encountered in serious "what not to do in business" articles.

Once I had a few employees, Mr. Fox became a standing source of entertainment. He was far and away the most talked about man in the neighborhood, predictable only in his complete unpredictability. He drove people crazy and appeared to relish doing so. We heard lots of stories from outraged customers; his asking pregnant women to leave because they were "taking up too much room" or refusing someone service in his back seating area for no discernible reason. And then he would nicely offer a child a cookie, or give someone coffee for free. Meanwhile, we enjoyed pretending he had a crush on one or the other of us, leaving notes in our logbook saying he'd come in. *Linda — Happy Birthday. This card entitles you to one all-expense paid date with Mr. Fox!* and *Nancy — Fox stopped in to ask for that hot blond chick that works on Sunday. I gave him your number — he said he lost the copy you gave him last week.* Response: *Emily — I really would prefer if you would not talk to Fox at all — you know how jealous I am.* And on and on...

In those first years, older customers would often ask "Who is the owner?" and show surprise on finding it was me. That secretly pleased me. I was not just a shopgirl! I had no formal business education, just my experiences working for others and I felt a bit like a prodigy. Young woman succeeds in business without really trying! In fact, I really didn't feel like I had to try too hard — though I certainly worked hard. In later years, as small businesses became scarcer, customers seemed equally surprised to find I was the owner, though by then I was certainly an appropriate age. "You are?" Subtext: You? The person gift-wrapping my wind-up toys? I sometimes got the feeling they thought I should be doing something more lofty.

A little glory came our way. We were written up in the *Boston Globe* and other local papers, and we won a prestigious Best of Boston award from *Boston Magazine.* "Joie de Vivre — Best Toys for Adults," (an award with more than a few unintended consequences.) That one got me an appearance on a midday TV show, along with other winners, where the affable host looked at a battered doll's head chained to a television screen, courtesy of the "Best Avant Garde Art Gallery" award winner, a dour young man seated to my right. "Is that one of your toys?" he asked me brightly. Horrified, I quickly pulled out my bag with the jumping mouse, a plastic bull dog gun and a few other items. "No!" I said. "These are!"

I wound up the mouse and put it on the table. As it started its flip-over routine, I picked up a pin screen, pressed my face into it and slowly stuck out my tongue. The host blanched slightly. Then he grabbed it and started to play. I felt bad for the gallery owner. It was hard to know what to say about his pieces and after that the host didn't try. I framed my Best Adult Toys award in a beautiful gilded gold frame and hung it in our bathroom where it no doubt confused more than a few.

The store became self-supporting relatively quickly. I had paid back my parents so Joie was debt free. One of my "employees," a friend who normally worked as an English and ESL professor, and who I had known since our college days, later confessed to me he was amazed things went well so fast. Maybe that's because though he worked for me on and off, he didn't care much about retail. His best feature was his ability to engage customers in interesting conversations that mostly had nothing to do with anything about Joie de Vivre. Business was good so I didn't care. He was often one of the people hanging out on the couch in the backroom at night, drinking wine and discussing everything under the sun. All of us were young and everyone got involved in everyone else's lives. We dated customers and went out for drinks with other shopkeepers on the block. It really was almost all fun and games for awhile. Yes, it was technically a business, but it was also a real community. That couch lasted only a few years, to be replaced by shelves of backstock, and maybe I'm glad the backroom walls never talked, but those early days hold a special place in the history of Joie, our "once upon a time" story.

TRUE CONFESSIONS #1

# *Woman Keeps Special Amazing Music Box Intended for Her Parents!!*

After I paid back the loan from my parents, I wanted to give them a special thank you gift. My mother loved music, and they both loved birds, and I had seen something in a booth at the gift show I thought would be perfect, a little box made of lapis lazuli with an oval piece inlaid with flowers on its top, concealing a tiny feathered bird. You wound it up, pressed a button on the side and the bird popped out, singing away while moving its beak and fluttering its iridescent wings. It sang for a brief ten seconds, then popped back into the box and the lid snapped shut. Magical.

Alice Sturzinger was the U.S. distributor for the storied Swiss music box company, Reuge. She had many wonderful pieces that I ordered and sold at Joie, from $18 "paperweights" to the classic dancing couples or high kicking Can-Can dancers in little glass domes. She had a nice selection of velvet lined wooden musical jewelry boxes as well, with marquetry inlays of flowers or instruments. These larger pieces sold for up to $250 and though we didn't sell lots of them, I loved having them in the store. But she also showed some of the high-end extraordinary Reuge offerings like the bird box, pieces that cost thousands. I found them mesmerizing. I loved music boxes.

The bird box was perfect for Joie de Vivre, but its retail price was $3000, and that seemed out of the question. Buying one for my parents was a different story. I might not have been able to open the store without their help. Being sensible non-extravagant types, they would have been horrified to learn the price, but I figured they would never know. As it turned out, they never did. They never received that wonderful bird box.

As soon as I unpacked it and held it in my hands, I instinctively knew I would not be able to give it up. I showed it to my friends, "Look what I'm giving my parents, isn't it absolutely amazing?" but every time that bird sang its short little song, I became more reluctant to part with it. It was relatively easy to justify keeping it. My parents didn't care much about "things," an admirable quality really. They wouldn't appreciate just how amazing this little automata was. It would wind up on a shelf somewhere and no one would ever see it. This had actually happened with more than one of my gifts to them. If that bird was mine, I would show it off to everyone.

And I did. It still sits on my piano, and I love it as much as I did the first time I saw it. I don't remember what I gave my parents instead, but I'm sure they appreciated whatever it was. When they eventually saw the bird box, they liked it, but I didn't see "I want one" in their eyes. I think I made the right decision. Didn't I?

CHAPTER 7

# What's In a Name?

I wanted to do something different with the store and adults were my intended audience. Joie wouldn't be a children's toy store nor would it be a serious craft gallery, Cambridge already had several of both. But I would carry products that might fit either one and if we sold a product that was technically for children, my criteria would be that it would have to please adults as well. My first business card featured a rubber stamp image of a man in a suit and tie riding a rocking horse. I wasn't sure "Joie de Vivre" would convey exactly what the store was about, so I decided to add a tag line. The card read "Joie de Vivre — Toys for Adults."

In the immortal words of someone, that was my first mistake. I would be in a booth at that first gift show, discussing the store or placing an order and the time would come to give my card to the sales person writing me up. This was thirty-seven years ago and a number of those staffing the booths were old school, older salesmen. As soon as they read the card and their demeanor changed.

I would get a wink, a nod, sometimes a leer. It may seem hard to believe but it took awhile for me to figure out exactly what was happening. Then "Oh no," I'd say, "not that kind of toys for adults, I'm going to be selling puzzles and kaleidoscopes, that kind of thing, nothing X-rated." After the twentieth or thirtieth round of this, my patience wore a little thin, and the explanation process began to seem somewhat tedious. I realized it was a problem but once back from the shows, I was engulfed in the practical details of opening and forgot about it. Until one day I overheard a few people standing on the sidewalk talking. They were discussing the shocking fact that an "adult" store was moving into the neighborhood.

A few months later — in advance of the next round of gift shows — I changed the card to read "Joie de Vivre, Diversions and Delights." That took care of that first problem, but there was another unanticipated and funny problem with the name. Lots of people had no idea how to pronounce it. New employees were afraid to answer the phone — they didn't want to have to say it. Or someone would come to the door with a package and announce that they were looking for "Joey D. Veevur." "Yeah, I got something for a Joey D. Veevur — where can I find him?" was one of the more memorable questions. Many of our Cambridge and Boston customers understood the name, but calling to place orders with companies out of the area was another story.

"Hello, I'd like to place an order please," I'd begin. "Please tell me your name or account number," the salesperson would request. As I obliged one of two things would occur. Dead silence or the evasive "are you at 1792 Mass. Avenue?" In either case, when I said yes, Joie de Vivre, there would be silence again, then "So that's how you say it," followed by "I was terrible at French." This often led to a nice conversation and frequently "What does that actually mean?" I spent a lot of time explaining the concept over the years.

At first I tried to translate it faithfully, explaining that it doesn't literally mean "The Joy of Life" as many would have it, but is more a quality that a person has — the quality of knowing how to enjoy life. But I soon realized my attempts to explain fell into the category of "putting too fine a point on it" and settled for "It means The Joy of Life." "Oh — that's beautiful," was the standard response. "I never took French in high school," was another. And sometimes, as I spelled it out for what seemed like the millionth time: J as in John, O as in orange, I thought of my runner up name, The Graham Cracker Club. Everyone would have known how to spell that. Of course, it would have brought its own set of questions.

We got a lot of calls for pizza. There was a Joey's Pizza in the area and information would give callers our number. There was the account who for months thought our name was "Spotted Zebra." Lots of mail came to Mr. and Mrs. Joie D. Vivre and for a while I kept a collection of countless botched spellings. I also learned that names can only be protected in the state one does business in. After the first ten years, other Joie de Vivres popped up. I had to bite my tongue when a salesperson would ask if we were in Florida, or in Cambridge, Maryland — an unnervingly similar address/location. "But I was the first!" I wanted to cry. "These other stores probably saw my badge and copied our name!" In 1989 we started to get occasional calls from people looking for their order of truffle oil or Herbes de Provence. It took awhile to figure out that there was now a French Food mail order catalog called — Joie de Vivre! Over the years there were several clothing stores with "our" name. I learned to live with it.

We made various promotional buttons to give away over the years. A favorite spelled out our name phonetically: "ZHWAH duh VEEV-ruh." One day I was behind the desk when a man came in, looking distracted. "What exactly is this place called?" he asked. "Joie de Vivre!" I replied. "Really?" he said, looking quite amazed. "And… what does that mean?" I explained. It was a lazy afternoon so I gave him the long explanation. "That's crazy," he said. "I had no idea what it meant, or that it was here. I was just walking by on my way to Harvard Square." He stopped, then continued. "I just had an argument with my wife. She said I had absolutely no joie de vivre." I gave him a few buttons. "Now you do!" I said. There is a little something in a name sometimes.

CHAPTER 8

# The Zen of Retail

Most people probably don't think of working at a store as a particularly Zen-like experience. Especially Joie de Vivre. Imagine the store on a busy day, a plush goat singing "The Lonely Goatherd," the plastic tiki drummer drumming away, someone banging on the xylophone or the steel drum, a few excited toddlers running around, some adults laughing over the button selection... and don't forget the yodeling pickle. I think it's fair to say for most people, this does not suggest what they might think of as Zen. But Zen can be found in the unlikeliest places. And some tenets of Zen practice are essential for those who work in stores, even stores like Joie. Compassion, kindness, diligence, perseverance, respect for all things and people, and repetition of form all come to mind.

There were many things in the store that needed to be explained. Over and over and over. Our square footage was tiny as retail spaces went so we didn't have room for large displays that "explained" products and in any case, I rarely liked the way they looked. Instead of a "dump" holding thirty-six talking parrot pens with a sign that explained: 1. They are pens, 2. They are mini flashlights, and 3. You can record your voice on them, we would keep a single parrot without its tag sitting on the front desk. When someone picked it up, looked at it and put it down without figuring out what it was, we would be there to say, "That's a pen. And you can record

31

your voice on it!" and do a quick little demonstration. "Polly wants to write a letter," we'd make it say, or just "Hello." Then we'd flash its light. We kept the items that needed the most explaining at the front desk.

Sometimes staff would complain about having to say the same things about products that "lived" at the front desk for years. Honestly, it could be difficult not to feel a bit like parrots ourselves. I would also find certain noisemakers hidden under the desk, and could tell customers must have been too enthusiastic with the crashing hammer or the screaming mirror, pushing an employee to the breaking point. I always put the offending items back out, sometimes to the distress of staff. But there was no getting around it. Customers needed to see how things worked, and they were usually delighted to find out. And all these front desk items were also conversation starters, even if they didn't result in a sale. Some long-time front desk denizens: the tiki drummer, the lady in the bathtub bank, the bandit box, the crashing hammer, the cat paw, and all our sound machines. And having them within arms reach, we could easily control their use or turn them off if a customer trying something out absent-mindedly wandered away.

Many things displayed throughout the store had functions not immediately apparent. A big part of our job was keeping an eye on customers and when a look of non-comprehension was detected, to step in and say, "That's actually a calculator, it works like this," or "That's a teleidoscope, it will make a kaleidoscopic image of anything you point it at — point it at me." Some people are naturally inquisitive and will figure things out or ask for information. But I learned that many will not, and I hated to see someone pick up a wonderful item, then put it down with a bored look because they hadn't quite figured out what it was or did.

We sold our favorite items for years so it was tempting to assume that everyone knew what a Chinese finger trap, a pin screen, the metal top with companion magnetic snakes or a kaleidoscope was. But not everyone did. Or customers picked up the dancing ballerina with her mirror and held the mirror upside down. Nothing happened. Some would think and figure it out but others didn't. They needed us to pick up that same mirror and make her dance; if we didn't, they'd walk away without knowing how well she could twirl. Even items that didn't require explanations could spur conversation. Engaging customers, making the little comment or joke about something, was a big part of making the store a place they wanted to come back to.

The Zen comes in when you realize you must have said "It's a cat's paw" at least a thousand times. But almost everything about a typical work day was repetitious. Every time customers moved through the store, they rearranged our displays. It wasn't their fault, sometimes we couldn't even remember where things went. And everything was consciously displayed in a very particular way. That glass shelf holding a couple dozen plastic wind-up toys? Those toys are actually placed there with intent — they are all facing forward, "looking" toward, not away. There was an even amount of space between them and there were often little plastic vignettes: the chattering teeth are next to the wind-up fruit tart, the animals that flip over are together, the little robot walks toward the fire-breathing nun. And every time customers played with those toys, they put them down in different places and we had to rearrange them maybe twenty times on a busy day. We had to make sure the kaleidoscopes were on the right stands. We had to make sure the pin screen had a recognizable image pushed into it — usually my face.

We tried to treat even the smallest item with dignity and respect, also part of the Zen of retail. We had a wide range of items and prices. Some customers never bought anything priced higher than ten dollars while others came in only for the yearly kaleidoscope or piece of jewelry and never looked at the other items. I felt I'd succeeded when someone bought an expensive item for a special gift and then added a few postcards or plastic fish. Respect for all things!

But the aspect of Zen that might have been the most useful to us at Joie de Vivre was this: No matter what happens, let go. That was the best way to survive the dreaded difficult customer. Most didn't mean to be difficult. It might have been a lonely kid with nothing to do, who came in every day for an hour or two and wanted to talk the entire time. It might have been someone truly anxious about gift shopping, who needed to buy something but was so unsure that even after an hour of suggestions they couldn't decide; nothing was right and they walked away unsatisfied. Or the person with minimal social skills who wanted to interact. These people could be trying, though they mostly didn't mean to be.

We did have customers who were more challenging. Some came in often enough that we gave them nicknames. Puppet Boy, Violin Man, Two Dollar Lady. Or bored babysitters who brought in their charges to play for an hour so they could chat with a friend. Parents who didn't want to watch their kids and bristled when we asked them to. Groups of adolescent girls or boys, out on their own having fun together — by the time they left you felt you'd been invaded by a particularly loud and excited army.

So yes, you wrapped ten gifts for someone that didn't say thank you, yes, that woman told her kids that "the lady doesn't want you to touch that" causing them to stare at you balefully, or burst into tears. Yes, that guy was kind of a pain, and yes, that woman who jumped into every conversation in the entire store was a bit trying. But they eventually walked out the door and left us alone. You had to remember what a small proportion of the total those difficult people were. And you had to remember whose day would be ruined if you held onto that annoyance for long. It wouldn't be theirs. No matter what happened, you had to let go. And move on to the next customer. "It's a cat paw." "It's a top," "Let me show you how that works." And move on to the next day for more of the same.

Some Japanese potters spend their entire life making the same teacups over and over, each one subtly and to most of us, not noticeably different. At the store, you could say the same thing a thousand times and get a thousand different responses because every interaction with someone, no matter how many times you've said "push that little button," is going to be different. You need the temperament to do that and not everyone does, including the makers whose work we showed. We often had to say "Sorry, she doesn't make those anymore" about one of our jewelers, or potters, or printmakers. Some did not want to make the same things forever, while others continued on and on.

Compassion, kindness, diligence, perseverance, respect for all things and people, and repetition of form, all essential to running a successful store. And I like to think that at Joie, we had our own versions of the Zen Koan, a statement or question posed to train the listener to "abandon ultimate dependence on reason and force a sudden intuitive enlightenment." One of the time-honored classics is "What is the sound of one hand clapping?" I like to think a few of our customers may have attained that enlightenment. After all, what is the measure of a pickle that yodels? What is the reason of a squeaking penguin? What is the sound of one hamster singing?

CHAPTER 9

# Core Beliefs and Aims

Paul Smith, the fabulously successful English clothing designer who opened a series of eponymous shops in Europe and New York, described his philosophy this way: "When you come into a Paul Smith shop, even if you don't buy anything, it should be a pleasant experience." Exactly what I aimed for at Joie de Vivre. I learned many things along the way, but I did go into the business with certain firmly held beliefs, and here they are:

*Don't make people feel that they must buy something to be welcome.*
Corollary: happy browsers often return as buyers.

*Have a wide price range so that no one feels "nice store, but nothing I can afford."*
A wide price range means anyone can leave with at least a little something.

*Treat all items, regardless of price, with equal dignity.*
The garbage man or janitor is as important as the doctor or professor, and the wind-up toy must be treated with the same dignity as the expensive kaleidoscope.

*The customer who spends $500 is not more important than the one spending $5 and gets the exact same treatment and respect.*
Corollary: Shoppers do not get a discount for spending more money.
One person's $500 is another man's $5.

*Until proven wrong, trust everyone.*
It's more important to treat the 99% of trustworthy people well, than to suspect them of being the 1% of people who are not.

*Don't sell things someone in the neighborhood is already selling.*
Don't try to take business away from your neighbors. (Exceptions — broad categories like greeting cards.)

*Our products are worth their price.*
Exceptions — discontinued items, mistakes (yes, we made mistakes) and celebration birthday sales meant to thank customers for their support.

*Always close on significant holidays.*
New Year's Day, Easter, Memorial Day, July 4th, Labor Day, Thanksgiving, Christmas.

*Don't have conversations at the desk unless anyone is welcome to join in.*
No whispering, make conversation inviting and open — like a nice cocktail party.

*Never try to "sell" things to people.*
Help them, engage them, show them new products, but no pressure ever.

*No tipping! Our wonderful gift wrapping and friendly service is free.*
If someone hands you a few dollars after you've gift-wrapped their purchases, hand it back!

*Don't sell knockoffs that are outright theft.*
I couldn't always tell if something was a copy, but if I knew for sure,
    I would not order it.

*It's always worth explaining things, even if you feel like a broken record.*
Aka the Zen of retail.

*Your business exists thanks to your suppliers, delivery people, customers and staff.*
Treat them accordingly.

CHAPTER 10

# I Can't Do This Alone, aka Employees

The last thing on my mind when I opened Joie was being a boss, but after six months working alone, I realized I needed help. My sister Nancy who had recently moved to town, volunteered to work Sundays. I was young and full of enthusiasm; if I kept the store closed Mondays, I could handle the rest. It was exciting having my own business, and besides, I had nothing much else going on. Being new to Boston, I had no close friends yet, and I now had no boyfriend, or even a pet to take care of. I'd close at 6:30 and spend the next few hours rearranging displays or doing paperwork. Working fifty plus hours a week? Easy. The store wasn't that busy during the day and I unpacked new merchandise right up at the front desk, pulling things out of boxes to the delight of the customers who enjoyed seeing this part of the operation up close and personal. I ate my lunch at the front desk too, and if I needed a coffee, stuck a "back in five minutes" sign on the door.

After a few months, I started to wonder if we should open seven days a week like the other neighborhood stores. Customers would tell me they had tried to visit on a Monday and how disappointed they were to find us closed. And Christmas was coming. I wasn't sure what to expect that first year, but I suspected that going it alone might not be the best idea. Shortly thereafter Patricia, a friend of an acquaintance came in, saying she was between jobs and would love to work part time. I liked her. She became my first official employee and stayed for several years.

Almost all of my employees were hired in this somewhat random fashion. Customers, friends of friends, kids of friends, employee's friends, my sister, my boyfriend's brother. There was the young guy buying a kaleidoscope one Saturday afternoon. I was looking for help, and as I wrapped his gift, he said, "Boy, I'd love to work here!" I jumped in. "You would? I need someone — want a job?" We arranged to meet a few mornings later to talk about the details and I proceeded to berate myself for the next two days. I didn't know this guy. Why had I offered him a job? He seemed kind of young. How could I get out of it? As the morning of our meeting approached, I couldn't even remember what he looked like. But he showed up, neatly dressed, on time, and I decided to give him a try. He was a little young and crazy, but he was good with the customers and had a winning way with our puppets. Sitting behind the desk, a bear puppet on his lap, he sold more of them than anyone has before or since. He stayed for a few years, occasionally showing up looking like he'd been up for days. "Oh, some friends and I drove to — fill out the name of a town four hours in any direction — last night to see a band. We just got back." He wound up becoming an investment banker and having two children.

A year after opening, I had a serious boyfriend and his brother Peter, who later became my brother-in-law, turned into one of my longest serving "employees." He started helping out when he was only fifteen and worked on and off for years, even after becoming a professional exhibit designer. He was always willing to lend a hand and was a huge help with technical issues and window displays. My sister, the first person to stand behind the desk besides me, years later joined me full time, not only working in person, but creating and maintaining our website. Two others who started young were high school students from Cambridge: Kate, very confident, and Julia, so shy she didn't talk much for the first year or two, though she later blossomed into one of our long-time all-stars, able to hold her own with anyone. Camilla grew up around the corner and haunted the store after school. She'd stay so long that her parents would call to say "dinner is served, please send her home!" She didn't actually start working until she was college age, but continued on and off until the end.

Some of my closest friends today are former "Joie-ettes" as we often called them. Emily first came in with her boyfriend. They both had bleached blond hair and crazy clothes, punk ragamuffins. They looked a little wild but they loved the store and were truly sweet, buying each other surprise gifts, and once bringing me homemade cookies. When I learned that Emily cleaned houses on the side to augment her salary as an after-school teacher, I asked if she would consider cleaning my house. To my surprise she didn't jump at the chance. "Well," she said diffidently, "I guess I could — but I'd much rather work here." She stayed for ten years. Danielle wandered in one fall just when I was starting to panic about the extra help I needed for Christmas. "I just moved to town and I'm looking for a job." Magic words. She was a quirky, intelligent, artist with retail experience, and stayed five years, leaving to my immense regret when her partner landed a good job out of state. Sarah from Mississippi, also known as Pleasant Darling or Daughter of Pearl, worked at Joie a few years and then moved to New York to pursue her dance career where she wound up working for a friend of mine in Soho. We hung out whenever I was in NY for a trade show.

Of course for all the hires that went wonderfully, there were others that didn't. The girlfriend of a customer's boyfriend's son, who sat behind the desk playing trance music, never doing a thing unless specifically asked to. She thought nothing of talking to me about her adventures jumping turnstiles and engaging in petty thievery. Needless to say, she didn't last long. Then there was the young man who despite his then fashionable multiple piercings and slightly sickly look, initially seemed reasonably presentable. On his first day he took off the baseball cap he'd worn when we met. He had messy, dirty green hair and I asked him to keep it on. I let the women on the staff wear the jewelry we sold as a way to show it off but when he started wearing our expensive necklaces and earrings, it didn't have the same effect. He would also disappear into the back to gift wrap something and when it seemed beyond all reason that he could still be doing it we would go investigate. Invariably, we found chaos, discarded boxes and tissue all over the floor and S. still wrestling with the gift. I agonized about how to get rid of him. Never good at being direct, I shrank from the idea of telling him he wasn't working out, but happily he solved the problem by moving away shortly thereafter.

For most of the year, I only needed a few people working, but in December, we needed more if only for a month or so. Luckily, a lot of former staff returned faithfully year after year to help out. They liked each other and the Christmas craziness was fun. But I often had to hire extra people fast and my instincts about who would be a good fit weren't as keen when I was desperate. There was the woman who turned out to have a large inferiority complex. She constantly belittled herself to customers with comments like "What do I know, I'm so clueless" when they asked for advice. Or the person who would go to the stockroom for something and return ten minutes later with an entirely different object. "What's this? I've never seen it before! What? Where are the flamingo salt and peppers? Oh, right, I knew there was a reason I was back there." To be fair, locating things in the stockroom was a bit of an art — there were theoretically logical "sections" — all the clocks here, the tin toys here, the kitchen things here — except for all the things that didn't fit, which were in an entirely different room. And some people had better visual memories than others.

Another Christmas hire would pick up the same item three times in a week, exclaiming how wonderful it was, as though she'd never seen it before. This person would get into long involved conversations with customers, responding to their questions but recommending a variety of inappropriate things: ballerina music boxes for teenage boys come to mind. Just take a deep breath and remember, after Christmas is over, they'll be gone, I told myself.

I had unexpected employees too. One fall my electrician JoeD, now a friend, asked if I needed extra holiday help. "I really can't afford you," I said regretfully, remembering his hourly rate. "I don't mind about the wages," he replied. "I've always wanted to work in a store like this." He worked many Christmases from that year on. Years later his daughter became the first child of a Joie friend to work in the store. Then there was my friend Rusty. On his way from English professor to ESL instructor to jewelry designer/importer, he worked part time for me for several years. He would often pick up an item asking "When did we get this?" "Ummm — I hate to tell you this Rusty, but that's been here for several years." He was at a loss when asked to recommend a birthday present for a five-year-old girl or a sixty-year-old woman, but he liked selling the kaleidoscopes. His real talent was starting interesting philosophical and political discussions. Joie was a store that often doubled as a salon.

The customers loved the staff as well. When Emily finally left I panicked, worrying that no one would come in anymore now that she was gone. And some customers were really quite disappointed, "Where is that wonderful woman who always wears cowboy boots?" but we survived, and she returned every Christmas. When others left, people would ask after them too, "Where is Katie?" Except for the ones I couldn't wait to get rid of, I thought of my employees as a wonderful gift. The Joie job was perfect for that in between time for the person who doesn't quite know what they want to do with their life. Or the recent graduate figuring out their next step, or an artist or musician who needs to be out of the studio a day or two a week and make some extra money. Or a good introductory course in retail for anyone thinking they might want a store of their own someday.

I knew everyone would eventually move on. No one could have made a career out of working for me, I gave them a generous discount but there was never enough money to pay them that well. As long as they didn't leave right before Christmas, I wanted them to find jobs that would be rewarding, financially and creatively. This happened naturally for most. People finished school, or fell in love and didn't want to work all weekend. Joie would begin to interfere with their life, rather than be their life. I understood. When occasionally someone stayed longer than was good for them, apprehensive about finding the next thing, yet bored, or just dissatisfied and unhappy, that was hard on them, and on both me and their co-workers. I wanted them all to find something, have their own careers, take chances and succeed. And they did. Besides our puppet loving investment banker, I now count a lawyer, a nurse, a real estate agent, a yoga teacher, two exhibit designers, a professional gardener, and more than a few educators among our alumnae. I'm sure there are others doing all kinds of great things. I was happy for them even if I hated losing them. I never forgot how nervous I had been about giving my notice at the gallery when I decided to leave. Lore's encouragement and understanding when I finally did was a tremendous relief, and that's the way I resolved I would react too.

Was I a good boss? I know at times I was not. I could be impatient and had a tendency to just do things myself rather than explain what I wanted done and how. I wrote up "What To Do When You Think There's Nothing To Do" manuals but shrank from directly dealing with potentially difficult situations and could then sent out slightly resentful vibes. (This was an even bigger problem in my marriage!) I was too timid about insisting on things I wanted — from no cell phones out front to one drink only per person at the desk, (there were often many more coffees, waters and bottle of soda or juice than people) to insisting that "would you like this wrapped?" is, except in moments of extreme busyness, a question that must be asked. And when I was nervous about money and sales, as I sometimes was over the years, I could be hard on people.

But small businesses like Joie are not easy to run in a formal fashion. All things considered, I think I was okay to work for and I think this partly because lots of people worked at Joie for years, and I'm still friends with many. We liked each other, and our staff parties were always fun. Over the years, they gave me wonderful, personal and thoughtful Christmas presents, and wrote me amazing notes, and poems. There were songs they adapted and performed at our annual 4 p.m. "The season is over" champagne toast on Christmas Eve. One time at a post-Christmas staff dinner at my house, the doorbell rang and I found a pizza delivery man standing at the door. "You must have the address wrong," I told him. "I just cooked dinner, I definitely didn't order pizza." He insisted it was for me, and finally said, "Just take it!" so I did. The box was curiously light.

I brought it in and to my surprise the pizza guy followed me. Someone said hi to him. When I opened the box, it all became clear — it contained a gift certificate for cooking classes by a favorite chef. It was a masterfully sneaky presentation — something they pulled off many times in various creative ways.

Different employees had their preferred tasks. Some loved to restock, roaming through the store, noticing what was missing, especially when it was busy at Christmas. Some enjoyed gift wrapping, others, not so much. Some loved to talk to little kids, others were better with teenagers or older people. Some liked unpacking boxes in the back, some wanted to be out front with the customers. Some were happy to go on errands around town, others preferred not to. But in the long run, everyone did everything, including me.

When writing this book I interviewed former employees, alone, or in a group, and I asked them what they remembered about getting the job, their best and worst experiences working, their favorite and least favorite items, and more. They remembered many funny little things I had forgotten, (and to my relief, I found that what they considered my most annoying trait was my habit of chewing on ballpoint pens.) But what stood out in every interview was this: Joie became a real community. One described our vibe as "positive and magical," adding that she loved instilling joy in the customers. Lifelong friendships were made, and there was a real sense of connection and love. It may sound corny, but this is what they told me, interview after interview. And it's the reason they returned to work at Christmas. One year I told Julia that I'd kept her on the "work at Christmas?" list even though I wasn't expecting her to. I knew she'd moved an hour away and was expecting her second child. Her reply? "Never leave me off the list!!" Peter drove down from his new home in Maine one year to work for one day, "just to keep his hand in." And every Christmas I thanked my lucky stars for my former crew. I haven't mentioned every single one here but I'm grateful to them all. We really became a family, a home away from home. Here is the closing stanza from a thank you poem I wrote for them one Christmas:

*You're a great bunch of people*
*and I love you one and all,*
*and wish you Happy Holidays,*
*I hope you have a ball,*
*and even when the time comes*
*that you can't come work at Joie*
*you'll still be in the family as*
*you really can't withdraw*
*and you'll always know the answer to*
*"Hey, what's with this cat paw?"*

(And for that last line to make sense… see Chapter 18!)

CHAPTER II

# A Crazy Little Thing Called Love

It is a truth universally acknowledged that when you have a bunch of women in their teens, twenties and thirties working at a store, and they're interesting, smart, nice and pretty, they will be in want of romance and flirtation, and relationships of various sorts will be a big topic of conversation and intrigue. The vast majority of Joie employees over the years were women; men were less likely to be interested, though over the years, we did have a few. I also count myself lucky that though there were dinners and parties and nights out in bars, I don't think there was a single case of two Joie employees really dating. That can complicate things. But there were more than a few instances of employees dating customers. And lots of crushes. Customers had crushes on some of us, and we definitely had crushes on some of them.

When a customer you really liked came in, it was good to be working alone out front. With no one else around to listen, it was easier to get into personal conversations. We helped each other out. If someone came in I knew someone else "liked," I'd think of a project that needed my attention in the back. Conversely, if the object of someone's affection came in and that person was working in the back, we'd be sure to let them know so they could casually wander out and pretend to restock something or ask a question, then, "Oh... hi." Sometimes I'd be in the back, sitting at my desk and the person working out front would come rushing in. "Can you go out there please? That guy I like is here. I can't act normal/talk to him!"

Happily, with a few exceptions, we all fell for different people. No need to fight. Someone would confess to me that they thought a certain guy was a dreamboat and I'd look at them blankly — hadn't even noticed him, or didn't have the same reaction. And vice-versa. But there were those customers we all agreed made us a little weak in the knees. There were one or two I couldn't wait on at first. Feeling too tongue tied and embarrassed, I'd run for the back room if I saw them come in rather than have to try to talk to them feeling like a blushing fool. But some of those people came in for years, and I eventually was able to not only get over it but get to know them as friends.

There were more poignant encounters too. One year, a quiet man began to come in to buy cards and little toys. He seemed extremely shy and when he spoke to me, his face flushed bright red. He mentioned that he was a photographer. One day he gave me a cassette of music box recordings to play in the store. "Thank you so much, I'm sure I'll love this," I said. His face got redder than I imagined possible as he mumbled, "You're welcome." A few weeks later he came in, handed me a small wrapped box, and beat a hasty retreat. It held another cassette, a poem, a chocolate — and oh no — a heartfelt love letter. Whoops! I had to let him know that I didn't feel the same way.

For weeks afterwards, I would sometimes spy him standing outside the store, looking in, his hand over his heart. Of course this made me feel terrible. Then, one day I was telling this story to a couple of artist friends, one who had worked in a photography shop. "What did he look like?" she suddenly asked. Hearing my description, she said "Do you know what? I know that guy. The exact same thing happened to me." This made me feel better. If he'd gone through this before, I couldn't have single-handedly broken his heart and wrecked his life.

For at least a few months after opening the store, love was the last thing on my mind, although I did fall for a French kaleidoscope maker I bought from; unfortunately, he was married — and lived in France. I'd recently split up with Bill and was still dealing with the repercussions of that. Then, some months later, I succumbed to a delusional Englishman with a fatally charming accent who lived right across the street from the store. My theory about that relationship now — I was subconsciously trying to assuage my guilt at leaving my boyfriend by choosing someone incapable of any real commitment. I even foolishly lent him five thousand dollars which I never got back, but I did learn a few lessons.

One Saturday morning, two couples who looked to be in their twenties came in. One of the men took my breath away and I know I didn't hide it. He was tall, with long wild curly hair and I felt that certain something that goes beyond physical attraction or so I romantically thought. I was still dating Mr. Trouble but had an instant electric reaction to this person. I was feeling good that day and though he seemed to be with someone, subtly flirted as much as I could without making a fool of myself, or so I hoped. A week later he came back, alone. I was happy to see him, but wasn't feeling well, and no sparks flew this time. He bought a few postcards and left. I saw him walk by a few weeks later. He didn't even look in the window, and I stopped thinking about him. (Although thirty-seven years later, I still remember what he was wearing when he passed by that day.)

One beautiful April morning, sunny and clear, I woke up feeling sure that I had finally left the Englishman behind. I had told him it was really over the day before and felt no regret. I was alone that day, feeling a little bored, not happy to be trapped behind the desk. I wanted to go outside and frisk, the lovely spring weather was getting to me. Late in the morning the door opened and in came the long-haired postcard man. No one else was in the store and we chatted for awhile. I lamented being inside on such a lovely day.

"Well, you know what?" he told me. "It's really only nice out right in front of your store. The rest of the street is grey with maybe a little rain coming." This was sweet, but when he returned an hour later and gave me a flower, I was a goner. The next time he came in, I screwed up my courage and asked if he wanted to go to the movies or do something and he said yes. He would become a very important part of Joie de Vivre; I had the good fortune of falling for a man who was, among other things, an artist and a builder. He made us many memorable window displays before returning to school and beginning a career as an architect. We had the usual struggles, but reader, I married him. And reader, we also divorced. But despite the unhappy end of our story, I count our twenty plus years together as a good thing and I'm glad he walked in the door.

Some relationships formed at Joie still endure. At least a few of our married customers met each other while shopping in the store, and told us so years later. One couple said they had come to browse for fun on their first date. When they told us that story, they had been married for twenty-six years. The store definitely had a friendly, conversational atmosphere. Another woman told us about meeting her husband at Joie. They had each been there alone and started talking about one of our products, then stayed talking about all kinds of things for an hour or so before exchanging phone numbers and going their separate ways. Now they came in each year to buy each other anniversary gifts.

Lots of couples came in together, with or without their kids, but some never did. A wife would come to buy things for her husband, and men came in for jewelry and gifts for their wives. The funny and fascinating thing to me was, eventually one day, I would see a man and a woman enter together, each of who I knew as a solo shopper. It would quickly become apparent that they were a couple, and I have to say, almost every single time my reaction was — yes, of course! These two people seem so right together!

One woman who worked for me became fast friends with another employee and met her handsome brother. Complications ensued but a few years later they married and now have three beautiful children, one of whom was very disappointed when I closed the store before he was quite old enough to work there.

There was definitely drama, especially in the early years. Some of the staff were worried about ex-boyfriends showing up. Or needed to talk — all the time — about their personal lives. I remember gift wrapping something for a waiting customer while an employee tried to talk to me about someone they'd met the night before. "So, I met this person and it was kind of strange..." "Not now!" I'd hiss. "Tell me later!!" And of course the inevitable break-ups required a lot of hand-holding and serious attention.

My own relationship with my eventual husband was quite tumultuous for some of the time before we decided to commit and I did things I blush to think of now. Wrapping myself around him behind the front desk in front of customers, focusing all my attention on him, not them, or after a breakup, locking the door for awhile to kiss and make up in the back room. Even at the time, I never would have tolerated this self-indulgent behavior from my employees, but I somehow couldn't stop myself, (and I sincerely apologize to anyone reading this if I ever ignored them or made them uncomfortable while in the throes of my desperate attempts to win him back. I also apologize to anyone who found our door inexplicably locked.)

I didn't write this note in our logbook myself, it was another unhappy person, but I could have.

*Note to Self— (and all those curious) do NOT meet up with your ex to "discuss" your relationship ON YOUR 30 MINUTE LUNCH BREAK. No Good. Don't recommend it. But hey, we live, we live some more and then some more — and then finally, one day, WE LEARN.*

Several women who worked for me were trying to figure out their own lives, not sure if they liked women, men, or both. It was hard on them, and hard on their partners, though everyone survived. Someone else had a former boyfriend she was kind of hiding out from and was afraid would find her at the store. And one day, a Chinese woman came in and asked for a former employee who was still a close friend. She was newly arrived in the states, searching for him and knew he'd worked at the store. She didn't know he had a girlfriend now. That created some serious drama.

As time passed and we all got older, social life at Joie got a lot more sedate. We still had our crushes, but most of us were somewhat settled down. And of course, most of us are less crazy at fifty or sixty than we are at thirty. Still, it was kind of exciting to think you never knew who might walk in the door, who you might meet. There was potential while sitting behind that desk. And after I decided to close the store I sometimes wondered — how will I meet someone new now?

## *I Dated Santa Claus*

I didn't know it was him when he came into the store. It was spring and
he was incognito. That morning I happened to be working alone. We
didn't really talk much but he spent a good hour browsing and he bought
a few things. He wanted a t-shirt we were selling, a takeoff on *Where's
Waldo*, it was "Where's Ralph Waldo Emerson?" He told me he was
related to Emerson — who knew? We didn't have the shirt in his size
though, Santa needed XXL. I told him I'd order it for him and he gave
me his number. He was using a fake name, Jonathan.

I called him when the shirt came in but he didn't answer so I left a
message. Then, later that day I was taking a walk and ran into him.
I was on my way out of town for a few days. I told him I'd left a message
about the shirt, and he said okay, see you later, I'll come in. "I won't be
there, just ask someone at the desk for it," I said. When I got back from
my weekend, I noticed the shirt was still there. It kind of confirmed a
suspicion I had. I thought he might be a little interested in me. I was a
little interested in him.

I had a profile on some dating site at the time. I'd been divorced
for awhile and was thinking maybe I should get something going.
I was down in NY at the Stationary Show when I got a message from
a Jonathan. It was him, still using that alias. "Why didn't you tell me

you were on Match?" he asked me. I let him know that I didn't exactly announce to customers that I was. Why would I do that? But we made a date to go out for a drink.

That's when he told me he was Santa. That first date. I can't say I was really surprised. He really did look exactly like Santa — white hair, big beard, twinkling eyes, big belly. I believed him. He told me some pretty interesting stuff too. Like about all the fake Santas. The guys who play the part at malls and events every year. Some of them thought Santas should be allowed to carry guns. It takes a lot to shock me, but that? I was shocked. He also told me that the most respected Santas had real beards. They called themselves Real Bearded Santas.

He told me that even though he was Santa, he had to work some of these jobs himself. He didn't mind though, he really liked people and making them feel good. One thing that surprised me? He said in Japan, Christmas is a romantic holiday. Kind of like Valentines. Couples get engaged and stuff like that. Crazy! He worked there one year and got to see it for himself. Later he got hired to pose for Coca-Cola. He was the first Santa of theirs that wasn't drawn. You'd see him on billboards around town and stuff. Pretty cool.

We started seeing each other once in awhile. People always looked twice at him, wherever we went. If anyone said something, he'd make some joke about how he just liked to hang out and relax the rest of the year, eating bagels, swimming, doing all the things regular people do. But he'd give them a hearty ho ho ho to make it clear that he really was who they thought he was. I liked when that happened, it was fun to watch. He also drove around with some sleigh bells in the back of his car. You'd hear them jingle some if he hit a speed bump or something. I could tell they were the very best quality bells. Of course they would be.

He and Mrs. Claus had been divorced for awhile. They had a kid. Having Santa be your Dad must have been weird. But awesome. I never got to ask her about it though, she didn't live in town. I really got pretty fond of this guy. At first I wasn't sure I'd like kissing him with all that beard but once I tried it — I liked it, no complaints. He was pretty busy around the holidays, but that was perfect for me. So was I. When you think about it, it was really pretty funny, me being the owner of a toy store and dating Santa Claus. Pretty good match. I gave him tips on what kids and grown-ups might want, the latest stuff, in case he didn't know. He had a lot to keep up with.

One time he had a private gig and I was going to be an elf. I bought some red socks to jazz up my look, and made a great neckpiece out of some decoration we were selling at the store. But the gig got canceled at the last minute. I never got my moment of glory. We also did a cool photo shoot at the store. He didn't wear his full suit, but with a red and white striped shirt, and red pants and suspenders and boots, it was obvious it was him. When I posted those photos, the customers were pretty impressed that I knew him.

In the end, things didn't work out between us. I was a little sad about it, you know, I liked the guy. But we decided to stay in touch, be friends. We definitely had some fun. We got each other. And if you don't believe we dated, you can ask him, if you catch him coming down your chimney or see him in a mall or something. Ask him if he knows Linda from Joie de Vivre. I think you'll get a twinkle and a smile.

CHAPTER 12

# Treasure Hunt (Where Do You Find This Stuff?)

"Where do you find these things?" This was a frequent question. The answer? Trade shows, craft fairs, and showrooms. Sometimes sales reps. Sometimes the time-honored tradition of snooping/shopping in other stores I liked out of town; if I saw something interesting, I'd buy it and try to track it down. Sometimes I just asked. "Where did you get that adorable collie purse? Can I look at the label?" Sometimes a customer started a business. And very very occasionally, someone just walked in our door with a great item they were looking to sell.

When I opened, I was lucky. The biggest and best trade shows were in New York, only four hours away. Even luckier, my sister Debra and her family lived there, on the Upper West Side, so I had a free place to stay, thus no reason to rush through in a few days in order to save a few hundred dollars at a hotel. I went down five or six times a year to shop shows and showrooms. A big bonus was getting to spend time with my three nieces. They particularly liked it when I came to attend Toy Fair, I got lots of free samples and they were the happy recipients. And they loved visiting me in the summer and helping out at the store.

I truly enjoyed shows. It was exhilarating to walk the aisles, a gargantuan treasure hunt, with treasures you didn't suspect existed. I never went looking for a plastic bulldog gun, or a wall mounted singing fish, a beautiful handmade photo album, a Godzilla cigarette lighter or a dancing coke bottle, let alone an actual coke bottle elegantly encased in lucite, but I found all of those and more. Some exhibitors had a whole booth full of wonderful items, from others I would order just one or two things. By the end of a show I would have walked miles and miles of aisles, returning home tired but inspired, and eager for the new orders to arrive. In all the years I was in business, I missed just one NY Gift Show — a summer when I tripped and broke my foot a few days before I was to leave. I hated to miss it and thought about going but I was just getting used to my crutches and scooter, strictly forbidden from putting any weight on my foot, so was forced to admit it would be too difficult.

The New York International Gift Show was the big one. You could find almost anything there, except, in the early years, American Crafts, which were found at specialized shows in smaller cities like Baltimore and Springfield. At its peak, the Gift Show filled every inch of the then brand-new Jacob Javits Center, spilling over into three nearby Hudson River Piers. Exhibiting companies might be huge and rent multiple booths to make one big statement, but there was equal opportunity for small businesses just starting out. (When I placed my first order with the now well known company Blue Q at the show, they had exactly one product, a cardboard cut-out "Flat Cat.") Some companies hired designers and made elaborate displays, others just rented a table and put out their goods. It was the mid 1980s, the economy was decent, there were lots of independent businesses and it was sometimes hard to get through the crowds of buyers walking the aisles. The show had an exciting buzz.

Some larger companies did not want to work with small stores like mine. One offered hundreds of toys and their giant inflatable Godzillas, over six feet tall and commandingly impressive, caught my eye. I really wanted to order some but they were inflexible about their $5000 minimum, which was not even close to the edge of the realm of possibility for me. I stood there distraught, explaining how small my store was, and a salesman took pity on me. "I'll tell you what you can do," he said. "You can buy them at Child World. They sell them at the same price as our regular wholesale."

At the time Child World was the second largest toy retailer in the United States, and they were rewarded with a very different pricing structure by manufacturers. I thought this very unfair but I wanted Godzillas. There were several of their stores in the Boston area, so I took a little trip. I created a bit of a stir, standing in line with my shopping cart, twelve Giant Inflatable Godzillas spilling out. The sales clerk gave me an inquisitive look. "Oh, I'm... making a movie!" was what I came up with. He blinked, nodded, and took my money. "Cool!" he said. "Come back for more anytime!" Back at the store, I worried for awhile that someone would be look at our price and say — Hey! I saw these at Child World for half this much! Happily, no one ever did, and really, no wonder, a giant inflatable Godzilla for $25 seemed fair enough to those who "needed" one. Our customers liked them so much I returned for more several times.

The Toy Fair was the most fun to attend, but at the same time, surprisingly serious. Toys were big business with a higher concentration of serious buyers walking around in suits than at the Gift Show. Mixing with these heavy weights were the rest of us, and always, a bunch of life size walking stuffed animals or characters — typically "inhabited by" unemployed actors or musicians. I loved having my photo taken with life-size crayons, fuzzy animals, eight-foot-tall rubber ducks. And though we didn't sell Legos, their booth was always amazing, built entirely of Lego pieces with a different themed character out front each year.

Through a friend, I learned that lots of inventors and magicians designed toys for big companies and attended the show. Sunday night was the annual Magicians/Inventors Dinner at a Chinese restaurant in mid-town and my friend brought me along. We squeezed around tables, sharing platters of food, while people pulled their creations out of bags and boxes and showed them off. I saw spinning tops climb out of coffee cups, tiny automata, an animated butterfly flutter in a jar, and a flip book that produced a visible rainbow hovering over its pages. I saw a man pour wine right into his hand and make it disappear, another solve a miniature Rubik cube in his mouth with his tongue, and untold amazing card tricks. I was the perfect foil, and could never help shrieking "How did you *do* that?"

when I saw real magic. Before a good magician we are all as susceptible as the youngest child and in my book, that's as good as it gets.

The Stationary Show, held each May, filled the Javits Center with cards and paper goods. It was more about making contacts and meeting sales reps. Few buyers had time to sit down and look through hundreds of postcards or cards at the show, so sales reps would visit our stores. A card appointment could wind up taking the better part of an afternoon and I got to know some of those reps well. But sometimes I sat down at the show, for smaller lines, or larger ones with reps that didn't carry the entire selection. And I'd always sit down at ArtUnlimited, a postcard company from Amsterdam, whose owner came over with many thousands of postcards, covering a wide range of subjects. He didn't bother with organizing them, buyers had to sit down and sift through them all. You'd be looking through sweet images of stuffed toys, photographs of animals, beautiful landscapes, and then pick up a rather disturbing and explicit "erotic" card. Those in the know shrugged and kept on going, but I saw some funny reactions from first time lookers.

There were smaller regional shows too. Boston had one spring and fall, perfect for smaller New England stores that did not want to go to the big city, but shortly after moving to the gigantic new Boston Convention Center, where it occupied a tiny portion of the space, it closed down, too close to New York to compete. I went to the Boutique Show in New York for years. It was mostly clothing, which we didn't sell, but had a small section of quirky jewelry and gifts. Alongside the conventional clothing offered, many funky and outré designers exhibited their wares, and it was hard not to stare at their provocatively dressed models as they roamed the aisles to drum up business. My best finds there were a man who made earrings out of miniature dollhouse food — tiny bags of potato chips or packs of Hostess cupcakes, and then the eccentric Steve of "Land and Sea" who sold the widest range of unusual items I ever came across, 50s lenticular of winking women, "Pino-Pino" alien dolls, alligator ashtrays, tacky snow globes, among them. After that show closed for good, he would pack some of his wares into a giant suitcase and meet me at the Gift Show where instead of renting a booth, he'd meet me in a corner so I could view his goods without the show managers noticing.

The American Craft scene was really blossoming when I opened the store and their wholesale fairs were like college reunions for me. I knew many exhibitors from my Vermont life and my life as a buyer for the Gallery before that. It was fun to be back and to get to tell friends I'd started my own business, and I loved selling things made by people I knew. When it made geographic sense I would visit and pick up my order right from their studios. This was a practice I'd started in my days as craft buyer for the Village Gallery. It was fascinating to see how kilns worked, watch a glassblower pull a rod of hot glass from their fiery "glory hole," or poke through someone's storeroom and see how their work had evolved. Still, since most of the country's craftspeople did not live within driving range, the shows were the way I found most of our artisans.

There were other, more specialized, shows which I attended off and on, but none became part of my regular circuit. The American Bookseller's Association annual show seemed like it would be a good resource, as we sold books that fit our Joie theme — some photography, a few kids' books, books of quotes, and joke and palindrome collections and silly books like *Mot D'Heures Gousses Rames* — Mother Goose in phonetic French. To my surprise, at the book tradeshow, most of the pages of the upcoming releases I looked at were blank. How could I tell if I wanted to order them? I learned the books I ordered mostly fell into the "gift" category, and were shown at the Gift or Stationary Show, and that publishers assumed that actual bookstores would order what they offered — the title and author all they needed to know. I attended the aptly titled Variety Merchandise show a few times too — but found it hard to keep a straight face when perusing the aisles of everything from irregular cedar clocks laminated with paintings of Jesus or cheese-cakey women, to booths of tube socks, condoms and batteries. Not quite our cup of tea!

Tea was found at the Fancy Food show. We sold a little "food," along the lines of Astronaut Ice-cream, champagne flavored gummy bears and chocolate cars, bugs, flowers and baseballs. I found these at the Gift Show where at the end of the day, the food booths were always crowded with buyers looking for a snack and the exhibitors did not look kindly on those who helped themselves too liberally, especially as most munchers had no intention of buying. When I went to the Fancy Food show I had my usual peanut butter sandwich and apple lunch tucked in my bag but from the first aisle I walked, I was urged to eat, eat, eat. There were at least ten aisles of booths from Italy, chefs cooking up dishes, flanked by huge wheels of Parmesan cheese and the show was a nonstop series of outstretched hands holding trays filled with samples. My peanut butter sandwich went home with me, but that was my only time at that show. It was fascinating and fun, but too focused on serious food to offer much I could buy for my silly store.

When walking the aisles of any show, you had to be very careful to be patient, to look everywhere and take your time. You might be reluctant to go into a booth with an overly aggressive salesperson, but you might then miss a great item. You might look the other way going down an aisle and completely miss a booth. You might not take the time to see what an item really could do. At Toy Fair one year, I walked by the Feisty Pets booth. Their "pets" looked like common commercial plush with oversized cutesy eyes. But I passed the booth again later and someone was demonstrating them. I watched their faces turn from cutesy/bland to snarling in a second and got in line to place an order. Smart buyers walked the whole show at least twice. Still, even after doing shows for years, and even when they got smaller, I'd have lunch with a friend/fellow buyer, and he'd pull something wonderful out of his bag and ask if I'd seen it. "No," I'd say, "Where did you find that?" "In the PlayVisions booth" might be the reply. "But I spent time in that booth — how did I miss it!?" Somehow, I would always miss something. So did he. Everyone did.

I mostly shopped alone, it helped me keep my focus. With another person, it was easy to be distracted by things we would never sell. I remember looking at a booth with Emily; full of hokey-looking sculptures of animals, plants, boats and things. A small sign labeled it "Art from Georgia." We read the big sign running across the back of the booth. It proudly proclaimed these sculptures were "Made Entirely of Crushed Pecan Shells." In an instant we were laughing too hard and had to leave. Walking with a friend wasn't usually all that productive though I had a few friends in the business I liked walking and comparing notes with, if only for a while. Inevitably I would want to spend more time in one booth than they did, and vice versa. My sister, my husband and my friends Danielle and Emily had great eyes, and I liked walking shows with them but only for part of a day. And of course my whole family was curious to see just what I was doing. They found it interesting, but after a few hours, they were more than ready to leave, even the most intrepid shoppers.

I kept a running list of booths I needed to go back to at a show, but I never crossed everything off it no matter how long I stayed. This was in part because a lot of time was spent just talking. I saw many of these people two or three times a year and some of my vendors became good friends. We talked about products, new ideas, what worked for us, what didn't, how business was going, fears, hopes, politics, the world, how your personal life was going, everything. I loved this part of shows. Those relationships were important to me. If I ran out of time, so be it. On some trips I had more luck than others, but I always found something and never left a show without feeling excited about getting my new finds onto the shelves of the store and introducing them to our customers. After days of walking, talking, looking, buying, going out to dinner, and more talking and walking, I was ready to go home. With my Joie de Vivre batteries recharged.

CHAPTER 13

# My Suppliers (Who Sells This Stuff to You?)

My suppliers were an extremely varied bunch. In the first years, I encountered a lot of old school long time professional salesmen, and I don't use the word salespeople because almost all of them were men. I was young, and they didn't take me as seriously as I would have liked at first, throwing around words like "honey" and "dear," though I wound up developing good relationships with many of them. These guys had stories to tell, as anyone in any business for years and years does. If I called one up to place an order, I could wind up on the phone for a good half hour, listening to tales of the way things used to be, and advice I hadn't asked for about how to price things, how to deal with special orders, and on and on. I often had to think of a quick reason to excuse myself, but I did enjoy their tales — at least the first few times I heard them!

Lydell Kahn, owner of Merry Thoughts in Bedford, New York was a sharp dresser, with an interest in music and culture. His company was based in Westchester County, NY, where I had grown up. We bonded over this, and became friendly. He was one of the "rent a table and just put your stuff out on it" guys, but it worked for his quirky selection of small toys from both Europe and China. We bought our bulldog guns, our Magic Gardens, our plastic ants, our bubbles and a lot of tin toys, German and Chinese, from him, and he was our source for Magneto, the company that made the magnetic Dancing Ballerina, the kissing spinning Scotty Dogs, the Seal with Ball and the strangely childlike kissing couple, Romeo and Juliet. He also ordered plastic Austrian snow globes just for us and, if a little perplexed by some of my special orders, he was always happy to oblige. But I was in business long enough for him to grow old, and eventually I realized he was asking me the same questions, not remembering much of what I said. He developed dementia in his eighties, and was forced to retire.

I became real friends with some of the sales reps who came to the store too, after weeding out the ones that didn't seem to get what I was aiming for with my merchandise selections. "But everybody's buying this," they would protest, when I glanced at something and said a quick no thanks. "It's going to be hot!" If I said "no thanks" to someone too often, I usually stopped seeing them. It seemed like a waste of their time, and definitely felt like a waste of mine.

Sales reps didn't seem important to me. It was just as easy to place my own orders directly with a company with one exception — greeting cards. Most large card companies did not go to the expense of printing complete catalogues, and this was years before internet ordering took over. Besides, that was a tedious way to order cards when it did. So, the sales reps I got to know the best were my card reps. I worked with one, Roger, on and off the entire thirty-six years. In the beginning, when I was still working alone, reps would show me their lines standing next to me behind the front desk. If a customer came up to buy something, we'd set down the deck and I would help them.

Eventually, card ordering happened in the back of the store. One of our best lines was Fotofolio, a New York company that represented photographers and artists, both current and past. At one point, they had over five thousand postcards, and Joyce Kennard, their Boston sales rep, would wheel in several big duffel bags full. When we sat down together, we didn't get up for hours. Within a few years, we timed our appointments so we could go out to dinner afterwards, and she was a guest at my wedding. I also learned a lot about art and photography going through that deck, flipping over an interesting painting, portrait or photograph to see who it was or who had made it. Joyce introduced me to Julie Galant, the owner of the company and we all wound up going out for dinner at least once during every show for years.

At least two of my suppliers started as customers. I met Rufus Seder, of Eyethink Inc. when he was a customer, buying all the optical specialties we had, including a collection of old Vari-Vue lenticulars, the flickery little pictures that changed when tilted, or had 3-D depth. They were common in the 1950s, found as prizes in boxes of Cracker Jacks and Cheerios, or as postcards of winking pin-up girls, political buttons and even record covers including the now highly collectible Rolling Stones LP, *Their Satanic Majesties Request.* I loved these when I was a child and was thrilled to be invited to the Vari-Vue NY warehouse where I sat on the floor and passed some happy hours going through their extensive collection, trying not to spend all the money I had. Rufus made similarly magical optical toys and we became and remain good friends.

Mark Weissberg had always been interested in movies and imagery and found himself drawn to our large collection of flipbooks. When he realized that a few of them were made by a guy from MIT that he knew, he started thinking — hey, maybe I could do this too. Here is an excerpt from a note he sent me after I told him we were closing up for good. "Without Joie there would be no Fliptomania. I remember like it was yesterday seeing that little flipbook showing a zoom-in to the Joie window, and realizing that THAT flipbook was made locally. 'Hey, Linda!' I asked, 'What's the story on this flipbook!?! It's local!!' To which you replied 'Oh, that's by Flipbook Eddie.' And the rest is the history of the rest of my life..." Mark's witty flip books became a staple for the rest of Joie's life. One in particular was quite the favorite with a certain young crowd, "How the Stick People Went Extinct." Its pages showed a couple of stick people getting intimate, and bursting into flames and I spotted more than one young boy drag in a friend to look at it, snicker, and make a quick exit.

Some of our craftspeople had rather eccentric philosophies. One maker of perfectly nice wood and metal mirrors and wall pieces had a personal statement that read: "It is our hope and goal, through continued refinement, growth, discovery and originality, to enhance the quality of life and the inner spirit of each man, woman, and child who comes into contact with an original Ivan Barnett design, bringing us, and the viewer peace, beauty, and a connection to his or her primal origins." I could never interact with him quite the same way after reading this. It seemed to be, let's say, a bit too lofty, as well as alarmingly grandiose, and we did not give out this "mission statement" when we sold his pieces.

One of our sales reps who became a good friend, Ellie, was wandering the streets of New York's Greenwich Village one weekend and noticed a man playing with some long-legged wind-up creature-like contraptions. She found them enchanting and bought one for herself and one for me. He packaged them in brown paper lunch bags and sold them for $28. They got to talking and she learned his name, Chico Bicalho. He was a photographer from Brazil and this little toy was a side project he sold on the street on occasional weekends. I loved mine and was thrilled when a few years later, a company I bought from, Kikkerland Design, teamed up with Chico to produce his pieces, leaving him time to invent many more, and also able to sell them at a lower price. We sold "critters" for the rest of Joie's life. They had many devotees and a few passionate fans.

A rather scruffy looking hippie, walked into the store one day, looked around a bit, introduced himself as Forkman and said, "I make something I think you'll want to sell." "I doubt it," I thought to myself, but before I knew it, he pulled two metal pieces out of his bag, placed one on top of the other and gave it a push. It spun around beautifully, simple and elegant. I looked closely. It was made from two bent and twisted forks. "Okay," I said. "You're right. That's really cool." We discussed price and I decided I would buy six. "Oh no," he said. "You have to buy twelve of them." I tried to be conservative on first orders, so began to press my case, and he finally agreed to sell six, "for the first time only." That seemed fair, so I wrote him a check, got his contact info and he left. I displayed one at the desk the next morning and in a few hours, had only that one left. I called him sheepishly. "You were right about the dozen," I admitted. He was nice enough not to gloat and soon returned with a dozen more.

Eventually Forkman moved down to Florida. He would call every few months to see if we were ready for another dozen and we usually were. A year or two down the road he had the dubious honor of being my only supplier to write me from jail. I hadn't heard from him in awhile and his letter began, "Hi Linda, As you can tell from this envelope, I'm in jail down here. I got a message from the friend who's picking up my mail that you had written to me. I got arrested with 5.5 grams of really good pot and one mushroom, so here I sit for a bit." He continued on, telling me he wasn't sure when he was getting out but would appreciate it if I could pay for my next order now. In cash. I declined. But he did get out eventually, and we remained his customer (for Forkmobiles only!) until the end. He was a lovely man, and his fork mobiles mesmerized many.

Another supplier arrived via *New York Magazine*. I was paging through an issue and stopped at their "Best Bets" page. Something that looked exactly like, and like nothing more than a spilled cup of coffee, was featured. I read the fine print; it was offered by an ice-cream/birthday party favor store called Jeremy's Place on the Upper East Side. I called and got Jeremy Sage, the owner, on the phone. "Do you wholesale these?" I asked. "I never have," he replied. "But I'd consider it. Where's your store?" When I told him the location he gasped. "I grew up a few blocks from there!" he told me. Soon I was selling his spills at the store and they were one of the most popular things we ever sold. And soon I found out that before opening his New York shop, he had been in theatre. "I was Jesus in Godspell for years," he told me. "Every night, I was Jesus." Now he was in the birthday party business. A few years later, he left that behind and concentrated on fake food full time. He eventually tired of that but another fake food company filled in so we continued to have a spilled cup of coffee on a display table leading at least one or two customers a day to tell us about it. They looked at us strangely when we asked if they would pick it up, but they always laughed once they did.

So many suppliers! I sold little bracelets made of telephone wire and crystal beads my husband made when we first started dating, back in the days when you could hit up a phone repairman and score strands of colored wire. Over the years, I sold some of his other creations too: drawings, collage, and amazing wind-up sculptures made from the pages of, and set in, old books. Two of my employees started a side business selling large earrings made from big plastic cherries and grapes. My friend Stuart Freeman, who I first met at the Gift Show where he sold his high design zany neckties and pillboxes, made an item for us for one Easter called Peep Show, a pink bunny peep wearing a faux leather bikini. We also sold his "Noel" necklace one Christmas, an alphabet in the shape of a Christmas tree, lacking — the letter L. And he made me dozens of small Joie related gifts, including a tiny pinball game labeled "Joie de Vivre, the best game in town!"

A glassblower customer regularly brought in a selection of teeny tiny vases and bottles made by his daughters for us to choose from. Another customer's very young daughter created something she called "Chicken-in-a-Blanket," using found slipper shells with a tiny rubber chicken tucked inside. She later added "Chicken Sleepover" — made with two chickens. I'm pretty sure we were the only store to sell her creations. Sadly, but not surprisingly, she tired of business at the young age of six and Chicken-in-a-Blanket was no more.

I made friends with many others too. Some of the artists I worked with rarely did shows themselves, I just met their representatives. But sometimes, we'd really hit it off over the phone and have long interesting conversations about work and life. I'd have to force myself to hang up and get back to the business actually at hand. But whether I saw suppliers and makers at shows, at the store, or only spoke to them on the phone, we developed real relationships. For many of them, we were one of their smaller accounts, but we ordered consistently, often for years, and always paid on time. They made it clear that they appreciated us. I know that I won't be able to keep up with all of them, but for the rest of my life, I'll be grateful that I got to meet all these interesting and talented people. I'll wonder about them, whether they're still making things or if not, what they're doing with their lives. And I know at least some of them of them will in some way remain in mine!

CHAPTER 14

# Oh No!

For years we sold a line of wooden puzzle boxes, handmade by an American artisan, shaped like hearts, moons, guitars, violins, and simple ovals and "beans." Each one had a small key piece, sometimes a tiny star, that pulled out as step one of the puzzle. Then you slid the top off, to reveal a felt lined interior, perfect for a special piece of jewelry, a favorite stone, a handwritten note, or some other special thing. Enough of a puzzle not to open easily, but not hard enough to be frustrating, they were made from an assortment of different woods, polished to feel as smooth as silk, and for their quality, very fairly priced. We typically ordered them several times a year.

I didn't know their maker well, but saw him once a year at an American Craft trade show, and we developed a friendly business relationship. His wife and daughter were often with him, and I think helped in the business some, but he always had a hard time keeping up with demand for his beautiful work. One year the daughter was in the booth alone. I asked after her parents and she told me her mother had died, and that her Dad wasn't yet up to doing all the socializing that happened at the show. I think (I hope) I wrote him a condolence note and he was back in the booth the next year.

A year or two later, I placed my usual order for the spring, but it didn't come. I called and emailed, getting no response, and finally

I got a note with an apology, saying it would ship by the summer, which it did. Then when I tried to do our Christmas reorder, I got no response. We always sold a lot of the heart boxes at Valentine's Day, so I tried again right after Christmas. I called, I emailed, I wrote a letter and finally I heard from him. He said he had decided to take a break from his production line and would be taking no orders for awhile. He thought he would start up again the next fall and I made a note to get in touch then.

I did. And it was the same story. Silence, no response. Now I started to worry about him. I had always liked this guy, and worried that the death of his wife was still a fresh trauma, several years down the line. But though I didn't know him that well, it seemed strange that he wasn't responding at all. We'd been his customer for at least ten years. Maybe he was ill. People our age were arriving at the "things suddenly go wrong" stage of health. Finally, after hearing nothing for a long time, I arrived at "maybe he died."

I started to google. He had lived in the same town for a long time, so I figured if he had died, there would be an obituary. And I didn't find one, but I did find something else, completely unexpected. A headline referencing a police report. Sex with a minor was mentioned. This was a shock. In connection with the person I knew, it seemed impossible, but of course I read on and it clearly was him. Oh no.

The details turned out to be a tiny bit less awful than I feared. He had been in internet contact with a minor, and they had arranged to meet. He had sent some explicit materials and a nude photo of himself. Her parents discovered their correspondence and the family was cooperating with the police; a detective posed as the girl online and set up a rendezvous. The police were lying in wait, but he had a crisis of conscience or nerve and drove back and forth in front of the house, then instead of parking, drove home. They arrested him anyway and he was sentenced to several years in jail for improper contact with a minor. That certainly explained his lack of communication. By the time I read about it, he was probably out.

Knowing what had happened shook me up. And now I faced a different problem. Should I try to order from him again? Part of me shrank from the idea and another part thought why punish him further? His wife had died, it had been hard, and though he had surely alienated family and friends, he'd served his time, and most important, he had not met the girl in person, but driven away instead. I couldn't really know why he had not followed through, but to me, that also spoke in his favor. I wrote him a letter, of course not mentioning that I knew anything, just saying we'd love more boxes if he was back in business but again, he never answered. I didn't pursue it this time. If customers asked when we'd get those beautiful boxes back in, I didn't tell them what I'd found out. "Sadly, we can't get them anymore," was all I ever said.

CHAPTER 15

# About The Things We Sold

Joie de Vivre's merchandise selection was confusing for some people right from the start. Inspired by both the Village Gallery, where you could buy an Eskimo soapstone sculpture for $5000 or a "Debbie Stone" for twenty-five cents, (a beach pebble with a flower, heart, etc. painted on by my sister Debra when she was in high school) and Mythology in New York, where you could buy a Japanese robot for $1000 or a flip book for $1.50 — price was not a determining factor in what I chose to sell. I made sure that much of our merchandise fell into a mid-range affordable category, but was as firmly committed to the postcard, the plastic fish and the flip over mouse, as the kaleidoscope, the Thomas Mann necklace and the porcelain teacup fairy. I remembered something Lore had told me about having special pieces in a store. "People may not buy them, but they will come to see them, bring their friends to see them, and often buy something else." Wise words that turned out to be true.

Looking at our handcrafted pieces, "Why does it cost so much?" was a frequent question. I found myself attempting to justify the cost of things made in America or Europe, often to someone who was clearly wearing a few thousand dollars worth of clothes and jewelry. Log book excerpt re $85 pair of earrings — *These are so expensive! says the woman who just told me she lost her 24-carat gold wedding ring in the Aegean Sea and is buying gifts for her trip to Moscow.* That could be annoying. Of course no one ever asked "Why is this alligator clicker only a dollar?"

Still, I realized that part of my job was to patiently explain, again and again. Other questions we heard a lot: What is this? (it's a cat paw, a kaleidoscope, it's a squid whisk, it's a mind-altering goldfish.) Why is this funny? (that one was harder to answer.) Does this thing turn off? (sometimes yes, sometimes no.) Is that twenty-five cents, or twenty-five dollars? (always dollars.) Does this really work? (Instant Irish Accent — ummm... sorry, no! Blue Q, the company we bought this from, and makers of Instant English accent, Look & Feel Canadian and other useful items, told me they had received more than one serious call complaining that their products did not deliver on their promises!)

We had many items people had not seen before, leading to one of the funnier questions we were somewhat regularly asked, "Do you make all this here?" I'd be so tempted to say yes. "Yes, yes we do! Right in our back room — we have a glass blowing studio, a book bindery, some woodworking tools, a potter's wheel and kiln, a printing press, and so much else back there!" But I never said that, because the question was if clueless, always sincere, and I think rooted in the feeling — where could all these cool things possibly have come from?

I was good at picking out the one item in a crowded gift show booth that would be perfect for us. "What's your minimum order?" I would ask. If it was $500, I would follow up, "I have a small store — what if I just want one dozen of one thing?" (This would total more like $100.) We did occasionally miss out on an item I wanted to sell but much of the time, as I explained why this and only this item would work for my store, companies were happy to accommodate. Because of this, we had hundreds of suppliers — one year I counted and we had placed orders with 453 vendors — spending $7955 with one, just $40 with another.

I seemed to be good at finding and selling things that didn't sell well in other stores. Acrocat comes to mind, a little plastic cat that sat on a sort of ping pong paddle. When you pressed a lever, the cat flipped up into the air, your goal to catch it and have it land back on the paddle, on its feet.

We kept one at the front desk so we could both play with and demonstrate it, and we sold a lot of them. One day when I called to reorder, I was told "We don't have any of those left." Assuming they were out of stock, I asked when they would be back and learned they'd been discontinued. "What?" I asked. "Why?" They were a relatively new item for the company and this seemed surprising, as they were so popular at Joie. "Oh, they didn't sell well," was the answer I got. "But — they sold really well for us!!" I protested.

I don't think it was because our customer base was so different than other stores. I think it was because if we were selling something that needed to be played with, we played with it. We pointed the bulldog "gun" at customers and made it bark. We squished the sticky wrestlers together so you could watch them slowly untangle. We scrunched and released the Boink so it flew across the store. Looking at an Acrocat in a clamshell package hanging on a wall is very different from seeing that cat fly up in the air while a laughing person tries to catch it. "But they sold so well for us!" was something I would wind up saying about many items, many times over the years, even cards.

I'd decided to sell mostly blank cards. We would have birthday cards, and greeted cards for holidays like Valentine's Day and Christmas, but I preferred the flexibility of the blank for everyday use. A beautiful shot of a waterlily floating on a pond? Could be used for sympathy or just a hello. A black and white photo of a young girl singing with her very large dog? Happy Birthday, or fun just to send to a kid or a music lover. Anything could be a birthday or a get-well card if you had a pen. Cards of couples could be anniversary, wedding, congratulations on your engagement — all you had to do was write a few lines yourself. This went over well with our customers, although unsurprisingly, people were the most reluctant to write their own sympathy cards. And I noticed something funny. Although our customers knew the cards were blank, they opened them and looked inside anyway. Presumably to see how blank they were?

Unfortunately, over the years some of our favorite card companies printed fewer and fewer designs as blanks. I would look at a new release and be bitterly disappointed to see that many of the great new images were only available greeted. When I'd call to complain, I'd hear that in fact, that's what 90% of stores preferred. "Our fifty best-selling cards are all greeted now." I of course was not able to convince card makers to ignore the cold hard financial facts. Happily, between our European sources, who no doubt because they sold to many countries with different languages, understood the value of a blank, and a few American companies who kept blanks in their line, we were able to keep our card racks filled.

A lot of our unusual stock sounded even stranger when discussed as though it wasn't. Speaking to a customer on the phone, we'd find ourselves saying, "Let me go in the back to see if we have a purple queen," or "You're looking for what? Three yodeling pickles and a Mona Lisa clock?" One day I called a man at his office to report on two things he wanted. I spoke to his secretary. What did I get to say? "Can you please tell Mr. X that the Zombies are here and ready for pick up, but the Pope has been discontinued. So, tell him we can't get the Pope but the Zombies are waiting." She went from serious to laughing in no time.

Also because of this, our sales slips often looked very, let's call it, enigmatic. We often abbreviated item names too and would wind up with lists like: positive spray, chocolate, one pencil, scrabble. Lost lions, point, keep calm. Eiffel cookie, gumby, fairy. Tooth erasers, tiny creatures, tin pins, moon. Another challenge — we all called things by different names. Sometimes I would look through the sales books and spend a good ten minutes trying to figure out what a "X" was. To add to the confusion, our penmanship suffered when we wrote quickly. Sometimes I just couldn't make a sales slip out at all and asked an employee to decipher their own handwriting. Sometimes they couldn't do it either. And in all fairness, they asked me as often as I asked them.

Sales of any particular item could be very unpredictable. I think most people are aware of the strange phenomena where the thought of a person you haven't seen in a long time flits through your mind… and then the next day, you run into them. That often happened with merchandise. I would glance up at something one morning and think, wow, we haven't sold one of those in a year. Later that day or the next, we would. There seems to be no scientific explanation for this. Some say it's just that you think about lots of people — or things you haven't sold — and then remember only the ones that actually wind up happening. It was certainly an uncanny yet not uncommon occurrence. But sometimes I would not have been thinking about a particular item at all and something strange would occur. From log book:

*We've been selling KitCat clocks for years, so long we even remember when they plugged into the wall with actual cords. We sell a few dozen a year at most, and can go for a month, even two, without selling one. Last weekend, I sold one on Saturday. It was the kind of sale where you don't interact with the customer beforehand — a man just walked up to the desk and said he wanted to buy one of the cat clocks. Later that day we sold a second one in the same fashion. That made two in one day after at least a month or more without selling any. Then on Monday, we got a phone call asking if we sold — KitCat clocks. This person wanted the more expensive jeweled version (genuine Austrian crystals.) We put one aside, and she picked it up the next day — the same day that another person called to inquire if we sold — KitCat clocks! This time I asked her if there had been any publicity recently about them as she was the fourth person in as many days to want one. No, she said; she already had one. It had been admired by a friend and she wanted it as a gift. On to the "hold" shelf went number four. And I swear I'm not making this up: an hour or two later a fifth person called. She wanted a red one, and we only sell black. I told her to call back if she couldn't locate one and we would special order it. That was a week ago. No one has called or come by for one since. It may be another two or even three months before we sell another. Strange...but true!*

The erratic nature of sales made it hard to decide how much to order of any one item. Another reason you didn't place big orders for any item is explained by the story of the programmable dog. You ordered that dog at the Gift Show, it arrived, and no one liked it, it was incredibly, annoyingly loud, the staff threatened to quit and you had to admit, you didn't like it either. You made some mistakes that could languish in stock for years unless you donated them or gave them away. That's one reason you never ordered the thousands of Singing Hamsters you eventually sold all at once. You learned to be cautious. Then you ran the risk of suppliers being out of a product as all their accounts desperately needed more at the exact same time.

I saw many things I thought were wonderful that just didn't fit our Joie de Vivre theme. Technically, I guess almost anything could have, because there is such a wide range of things that could bring any one person "joie." But we couldn't sell serious photography books about war torn countries or poverty, and how to manuals and Russian novels wouldn't have made sense either. Ditto serious kitchen equipment, bath towels, skin creams or slide-rules. Shoelaces would have made no sense — unless they glowed, and we did sell some of those. Ditto rubber bands unless they were in the shape of animals and we sold some of those. Or tape dispensers that were frogs or otters. We did sell some of those. And then, there were things we loved but didn't sell for other reasons.

CHAPTER 16

# About The Things We Didn't Sell
# (Or Hid In The Backroom!)

Some things just didn't fit into our Joie de Vivre theme, but there were others I decided not to sell. Included was anything featuring what I thought of as "bad words," whether scatological or just mean or disrespectful. Part of this was no doubt due to my genteel 1950s upbringing, but I also didn't want to offend anyone or have a younger child read a magnet and ask, "Mommy, what does f___ mean?" I could appreciate certain uses of that word, but I knew many people did not. And I was never comfortable with the word "bitches" unless applied to female dogs. even when I thought it was funny, as in "Namaste, bitches!" If you wouldn't see a word printed in the *New York Times*, chances were you would not see that word on something at Joie. This concern about words led to the occasional Joie-censored item — usually a magnet too funny to pass up. We would designate one as our display and carefully obscure the last three letters of "f___" with black tape, then give the customer an uncensored one from "behind the desk." We didn't do this often though; it was too easy to absent-mindedly put an unaltered magnet out.

Blue Q, one of our all-time favorite companies had, (and still has!) a winning way with various "bad" words, proudly peppering their socks, chewing gum, oven mitts, carry bags and just about everything they made. Luckily, they offered plenty of g-rated funny things, but it killed me sometimes, looking through their latest catalog, to see the many items I thought were funny but felt I couldn't order. The same thing occurred with our button companies. One button I remember was "If we really learned from our mistakes, I'd be a f____ genius by now!" "Why not just leave that word out? It's still really funny," I'd ask, but they just couldn't see it my waspy way. When little squeezy pooping animals were all the rage I also declined to sell them. I just couldn't imagine listening to jokes about them all day, as I knew we'd have to and I felt the same about farting toys. Just — no thanks.

Next, the disrespectful items. I think the first time I articulated this concept to myself was when a favorite vendor came out with something called "Pin the Ear on Vincent Van Gogh," a version of the classic birthday party game. Customers heard about it and several asked me when we would get it, thinking it was the kind of funny thing we would sell. But I didn't like it at all. Vincent Van Gogh had a tortured and difficult life. The idea of making money from and making light of his cutting off his own ear, when he barely made a dollar from the artwork that made him famous later just felt wrong. And though I had no similar respect or sympathy for George W. Bush, when a supplier made a Bush magnetic dress-up set that included a terrorist outfit post 9/11, that felt wrong too. The rest of the outfits were funny, but no one would see that product at Joie. Sarah Palin condoms were funny too, "as thin as her resume" but there was no way we would sell those.

Another awful product, regardless of your political persuasion, was toilet paper printed with the face of your most disliked politician. (The companies making this merchandise tended to be equal opportunity, offering both Republicans and Democrats.) For so many reasons — no, no, no!! Also no to "nerd glasses" — thick bottle style eyeglasses that are not so secret code for someone supposedly socially impaired and boringly studious. We had customers who wore glasses like that.

Sometimes an item didn't work for a very different reason — terrible packaging. I ordered a very cool and innovative clock, as an excerpt from our blog explains:

> *These clocks run on water! And they are also alarm clocks. Simple elegant design. They arrived, and on each box was an incredibly cheesy and embarrassing (to me anyway) picture of a very well-endowed young woman. Why?? Now I have to figure out a way to cover that part of the box so that if say, a mom wants to buy it for her son, or an aunt wants to buy it for her nephew, or a girl wants to buy it for her boyfriend — the box won't be a deal breaker! See below and pick any picture — would you want to see this on a box displayed at Joie de Vivre? Sorry, but I don't think so. Or, in the immortal words of a favorite website of mine: FAIL!*

I complained about this to the company and a few months later, a subsequent blog continued the story:

> *If you read this blog you may remember a post titled "Inquiring Minds Want to Know." Those minds were wondering why a nicely designed water-based clock would be in a box covered with cheesy pictures of bosomy girls. Update! Yesterday at the Gift Show I saw the company that makes the clocks, and noticed the clock was now packaged in a simple clear box. The company owner recognized me and said "I'm glad you came in, we wanted you to see this new box." (They had previously sent us large stickers to cover the girls.) He told me he had changed the packaging in large part because of my complaint. That made me happy. Sometimes I feel like I'm always complaining about things... it's nice to know that people are listening at least some of the time!*

I was definitely a complainer. I complained about things I liked that I thought could easily be better as above, or items we ordered that just didn't work. I never complained to the toilet paper type companies, they had their audience and I wasn't their customer. But if a company I bought from regularly offered something that I thought was out of line, I had to let them know. Sometimes they appreciated the input, other times not.

I ordered bath salts from a vendor we worked with. They were nicely packaged, printed with bath or water related sayings. "A woman is like a teabag, you don't know her true strength until she gets in hot water," was one, "There must be quite a few things a hot bath won't cure, but I don't know many of them," another. When they arrived I saw that each one had its quote source listed: teabag Eleanor Roosevelt and hot bath — Sylvia Plath. ?! Sylvia Plath struggled with both mania and depression and took her own life. Reading the quote again knowing it was hers I thought, well, she definitely found something a hot bath couldn't cure and couldn't bring myself to put her bath salts on display. I called the company. "Has anyone else mentioned it?" I asked, met with silence after explaining why I'd called. "Uh, no, no one has mentioned it," a customer service woman replied. A pause. "Who's Sylvia Plath, anyway?" I thought of the Bell Jar, the searing books of poetry. I tried again. "It's fine if you want to return them for credit," she said. I did. Win some, lose some, but I had to try.

We briefly had a couple of items that we absolutely loved but equally absolutely could not display out front. For them, we invented the "back room only" category. One of our French kaleidoscope makers also bought and sold antiques. He purchased an old desk and reproduced a tiny set of six lithophanes he found inside. When you held each porcelain rectangle up to the light, you saw an extremely instructive way of spending time with the opposite sex. It was quite the optical novelty, though the price was high and we sold only a few.

The all-time winner of best back-room item was the Surprise Chicken which sold for a very reasonable $10. I found Surprise Chickens in a small booth of Mexican goods at the New York Gift Show, very early on, cute ceramic chickens, about an inch and a half high, sitting on a base. I picked the little chicken up to find the base held — an extremely tiny, extremely graphic nude couple engaging in, we'll call it, a little fun. This chicken was a surprise indeed, managing to be adorable and provocatively sexy and I had to order some. They were later joined by a surprise bride, the little couple hidden under the tiny but voluminous white skirt.

Again, I couldn't display these chickens out front, so we took to telling customers who were friends that we had something to show them in the back room. Off we would go, and unsurprisingly, we sold a lot of those chickens and brides. But there was a problem with back-room specials. You couldn't be sure who might want to see them and it felt odd to go off into the back with one customer while leaving another standing behind, wondering why they had been excluded. And they really were quite graphic. I began to realize I might feel strange if an unknown to me male customer asked to go into the back to join the party. But while I was deciding what I should do, my Surprise Chicken vendor stopped selling them Their little angels and other ceramic figures were more popular and who knows, maybe they felt uncomfortable too. I have three chickens at home and treasure them, but the back room only goods era came to an early end.

It was briefly revisited awhile later when a European friend introduced us to the "Bougie Magique." We suspected this crazy birthday candle was illegal because it shot a fairly large flame a good foot up into the air before opening, transforming into a flower with pre-lit petals, that burned down while it played Happy Birthday. It was truly spectacular, but knowing even simple sparklers were illegal in Massachusetts, I couldn't imagine this candle wouldn't be. Its initial flame alone was way more intense than a sparkler. Still, it was amazing, and I thought the sparkler ban was silly as they are legal in almost every other state, so we told people about it, warned them to be careful, and kept the stock in the back. They were very popular, despite people driven crazy by the unending Happy Birthday tune (which would play for up to a week if directions to disable it weren't followed!) Someone we didn't know would call and ask if we had any of "those" candles and I would panic, thinking what if it's a trap? What if this is the sparkler police and I'm being set up? But it was always a customer who wanted something spectacular for an important birthday and just knew to keep it on the down low. A few years later I saw one in a big chain grocery store and thought — if they're selling it, it can't be illegal. A little research revealed that if a flaming sparkler — or a Bougie Magique — was set in a cake, it fell into a different category and became legal. Hold a sparker in your hand — illegal, stick it in a cake — fine. The candles went out front and that was the end of the era of back room only goods. Although... if I had ever come across those chickens again... I think I would have revived it!

CHAPTER 17

# Trends, Sensations, Singing Hamsters, Fads, Crazes and Classics

*Trend:* a general direction in which something is developing or changing. I often returned from a show with a trend report: *Matroushkas have become amazingly popular and everyone is making cute flash drives. Octopuses are on the rise, with owls and birds still holding their own. Squirrel and bacon related items appear to be on the decline.* Fish were on everything. Then everything would be southwestern for a few years, followed by Florida and flamingo themes. Color trends! Unicorns! Fifties women saying smart-alecky things! Quotes on everything! How and where these trends started was always a bit of a mystery — not unlike children's names. Suddenly everyone is Isabella, or Emma, or Joshua or Mason. People who think they're choosing an unusual name later discover just how many others chose the same one, it was just in the air somehow. In retail there was more overt copying, but a similar "in the air" explanation was doubtless a factor as well.

Trends begin slowly and last a while. They're broad; if owls were a trend you'd find owl jewelry, owl coffee mugs, owl wallets, and pens, and maybe an owl lamp, snow globe or owl shaped serving bowl. When quotations started trending they were on greeting cards, posters, compacts, cocktail napkins, mugs, magnets, everywhere. I ordered from a company called "Quotable" whose entire line was based on quotes, some of dubious provenance. I never really believed that Ralph Waldo Emerson said "Be Silly, Be Honest, Be Kind," or that "Thank you from the Bottom of my Heart" was a Latin Proverb. (When I asked the company for the source of the Emerson quote, they were — vague.) Trends might leave and return, not unlike skirt lengths and fashion styles in general. Unicorns were one, tremendously popular in the 1970s, only to fade and return with a vengeance (if such a term is applicable to a unicorn) decades later.

*Sensation:* something very exciting or interesting.

Other categories were shorter lived. Billy Bass, the wall mounted singing fish is a perfect example of a sensation. When I walked by one the first time and it spontaneously started to move its lips, singing "Take Me to The River," I stopped dead in my tracks. It was "intended to startle the passerby" and it certainly startled me. It was a rubber fish. How was it doing that? Its lips were actually moving to the words of the song. I was mesmerized — but did I actually like it? Did I want to order it? I couldn't tell. I kept returning to see it during that show, testing my response, and finally decided I had to order some. A dozen was the minimum order, and when they arrived at the store, we hung one on the wall right across from the front desk. The first person to walk by it stopped and stared, just like I had. They didn't debate as long though — they bought one instantly and we sold the entire dozen in one hour. I ran to the phone to order more. Billy Bass was a sensation. There had simply been nothing like it though animatronic singing animals eventually became more commonplace as the technology developed. (Interesting side note — Al Green said he received more royalties from that singing fish than from any other recording of the song.)

Billy Bass was how I learned about a distinction in the retail world between "specialty stores" and "the majors." Specialty stores were small businesses. They might have more than one location, or even a dozen, but they were owner run, highly individual stores. The majors were — major. Department stores like Macy's, mail-order catalogues with huge reach like Lillian Vernon, and the big chains, Toys-R-Us, the Home Shopping

Channel and QVC, Walgreens, Target and Walmart. These businesses got discount pricing and sold below "keystone," the wholesale price times two that was the industry standard. When I ordered Billy, I was told that the specialty market would have an exclusive on the talented fish for the first few months, but then it would hit the majors. I could still buy it, but it would be widely available at a cheaper price. It wasn't quite as dramatic a difference as it had been with Godzilla, but I was forewarned and they did let us continue to order our dozen here and there, even while sending thousands out to bigger stores. Once again, no one complained, though several customers did tell me that they had spotted Billy elsewhere.

*Singing Hamster:* a series of fuzzy singing and dancing hamsters made by Gemmy Industries and Funtime Gifts/Funtime Inc.

The Gemmy Industries booth, home to Billy Bass, was big and not a booth I spent much time in. Their offerings were very commercial, more than a little on the tacky side, the bad design side, the copies of better things side. Their displays were terrible and the second you walked in, a salesperson was on you. You had to fight them off just to take a look around which was annoying. But every so often they had a truly great item there, hidden among the decidedly less than great. And that booth was where I saw my first Singing Hamster, an item we would wind up selling several thousand of. Everyone who worked at Joie would fall in love with them and so would our customers.

Again, I didn't know it at the time. I looked at the little rubber creature, maybe eight inches tall, standing on its hind legs, wearing a bright orange knit hat. It wasn't doing anything but I'd always liked rodents and it caught my eye. Just as so many would later on in the store, I had to ask, "What does it do?" An obliging salesman squeezed the hamster's foot. It started to move its little front paws, singing Rapper's Delight. I didn't know the song (though I would soon find out that all my younger staff did) but I had to admit it was… arresting. I couldn't tell if it was great or awful but it wasn't a big investment and I placed an order.

Soon, we'd unpacked our first dozen and displayed one on the front desk. No one knew quite what to make of this little rubber rodent at first. He was not an instant sensation a la Billy Bass, but he began to grow on us with his high little voice and spasmodic movement. It began to be hard not to dance a little when someone squeezed his foot and he started to sing. Our feelings evolved, and soon, we knew for sure he was one of the greats and we started to love him. Someone would press his foot and two or three of us behind the counter would dance and sing along. We were powerless in the face of the Rapping Hamster's infectiousness and customers began to catch on as well.

Our second hamster was furry — a Kung Fu master, spinning nunchucks and singing, of course, "Everybody was Kung Fu Fighting," in an extremely cute and catchy way. He was an instant hit. Fuzzy was in. More fuzzy hamsters followed: Larry Love, Sexy Rex, Fly Guy, Wild Willie, and Wild Critter Cody Jr. who sang "I want to be a cowboy, and you can be my cowgirl" while twirling a tiny lasso. Sadly, the advent of all these fuzzy singers brought a tragedy. Gemmy replaced the original rubber rapper with a fuzzy version and it just wasn't as good, it lacked that tough rubber "street" feeling. But fuzz and fur worked well for the rest. They were ridiculous, funny, adorable, and affordable — the perfect ingredients for a Joie de Vivre smash hit and they were doing well in the wider world as well. Sadly, what typically happens when a very large company has a very successful product, happened. They ran it into the ground, adding new ones at a faster and faster pace, eventually making over ninety-six different Singing Hamsters. Inevitably, most of them were not so great. We only ordered the twelve hamsters we thought were worthy, though looking through their archive, I see I missed a few good ones. All ninety-six were never available at the same time, different styles came and went over a three-year period, and then they faded away. That's another thing about big companies. If they're not selling a LOT of something, out it goes. Too bad for stores like mine that would have happily sold those hamsters forever. (Perhaps realizing they had messed up a good thing, Gemmy tried to revive them several times but made them larger and "cuter" and they never really caught on again.)

*R.I.P.*
*Phat Daddy Mac – Rappers Delight*
*Kung Fu – Kung Fu Fighting*
*Wild Critter Cody Junior – I Want to be a Cowboy*
*Teddy – Take Me Out to the Ballgame*
*Nigel – I Want You to Want Me*
*Sexy Rex – I'm Too Sexy For My Shirt*
*Larry Love – I Think I Love You*
*Jacques – Ice, Ice, Baby*
*Wild Willie – Born to be Wild*
*Fly Guy – Hooked on a Feeling*
*Princess – Dancing Queen*
*Carly – She Works Hard for the Money*

(Note — the female versions were never as good. There was something disturbing about their make-up and hair… they were, in the immortal words of the Kung Fu hamster — "a little bit frightening!")

*Fad:* an intense and widely shared enthusiasm for something, especially one that is short-lived and without basis in the object's qualities. A temporary fashion, notion, manner of conduct, etc., especially one followed enthusiastically by a group.

*Craze:* an enthusiasm for a particular activity or object which appears suddenly and achieves widespread but short-lived popularity. An activity, object, or idea that is extremely popular, usually for a short time.

A true fad was popular everywhere, and usually inexpensive. Suddenly every school age child wanted the adorable Japanese erasers, or the rubber bands in the shape of animals, cars or dinosaurs that snapped back into shape after being stretched. Every kid and more than a few adults wanted squeeze foam balls or squishy cupcakes. Fidget spinners were a big one, a fad and craze that seemed to come out of nowhere. I saw them at a show, ordered a dozen, and they just took off — we reordered and soon were selling a dozen in a few hours, mostly to kids but again, also adults. We initially sold them for $10 and one mother said she had seen them for $20 elsewhere and online. Quite quickly they were available in tons of different colors and styles as companies competed to cash in. Then, like most true crazes, within a few months, they were everywhere — three for $5 on subway platforms and at street fairs in New York.

Every store has unique crazes. I don't know if other stores sold as many of the Little Fridge stationary set as we did, a cute plastic refrigerator, filled with "food" that was all something else; fruit and vegetable erasers, a milk carton measuring tape, maple syrup glue. It was the must have birthday present for our junior high customers for a good year or two, selling for about $15. (I just spotted one on Etsy for $250!) Other Joie crazes included the wind-up rolling truck that turned into a running dog, the mini movie viewers and the Backwards Bush countdown calendar, which ran down the days, minutes and seconds until George W. was officially out of office. But I'm quite sure no other stores had a Stardust craze. There simply weren't enough Stardusts in the world for that to happen.

Stardusts were "sound sculptures" and arguably the most magical thing we ever sold, small round pocked metal objects that chimed when picked up, and resonated deeply when tapped. They were made by Reinhold Marxhausen, an art professor from Nebraska. He made them all himself, so there was a very limited supply. Phyllis Morrison, a scientist who lived near Joie and had worked with Marxhausen at the San Francisco Exploratorium showed me hers, and told me how to contact him, and he agreed to sell us some. They qualified as a sensation too as no one had ever seen anything remotely like them before. Their $125 price, back in 1986, initially kept them from flying off the shelves, but then we started selling them rather quickly to a group of somewhat new-agey customers who glancingly referenced "the airplane game." We soon found this game was a glorified pyramid scheme and a stardust had become a prize trophy for local participants who did well. The airplane game crash landed, as pyramid schemes do, and our sales slowed back down, but Marxhausen was invited to appear on the David Letterman show and could not keep up with demand after that. Still, he sent us a dozen now and then until he developed dementia and could make no more.

*Classic:* Judged over a period of time to be of the highest quality and outstanding of its kind.

We had many items we sold through all our years in business. Some were classics already, the Etch-a-Sketch, Jacob's Ladders, fortune telling fish, the Magic 8 Ball and the Magic Garden. Some started as fads and ended up with staying power like Koosh balls and space tubes, thus entering the classic pantheon nationwide. Some were never quite a fad or a craze but just so good we sold them the entire time we were open, so they became our classics: the White Mouse Puppet, the Playful Penguin Race, the Rainbow Maker, the Pinscreen, the Devil Duck, the Dancing Ballerina, the Buddha Board, the Stylish Mustache set. Some things would certainly have become classics if they had remained available and we could have kept selling them. Sometimes a company would cease production of one of these items, underestimating its staying power, only to capitulate to customer demand and bring it back. Our "never say never" philosophy developed over time, as certain items "gone forever" unexpectedly returned. When we closed, I still had a file of special request cards, some dating back over ten years. A particular cat puppet, a tiki drummer, a microcopter, and ever so often, I got to call someone, say, "a long long time ago, you wanted to know if we ever got X in again," and hear a shriek of joy.

CHAPTER 18

# Our Most Unusual Product

The award for the "Most Inscrutable" item ever sold at Joie de Vivre goes, hands down, to the "Purrfect Paw," a life size mechanical cat paw made by Bandai in Japan that was discontinued before I ever set eyes on one. "What IS that?" was a frequent question when customers saw it for the first time, and our simple fun to say answer, "a cat paw!" didn't always satisfy them. "What do you *do* with it?" often came next. Sometimes we'd give them suggestions. Pretend you're a cat, play with your cat, pull it up your sleeve and pretend to be the victim of a transplant gone wrong. Sometimes we'd look them in the eye, pick it up and pull the little trigger that made the paw bend as if waving. Then we'd make it push something off our front desk. "Play with it," we'd say.

I saw my first cat paw at a branch of The Last Wound-Up in New York, a few years after I opened the store. It had been a favorite haunt of mine for a while, and years earlier, I'd bought myself my first plastic wind-up toys at its original location on Columbus Ave uptown. I'd heard they were going out of business and wanted to pay my respects. Browsing around the store, I noticed these... cat paws. They were packaged on cardboard, the "Purrfect Paw," and it was love at first sight. A perfect Joie item but I had never seen one at the Toy Fair or the Gift Show. Where had they come from?

I approached the man I took to be the manager. "I have a store in Boston and was wondering if you'd be willing to tell me where you get these paws from?" I asked. "I'd love to sell them." "They don't make them anymore," he said. He looked me over. "We're closing this store. I can sell these to you if you want them." And that's how I met Steve Agin, who was our cat paw source for the next thirty years. He had a lot of them though I didn't know that at the time. He was sparing with the details.

Our first "order" arrived, and everyone was quite taken with them. They quickly became a Joie favorite, though some customers found them creepy; not everyone thought they were "purrfect." Steve lived in New Jersey and had a garage and storeroom full of toys. The cat paw was a bit of an anomaly for him; his specialty was rare and collectible Japanese robots and character toys of all kinds. I'd call him and order a few dozen paws at a time. He would warn me that he didn't know how many he had left, usually inch up the price a bit. This became our standard routine. I was always a little afraid of the day he would say, "Sorry, they're all gone," and one day when I called, he warned me that there were very few left.

"How many do you have?" I asked, feeling that Joie de Vivre without these cat paws would definitely be a lesser place. "I think I have twenty cases left," he told me. "Think about it. You should probably just take them all." I agonized about this for a week or two. Did I believe him? Was that really it? Twenty cases was — a lot of cat paws. But I was pretty confident I'd be in business for awhile and the idea of not having them was terrible to contemplate. I'd been buying them for a few years now, surely he was telling me the truth. I called him back. "Okay, I'll take them all," I said. *Logbook entry: "I have to mail out a postal money order for $1300 to buy the last twenty cases of cat paws! Am I crazy?"* (Two responses to this from the future — nope, not crazy at all — and nope — those were not the last twenty cases!)

A few weeks later, twenty boxes were delivered to the store. New problem — where was I going to put them? Our stockroom was pretty full. And it would take years to sell them all. I decided I'd have to bring the bulk of them home and store them in my garage. I managed to cram the boxes into my little Toyota station wagon. They filled up every inch of space, but I lived nearby, so I figured my limited sight line was no problem, and hit the road. A few blocks from the store I drove through a yellow traffic light, and a few blocks after that, a police car pulled ahead of me and blocked my way. "Didn't you see me back there at the light?" he asked. "Umm, sorry, I didn't," I told him. There was no way I would have noticed. With the car so filled with boxes I could only see straight ahead. He looked in the car. I wondered if he noticed that all the boxes were labeled "cat paws" and if so, what crossed his mind. But he didn't mention it. "I'm only going to give you a warning," he told me. "But you go directly home and clear out this car."

Those twenty boxes lasted us a long time and cat paws became an iconic Joie item. Of all the things we sold, they were probably the one thing you absolutely couldn't find anywhere else. One day a little boy came in with a $20 bill clenched in his hand. He looked about nine. "I want to buy a cat paw," he told me. I got one from the back and handed it over. He beamed. "I've been wanting this my entire life!!" he confided and instantly became my favorite cat paw customer ever. We used their image on our anniversary party invitations, and on the front page of our website, even dedicating a whole webpage to them there. Suitably inscrutable. You clicked on "It's a cat paw!" and it took you to — a photo of the cat paw. That was it. No details.

One of our employees was a talented cartoonist who filled our logbook with his creations when it wasn't busy, and the cat paw became a staple of his work. His futuristic drawing of a couple buying a cat paw in 2013 (a date that actually seemed futuristic to us back in the 1980's) was an instant Joie classic.

We finally did sell the last one. Joie without them just wasn't right. I decided to call Steve in hopes that another box or two might have turned up and that turned out to be a good call. "Yeah, I've got a bunch," he told me. "But I think I'm pretty low." "That's what you told me last time!" I said, a little indignantly. "Don't you remember? I bought the last twenty cases!" "Well, I found some more," he replied calmly. "You have to understand —

I have a lot of inventory. I'm never quite sure about what might be where."
I couldn't stay mad. Eyes on the prize. We had sold them all. The important
thing was — we needed more and he had them. I started doing small
orders again, and this kept up until the year before we closed.

"I'm pretty sure I have only six boxes left," he told me when I called
for the last time. "For real." I decided to buy three of them, and they saw
us though our last day. We had maybe two or three left after I gave some
to friends and a few customers, and they are in my basement, backup for
the two I have upstairs. It was indeed an odd item, the very definition of
quirky, and we loved them and completely agree with spokesperson Izumi
Nagano at Bandai headquarters in Tokyo, who explained: "It is something
that is unique and brings both playfulness and joy."

*Author's Note: One morning while indulging my quaint habit of looking at
the actual Sunday newspaper, I saw a photo and mention of a cat paw letter
opener belonging to none other than Charles Dickens, soon to be on display
at the New York Public Library. It was an actual cat paw handle, made
from the paw of a beloved (& deceased) cat. And it's engraved "C.D. — In
Memory of Bob, 1862." Quite a strange way to honor a pet. And quite possibly,
the original cat paw item? Perhaps the first in a series that led to our
Purrfect Paw??*

# CHAPTER 19

# Kaleidoscopes

From the logbook: *Customer looking at kaleidoscopes — "What are these? Flashlights?" (Actually, most people think they're bongs...)*

When I opened the store in 1984, we had some beautiful kaleidoscopes on the shelves, the work of four different makers. I was lucky to begin my business just when these optic wonders were being rediscovered and re-invented by American and European craftspeople, transitioning from inexpensive kid's toys to sophisticated and beautifully made objects. I displayed them right by our front desk as I knew I'd not only need, but want to talk about them a lot. Hardly anyone knew what those cylinders made of metal or marbled paper were. When customers looked through one for the first time, they were entranced. A common sight in the early days of Joie? A bunch of adults standing by the desk with tubes of various sizes held up to their eyes.

As a child, I loved looking through the simple cardboard scope I'd found in a basket of toys at my Nana's house. That was the only kind of kaleidoscope you could find back then, unless you were an antique dealer with a good eye. Some of the original scopes made by Charles Brewster and the later American maker Charles Bush, were still out there, packed up in attics or sometimes on shelves, but the art had died out. No one was making anything like those beauties in the 1950s.

Charles Brewster had almost accidentally invented the kaleidoscope in 1815 while doing experiments on light polarization. He created the term from three Greek words: kalos (beautiful), eidos (form), and skopeo (to look at). Once he had perfected his invention, he believed it would not only be used by artisans designing Oriental rugs and other ornamental goods, but become popular "for the purposes of rational amusement." He was right about both. Kaleidoscopes became a huge craze. They were small and portable and people took them everywhere, resulting in complaints of distracted people immersed in their new devices, walking into walls or bumping into cyclists and pedestrians on the streets of London. For many years, manufacturers couldn't keep up with demand.

For awhile, keeping up with demand was hard for us too. These new kaleidoscopes were all made by individual craftspeople and there was a limit to how many they could produce. By the late eighties, there were almost a hundred individual makers in the United States, and just as in every world, some rivalry and politics crept in. When one maker branched out, opened a small factory and started manufacturing their own line of scopes and other optical objects in Massachusetts, many of the purists were taken aback. Mass production — sacrilege! Still, for the most part, it was a very caring and lively group of people, makers and retailers alike. I made some good friends and knowing kaleidoscope makers personally made selling their work even more rewarding. I loved to talk about them with customers, some of who were on their way to becoming serious collectors.

One day a woman walked in. She said she was looking for a little something for her nephew and noticed the kaleidoscopes. "What are those?" she asked, and after an hour or so, left the store with four of them. This was a big sale for us and I was quite excited, but a few days later, I spotted her outside the store with our shopping bag. Oh no, I thought. She's regretting her quick decision to buy, and is going to ask to return them. Anticipating resistance when I said we only gave store credit, I watched her apprehensively as she entered the store. And yes, "I bought these here the other day and I'd like to return a few," she began. But then she continued, "I love them, but I'd like to trade one or two back for different ones." "Of course," I said, and she walked out of the store with not just the exchanges but a few others. And she became our first, and our biggest collector, buying pretty much one of every scope I ordered.

Within a few years of opening, we were selling the work of at least twenty-five different artists, and new ones were arriving on the scene all the time. We never because a true collector's paradise though, because I only wanted to sell scopes I liked, and there were some I just didn't. The outside might be spectacular, but if the inside was boring or blurry, I said no. There were plenty enough scopes I liked to fill our shelves. And some scopes retailed for a thousand dollars or more. We rarely stocked those though I did order a few, all of which eventually sold. My rule of thumb was, would I be happy taking it home if it didn't sell? If the answer was yes I'd risk it. But I wasn't obsessive about selling everything ever made, so while we sold to collectors, we were rarely the first place they'd look.

I always tried to have a good selection of cardboard scopes for kids too. Naturally, few customers wanted to introduce a child to a first kaleidoscope that cost serious money. Happily it wasn't that difficult to find good, inexpensive ones. I was fussy about mirrors though, the image had to be clear and many inexpensive scopes were not. I never understood why as there were companies making them for the same price with decent mirrors. Giving a child a blurry scope seemed the same to me as giving a xylophone that was not in tune. Would you try to spark an interest in music that way? Many of our "kids" scopes were really quite lovely, and I know some wound up in adult hands.

After a few years, our first collector invited me to her home to have dinner and see her collection. She had acquired a rare contemporary parlor scope and I was eager to see it, and to revisit the many pieces she had bought from us. I wondered how she displayed them all. When I got there I found out. It was kaleidoscope chaos. They were all over the place; shelves and side tables filled with them, and an overflow just sitting on the floor. It was not what I was expecting, and "Wow, you really have a lot of kaleidoscopes!" was about all I could think of to say. We had a nice meal and fun discussing her collection. Her prize parlor scope was not on the floor and we spent a lot of time looking at it that night. It was a real beauty. Eventually though, like many collectors, she got to a point where she had enough, and we didn't see her as often after that, although she never completely lost interest and did come shop for other things.

A kaleidoscope organization, The Brewster Society, began to run an annual convention for makers, retailers, and collectors and fans. It was a multi-day event that took place in a different city each year, and I went when I could. One year it was held close to Boston and a few attendees came afterwards to visit Joie. One was a Japanese man who spoke little English. He was planning to open a kaleidoscope museum in Japan and had come to the store to see an antique scope I had for sale, but was very interested in all the older pieces I had in the back. We wound up in the stockroom, I pulled them all out, and soon the floor around us was littered with kaleidoscopes.

We weren't able to communicate too well, but eventually, I wanted to get them off the floor and back to their places so I asked which ones he wanted to buy. "All," he said. I blinked. "All?" I said. I pointed down to the floor. "All these?" "Yes," he said. "You will ship to Japan." "Ummm, okay," I said. "I will pay later," he said, gave me his business card, and left. There was a lot of back and forth over the next few months about final pricing and credit cards. I set the scopes aside but didn't pack them up, not at all sure this huge sale would go through. But finally it did and at $9,000, it remains the biggest single purchase we ever had.

Interestingly, Japan became a hotbed of kaleidoscope innovation and makers. Artists there made incredibly intricate creations, most so expensive that I would never be able to sell them, not even counting the cost of shipping them from abroad. At the same time, many American makers I bought from were retiring or moving on to other things. And our customers who had collected scopes found their disposable income had changed. Or that maybe twenty or thirty was enough. Or that they weren't looking at them as much anymore. We had one collector who visited us faithfully every summer from Philadelphia and always bought a few, but eventually he just wanted to tell stories and talk about the scopes he had bought in the past.

The wave of interest that started in the 1980s lasted maybe twenty years but I never lost my love for kaleidoscopes, and we were able to maintain a good, if smaller selection until the end. We always had customers discovering scopes for the first time, and I never got tired of talking about them with anyone who was genuinely interested. Helping a customer pick one out provided me with the chance to stand there and look at them too, and that never failed to remind me just how beautiful I found them. Just a few months before we closed, one of our regular customers suddenly picked one up and got hooked. He'd been in the store numerous times, but never really looked at them, and it was a nice "last time" for me, turning him on to various styles, and having a chance to look through them all yet again myself.

I have a small collection at home now, along with a list of "wish I hads," but older makers retired, and many of the scopes I always thought I'd take home "someday" were suddenly no longer available. And I didn't want them on the floor and under the couch so I chose carefully. I don't look at mine often but when I do — the years between me and that little girl with her cardboard scope at Nana's house disappear. Metal, wood, or cardboard, the magic's still there.

TRUE CONFESSIONS #3

## *Devil Duck*

*(Editor's note: It appears this page was not in the original manuscript, in fact, was not even written by the author, but we were contacted by someone claiming to be a representative of its writer who said we'd put it in the book — if we knew what was good for us.)*

I was the true icon of Joie de Vivre. Forget the white mouse, the cat paw, or that little blue fairy. It was me! The devil duck!

I was born in 2000, pretty far away, in China. I got lucky — I was delivered with eleven of my siblings to Joie de Vivre. I would disappear when someone "came to the back" to get a new devil duck for a customer, so I never had to leave. I was at the store for years and years and years. No white mouse can say that. I was king of the stock room. We had a blast back there, we rearranged stock, made the printer go haywire, loosened up the overhead lightbulbs, anything to bewilder the people working there.

I was really popular. Everyone wanted me. The place that made me figured they could make a lot of money if they made a lot of different kinds of me. You know, camouflage devil ducks, pirate devil ducks, a tattooed devil duck, different colored devil ducks. One was spotted like a leopard. And get this — one of them glowed in the dark and one of them — invisible! Then they made other stuff, inspired by — me. Pencil toppers. Bandaids with pictures of me. An air freshener for a car — in the shape of me. Oh yeah, and a Christmas ornament too. That was pretty sweet... but you know, I am still the best.

Personally, I think the greatest thing they made was these little tiny versions of me. Really small, smaller than a dime. I liked those. I could blame all the store "accidents" on them! It was almost like having a bunch of kids, but then they had to stop making them. Too dangerous or something. Real kids could eat them. Someone at the store ripped the wings off a fairy and glued them on one of those little guys – pure genius! It flew over the register and everyone wanted it, but they wouldn't sell it. Or make more. I think the fairies complained.

I'm a bona-fide classic. Proof? In the end, I'm the only one that company still makes. No big surprise. After all, I'm the best. Everyone at Joie de Vivre was pretty darn fond of me, but this one woman really a lot more than the rest. I think they called her Nancy. She took one of my best friends home and I'm telling you that duck lived like a king. Every Sunday he got to go for a drive, get an ice-cream soda. Every Sunday. I had to make do with chocolate kisses at the store. And he got his picture taken a lot too. To this day, he still gets the royal treatment. Maybe not every week now, but often enough for my tastes. Hmmm... perhaps I will pay him a visit now that I am retired.

I was on the front page of the website too. I was pretty much into everything. On the fax sheet, on lots of posters and postcards too. Always at the end of the newsletter, every single month. I got to pose in lots of different situations. On the beach, in an ice-cream cone, with a bunch of rabbits, taking part in a maypole dance. Sometimes this yellow duck joined me. She was pretty sweet, but I don't know what happened to her at the end. I hope I see her again sometime.

I really had a lot of fun living at that store. I had plenty of time to think up fun things to do and couldn't resist. Loved taking the price stickers off all the other rubber ducks. Someone would bring one up to the register and ask how much it was. They'd have no idea and it was fun to see them try to figure it out. Or I'd mark one $50. People would ask what the deal was. The staff didn't know what to say. Hiding the scissors or the hammer was good too. Sometimes it took them a day or even more to find them. And maybe this was a little mean, but there was this one lady working there, she was terrified of mice. Real mice, not those white puppets. I'd take the tops off the food containers in the backroom to encourage the mice to come by for a little snack. This lady, I think her name was Jenn, if she saw a mouse, she would scream and run. No one ever suspected me, they always thought it was one of them who did it.

When the store closed up, I got put in a box and brought back to the owner's house. I'm living in a basket with a bunch of old Happy Apples now. They're pretty cool. We get along. I kind of miss the store though, I was a lot more famous there. It's quiet here. Sometimes people don't even see me in that basket of apples. And I got quite a shock the other day. I overheard the owner talking on the phone with a friend about me, saying my family had been discontinued. No more devil ducks. Has the world gone mad?

But remember that woman I mentioned? Nancy? The one who my cousin got all the ice-cream from? She made a whole book about me. I'm right on the cover. And it has all the pictures from over the years. I think it's going to be a best seller. They're going to want interviews. And probably some travel, appearances, that kind of thing. I'm up for it. I think the best is yet to come.

CHAPTER 20

# Customers, Part One — Adults

I can't possibly do justice in one chapter to our wonderful customers. An interesting, thoughtful, eccentric, captivating, occasionally annoying, and great group of diverse people. Some lived in the neighborhood, some worked on the block, some came from afar just to visit the store. Some shopped at Joie the entire thirty-six years we were open, others found us years later, after moving to town, or simply noticing us for the first time, "discovering" the store after living across the street for ten years. We had customers who moved away, but came to shop and say hello on every visit back to town; some of them we saw more often than our local patrons. When a person said, "It's so nice to be here, I moved, and haven't been in for awhile," I would ask, "Where did you move to?" The answer was equally likely to be Lexington, a mere few miles away, or much farther; New York, California, Paris or London.

Joie was just outside of Harvard Square, and many assumed our customers were mostly students but that was never true. We had students of course, but also teachers, artists, grandmothers, chefs, scientists, musicians, old, young, women, men — I was never able to characterize them as any one type. And they all saw the store in different ways. Some would walk in, see the rubber ducks and wind-up toys and immediately, we were a kid's store. Others would buy a kaleidoscope, print, or fragile piece of glass and say, "I would never bring my kid in here!" Some never looked at the "nicer" merchandise, only the silly stuff, while others just wanted the handcrafts. I understood, but I was happy when people liked our whole range of goods. One sales slip I kept a copy of featured a necklace for $250 and a rubber chicken for seventy-five cents, and the customer who appreciated both was our kind of person, though we appreciated every purchase, whether a postcard, a fortune fish, or something bigger.

People had very different shopping styles. Some were serial purchasers, always buying the exact same thing; the wedding scope, the birthday bear, the rainbow maker. They liked it, it worked, so they gave it to everyone. One MIT professor bought fuzzy singing animals for his graduate students when they finished their studies though to his sorrow, the company could not be convinced to make a fuzzy singing fruit fly — his field of expertise. Another professor bought multiple tin wind-ups for his students to dismantle and put back together. One customer could pile up a few hundred dollars worth of things in five minutes, while another took an hour to choose one card or small toy. Some could easily make up their minds, for others, it seemed more like torture.

We once had a woman spend almost three hours choosing a few glass Josh Simpson planets. It's true we had a dozen or more, and true, they were all quite different, but three hours of indecision is a long time and we breathed a sigh of relief when she finally made her choices. Another was having trouble choosing between the three Cat on a Couch salt and pepper shakers out on display. I knew we had more in the back, all slightly different, but decided not to overwhelm her and she finally chose one and left. A few hours later she stopped back in and asked to use our bathroom. Quite a bit of time went by. I went to check on her and found her standing almost paralyzed, staring at the back stock of cats she hadn't seen. I made up some excuse, "these just arrived," and she snapped back to life and went on her way.

Another interesting phenomenon was the question, "Do you have more of these?" Sometimes it meant the person wanted five or six, and other times they just did not want the one that had been on display.

Of course, it never helped when a staff member said, "I'll get you a nice new one from the back," only to return empty handed saying — this is our last one — inescapable subtext — since we don't have a nice new one, would you like this old thing? Some customers' response would be "Wow, the last one, I lucked out!" while to others it was the kiss of death and no matter how perfect its condition, they didn't want it. We learned not to try to convince them the item was fine; their desire for a new one was not necessarily rational.

Sometimes a regular customer would surprise me by picking up an item saying, "Wow, this is great, when did you get this?" It was often something we'd been selling for years, something I never would have pointed out to them because I'd assume they'd seen it many times. On a single day, two customers who had shopped at the store forever "discovered" that we sold wind chimes — an item we'd had almost since day one. This was why it was so important to talk to people, try to make suggestions even if they said they'd looked around and found nothing. Of course there were times when someone could not find the right thing. I expected that. But they usually had not "seen everything." I once sold a woman a poster she loved. She was standing right next to it but hadn't turned her head that way.

One fun thing about having a store in Cambridge was the annual influx of visitors, students and academics in town for summer programs. They came from all over the country and the world. It was a good opportunity to play "guess that language," or practice your elementary French or Spanish, though we had to resort to drawing pictures more than once. Some returned a few summers in a row, becoming temporary "regulars." And there were plenty of American visitors too, coming to Boston for a little history or to visit family or friends.

Of course all our customers weren't fun. Often it was obvious that someone had real problems, making it easier to be patient, although I guess that others we found trying had problems too, if a lesser sort. We gave nicknames to some. Violin man, a middle-aged guy never without his violin, stood at the counter for what seemed interminable amounts of time, especially when certain female employees were working. Or "Oh no, it's Puppet Boy!" Puppet boy had a talent for making the most innocent bear, mouse, or raccoon puppet seem unbearably lewd, manipulating them while staring directly at you in a suggestive manner. One guy came in for years with a succession of different women that we eventually concluded must be Match dates. (The store was a fun place to meet on a first date.) He dragged every single one over to the Porn for Women book, a harmless volume with photos of handsome men washing dishes and bringing home flowers, but I don't think he ever found love. There was $2 Lady, who despite her expensive clothes, wanted to spend "about $5" on a "nice gift for a psychologist." She once found something for $2, hence her name. We were generally happy to try to find something in any price range for anyone, but she typically shot down most suggestions and was a pro at trying our patience.

Some customers were just eccentric, delightfully or otherwise. We had a magician who would astound us every time he came in, bending quarters, reading our minds, making dollars appear and disappear from our outstretched hands. Rabbit Man bought every rabbit item we had for his rabbit-collecting wife. Chicken Man pulled a clear trailer behind his pick-up, filled with silly chicken items. Another customer amazed us making teeny tiny origami animals for us, hands behind his back. And we met Pete and Fred, two guys who worked at the local grocery store. Once a week, after getting out of work, they visited all the stores on the block. They were decidedly odd and we found them rather alarming at first — were they casing the joint? We soon realized they were harmless and got used to their rituals; they walked around the store, picking up the same few items each time, making the same comments, saying hello to us by name — and if one of us was maybe at lunch, they would always ask, "Where is Jenn?" or "Where is Nancy?" Once a week, every week, for years.

Every so often we became aware that we were seeing a lot of a particular customer. Actually, "customer" in this case was not quite the right word as they generally didn't buy anything. But someone would come in, head for something — our fortune telling Q cards, or often the big xylophone on our front counter. They rarely looked at us or responded to our hello, but suddenly we would realize we were seeing this person almost every day. And that they were doing the same thing every day. We had a gentleman who came in each morning, played the xylophone awhile, wandered to the back of the store, put on the hologram eyeglasses, then took them off and left. He did this daily for a month, then must have found a new ritual, and we didn't see him again. One woman came in daily to consult the Magic 8 Ball. Just an odd little part of the retail biz.

Hypochondriac lady could talk about her various ailments for a good hour, and often did if it wasn't busy and you couldn't get away. Another customer invariably came in shortly before we closed. She always seemed dissatisfied, would take her time finding gifts, asking for help but rejecting our numerous suggestions. Then, though forewarned about the time, she wanted them wrapped, acting put out and surprised when we said we needed to close. (We did stay open late at Christmas. One year she came in at our usual closing time, and asked what time we closed. When we said 9 pm she looked disappointed!)

Some created chaos. One woman in particular left a trail of destruction everywhere she went. She took things apart and left them lying there, or carried things to the other side of the store and abandoned them, almost never buying anything. But without actually following her around and taking things out of her hands, there was no stopping her so we just took a deep breath when she came in. And spent a half hour straightening up when she left.

Our last memorable eccentric was youngish, normally dressed, and started coming in maybe two or three years before we closed. She entered and stood near the front door, staring fixedly in one direction, without appearing to focus on any particular object. We'd ask if she had any questions but she never responded. She would sometimes stay as long as twenty minutes, sometimes just five. We began to refer to her as Quiet Girl, and though we tried to greet everyone who came in with at least a hello, we knew something was off and stopped greeting her. Then, one day, she became, dramatically, Quiet Screaming Girl, suddenly shouting, "Fuck off!" and "Nazi Regime!!" The other customers slowly moved towards the back of the store, as far away as they could get. She then stormed out. It never happened again but from then on, whenever she came in, we were quite on edge.

We had famous customers too, though I didn't recognize all of them. One busy day, I looked up and the tallest man I'd ever seen was coming in, bending his head just to get through the door. I nudged Barb, working beside me. "Look how tall that man is!" I whispered. Her eyes widened, but not for the same reason. She came from a sports family. "It's... Bill Walton!!" she exclaimed, "Of the Celtics!" This was Boston's pro basketball team but meant nothing to me. "Oh," I said. "He sure is tall." He turned out to be living around the corner and bought himself some of our kaleidoscopes. He was a very interesting guy, though I was always quite distracted by his height. He was almost two feet taller than me.

Aerosmith shopped at Gypsy Moon on our block and stopped in several times. I was actually a little fuzzy on them too, but everything about their demeanor and presence screamed "Star!!" Others were more under the radar — at first. Two regular looking middle-aged men were in one day, browsing with a friend, and clearly enjoying our selection of goods. Suddenly a laugh rang out. Everyone in the store snapped to attention including me. It was so familiar, where had I heard that laugh before? The guy laughed again, and a bell went off in my head — Car Talk! It was the brothers from Car Talk! I loved that show, listened to it all the time. And I felt acutely how difficult it is to act normally when a very well-known person approaches the desk to pay. I guess I didn't act like a complete fool as they came in again many times.

It was easy to act normal if you didn't recognize someone. One Sunday there was a cute young couple in the store, and the woman asked me about an embroidered pillow. It was on the expensive side, but I told her we had a few more, and asked if she'd like to see them. She looked them over. Much to my surprise she said, "I'll take them all. Can you hold them at the desk while we look around?" Later I noticed a pair of young women approach her. "I never do this, and I don't want to bother you," one began, "but I love your work." Oh, she must be in a band, I thought. I was long past knowing who was who in the music world, but that made sense. She selected a few more things and checked out. When I ran her credit card, I looked at her name. Emma Watson. The Harry Potter films! Hermione!

Another famous customer I somehow didn't recognize at first: Yo-Yo Ma. He came in occasionally, an extremely gracious, kind (and handsome!) man, who bought a few things with a minimum of attention from us. When I finally ran his credit card myself for the first time, I'm sure I lost my composure somewhat. Oh! That's why he looked familiar. We got friendly enough to joke around over the years, and one time he told me, "You know, I think I'd be pretty good at working here." I knew he meant it and he was right — he really enjoyed the store. I was encouraging. "If you ever find you need a part time job, we'd be more than happy to give you a try." Sadly, he never applied.

There were Timothy Hutton and Robert Reich, John Malkovich, and many well-known authors, scientists, and professors, but the person I was the most nervous about meeting was my cartooning idol, Roz Chast. For once, I was forewarned. One of her close friends had given her gifts from Joie (thrilling enough!) and she wanted to visit the store. I was terrified she wouldn't like it, might look around for a minute or two and leave. This happened sometimes and it didn't usually bother me, but if it was Roz Chast, crushing. My second-choice name for Joie had come from one of her cartoons, The Minutes of the Meeting of the Graham Cracker Club. Happily, she loved the store. She was quiet, likely shy, but spent a good hour, bought some things and was gracious with me when I tried to express how much I absolutely loved every single thing she had ever done.

All told, the vast majority of our customers, the ones that got us through thirty-six and a half years of business, were wonderful. They brought us cookies, meringue mushrooms, birthday cakes, flowers and books. We had fun, and great conversations with them, getting to know some of them quite well. We'd call out their names when they walked in the door. "Bob Purdy!" Linda!" Kitty!" "Lisa!" Many families shopped at Joie, and being in business so long, we got to see their children grow up. Some of those kids came back years later with their own kids. Hearing someone say, "This was my favorite store when I was your age," to a five-year-old was both mind blowing — where did the time go? — and heartwarming. I loved the shows, and finding new things, but most of my working days were made interesting and rewarding by the people who walked in the door.

CHAPTER 21

# Customers, Part Two — Parents & Kids

Observing customers from behind the desk at Joie, I sometimes felt like a social scientist, collecting data on various psychological experiments. How did people make decisions? How did they think about buying gifts for others and why was it so difficult for some? Could I make an unhappy person happier? How did gift-shopping couples relate to each other? And maybe most interesting, how did parents interact with their kids?

I did not conceive of Joie as a children's store, and there were many breakable objects within easy reach of young hands. However, we wanted people to feel free to touch and pick things up, carefully of course, and the same went for younger kids. If a parent was next to their child, helping them to hold or look at something, that was fine with me. But Joie de Vivre was decidedly not a place to let your two- or three-year-old do whatever they wanted — not that any place outside of a supervised playroom really is. And most kids found the store fascinating. More than one was dragged out screaming because they did not want to leave.

Sometimes we would see a very young child reaching for something high on a shelf and we'd look around. Uh-oh. Who was this kid with? Sometimes we just couldn't tell. If there were several customers in the store and it was not obvious who the parent was, that was a bad sign. I would try to get around it by speaking directly to the kid, saying "It's okay if you touch that, but only if your mom or dad is helping you," intending that the parent would overhear and come to the rescue. They usually did, especially if I had to say it more than once, though sometimes the parent then forcefully said to the child, "The lady doesn't want you to touch that!" The child would then look at me and start to cry, instead of at Mom or Dad. Gee, thanks!

As our neighborhood transitioned away from rent control, we had more families where both parents worked, and started to see more nannies and babysitters. They often used us as a sort of entertainment center, bringing the kids and letting them play for an hour. I frequently had to play detective with them as well. Who was with who? You had to feel sorry for those who were clearly overwhelmed by their energetic charges, but letting a kid run wild did create difficulties beyond danger to the kid and our merchandise. One parent might be telling their child not to touch anything while another kid the same age was happily wreaking havoc with the penguin race. "Not fair!" It was also confusing for kids told not to touch anything because "These are not toys!" That was all well and good when looking at ceramic coffee mugs or salt and pepper shakers, but rubber ducks? One day I overheard a very young boy object to his mother. "But... rubber ducks are toys!" I had to give him credit for pointing out the truth.

The "I want this!" scenario was also interesting to observe. Of course little kids wanted things. Who wouldn't want a squeezable octopus or a tiny slinky? Some parents would let their child choose a small toy, we had plenty of choices for a dollar or two. Others would say no, we're going to find something for Daddy today, and stick to their guns. But many caved in, saying no, no, no, then capitulating to an increasingly demanding and agitated kid. I silently applauded those who were consistent, who said, "Today we're just looking around for fun. Maybe next time we'll buy something."

"I want this!" created other problems too. Even in politically correct Cambridge, I noticed some parents did not want their son to choose the pink version of anything. It was interesting listening to them say both "Choose the one you like," and "No, no, not the pink one!" No surprise, by the time they were older, most boys did not want the pink one. I remember one day we were down to one of our much-coveted fidget cubes. It was pink. A ten-year-old boy and his father came in asking about them and I directed them to it, thinking good chance he won't want it. But surprise, he happily took the pink one without even asking if we had other colors. In later years, pink became a different kind of problem. Our customers still didn't want to buy pink things for boys, but not for girls either. Too stereotypical.

Some kids were very very careful. I remember one little girl, in with her nanny, who spent a good hour pulling out every floaty pen, carefully looking at it, and putting it back in its place. Some were slyly defiant. Their parents told them not to touch, and I watched them stick out one finger and sneakily touch almost everything when they thought no one was looking. Some kids loved to talk, and would tell you all about their birthdays, their sister, their school, their favorite animals. If you asked another "Do you like cats?" or said "I like your shirt," they were terrified and disappeared behind their parents' legs. It wasn't easy to predict.

Coming to Joie without your parents was a rite of passage for neighborhood kids. Once they got up the courage, some would come in often, alone or with a friend. Some wanted to talk, talk, talk to us, and others just looked around quietly. Eventually, most moved on to the next step — going without their parents to Harvard Square, where there were more stores, more people, more places to hang out and figure out the world. But at least two of our young devotees wound up working at Joie later on in their lives. And I don't know who was more pleased by that — us, or them!

This chapter ends with stories written for our blog or Facebook over the years about some of our younger visitors. In honor of the 1950s book I loved as a kid, we present: Kids Say the Darnedest Things!

It's like a Party!

*A young boy, probably five or six, was killing time while his mother chose a gift for a friend. He was looking through a glitter wand kaleidoscope —*

*the kind where the glitter floats down through liquid and forms a kaleidoscopic image. "It's like a party!" he cried, and I told his mom that I just might have to use his quote.*

I love it!

*Three teenagers were looking around at everything, having fun with our stock and with each other. Sometimes three teenagers can seem like about a dozen people — they get excitable and crazy around each other, all in good fun, but these three were very easy to take. One of the girls looked at a miniature coffee creamer and said "I love this even more than I love myself!"*

I hate it!

*A little girl, maybe three or four, was in Joie de Vivre with her mother and had very definite opinions on most of the things she saw. She didn't like them. She particularly did not like the singing animals many kids her age love; she put her hands over her ears and said "I hate that." Eventually I realized they were looking for a present for the little girl to give to an older woman — her grandmother? They looked at the Aqua pets — cute little Japanese toys and these got the same reaction: "I hate that." They continued through the store and I heard the phrase "I hate it" several more times, realizing I had never in twenty-seven years heard anyone say it that often. I caught Mom's eye. "Guess she's going through a phase?" I asked as quietly as I could so the little girl would not hear me. Mom nodded. "Oh yes, this is a new thing." The daughter was temporarily distracted by a spinning tin toy — she actually liked it and it was briefly considered as the gift. "You could play with it when you visit her," Mom suggested helpfully. It was finally rejected, but without the usual condemnation. They wandered back to the singing animals, and the daughter noticed that the singing birthday bear was wearing a birthday cake hat that lit up. She became a little intrigued. "I think she might like this," she said to her surprised Mom. "I think she'd like that too, but it sings," said Mom, who though extremely nice and patient, was beginning to show signs of wanting to get this over and done. More discussion followed, and — to my surprise, little "I hate it" girl agreed to the bear — "if we don't make it sing." Into the bag it went, and out they went. I hope it's a long time before we hear another customer say "I hate it" that much again!*

## I am awesome!

*We have a new item at Joie de Vivre that we're all a little in love with — and we've decided to make it our item of the month — The Emergency Affirmation button. Push the yellow smiley face on its front and it says "You are awesome!" And there was a little girl in the store the other day, probably about 4 years old. We pushed the button for her, and she smiled and said, "It's right! I AM awesome!"*

## Darnedest and Sweetest

*One busy Saturday, two boys, probably thirteen or fourteen years old, entered the store. They were a bit loud, and clearly excited to be there. I was helping another customer when one of them grabbed a brass kaleidoscope. "How much is this?" he asked me, and looked rather taken aback to learn that it cost $150. But he and his friend both looked through it, then returned it to its stand. I kind of kept an eye on them, but soon got caught up in helping customers. In the middle of a transaction one of the boys approached me again. "Excuse me," he said. "I just wanted to tell you that this is a really wonderful store. I really like it." My heart melted a little. "I came in here a few weeks ago and I just brought in my friend." My heart melted a little more. He was so sincere, and so polite. "Well, thank you," I said. "I really appreciate the compliment, and I'm glad you like the store." I wasn't kidding. That kaleidoscope grabbing adolescent boy made my day!*

## Hi ho! Hi ho!

*A very little boy was in the store with his grandmother today, maybe two years old? He loved to talk and identify things, and had one of those adorable little kid voices — excited and sweet. They had made it almost all the way around the store when he spotted the Snow White musical snowglobe sitting on the front desk. He got very excited, pointed at the base and said in his little voice "hi ho! hi ho!" I asked his grandmother if he had seen Snow White. "I don't*

*think so," she told me. But I wondered... how else would he associate "hi ho"
with a dwarf? Later, he spotted our much larger yard gnome, and instantly
started with the excited "hi ho!" again. Further questioning solved the mystery.
He had seen a video of Snow White. Someday, probably soon, he'll discover the
words dwarf and gnome. But I kind of like "hi-ho's" myself...*

## Play with it!

*A mom and her young daughter were in the store today. I'd guess the daughter
was maybe three years old. She picked up a mini slinky and carried it around,
occasionally asking if she could have it. When they were ready to leave, this was
still under debate, and the mother asked, in a slightly exasperated tone: "If I get
this for you, what are you going to DO with it?" The daughter seemed slightly
confused by this but with impeccable logic, quickly came up with her answer:
"Play with it!" The slinky was purchased and out they went.*

## Can I have Yours?

*We have a musician customer who gives piano lessons in her home. She recently
bought a couple of our mini robot necklaces and told me she loves them, but
can't wear them while she is teaching because her students like them so much
they become distracted. A seven-year-old girl asked her where she got them,
then asked if she would buy her one. "No, I'm afraid not," was the reply.
"Can I have yours?" responded the girl. There's something compelling about such
forthrightness of desire! Sadly, the answer was once again no.*

## Kid asking Magic 8 Ball questions

*Will humans ever colonize Mars? 8 Ball answer — Yes!
Will things ever go back to normal after the coronavirus? 8 Ball — Yes!
Kid: This is a very optimistic Magic 8 Ball!*

## Is it for Me?

*I had just closed the store. The lights were off, the door was locked, it was
probably 6:35. As I walked up to the door to let myself out, I saw a Dad and
a very young girl, maybe three, standing at the door looking in. I said hello*

*and the Dad told me, "This is our favorite store." I said hello to the little girl who was staring at the small gift-wrapped present I had in my hand. "What's that?" she said. I told her it was a present. Completely genuinely, she asked, "Is it for me?" I told her no, it was for a friend who was moving out of town. "What's in it?" was her next question. I described the contents; a pack of gum, a wish token, a globe marble, an ice-cream eraser and a note, all wrapped up with festive ribbons in a little coin purse. She sighed. As she and her Dad walked away, I heard her begin "When I grow up…" but couldn't hear the rest of her sentence. Maybe she was thinking I'll own a store. More likely, she was thinking — someone will give me a present like that. In any case, she gave me a present — there's just something so delightful about being young and innocent enough to think that a complete stranger emerging from a store with a wrapped gift might have gotten it for you.*

CHAPTER 22

# Customer Quotes

Kids aren't the only ones who say the darnedest things; adults can more than hold their own.

*Questions:*

"Is this a funny shop?"

"Is this easy to read?"

"Do you think this is colorful?"

"Do you have anything for an electrician?"

"Do you have anything that would make the flames higher in a chalice?"

"Where would I buy batteries?"

"She plays the violin — what color do you think she'd like?"

Looking at fruit bowl made out of a 33rpm record: "Do you think it still plays?"

Playing our pipedream/gamelan: "Is this a catatonic scale?"

To Magic 8 Ball: "Will I die in one second?"

Re yodeling pickle: "In your opinion, is this X-rated?"

Looking at a globe pillow: "Is the United States on here?"

"Do you have anything for a white kid who wants to be black?"

Looking at snake top: "Are these intestinal worms?"

"He's on medication — would this be too scary for him?"
    (squeaking bulldog gun)

"Which is more appropriate — the mouse puppet or the communist
    breath spray?"
    (she bought the breath spray)

"Do these glow sheep glow?"

Holding mug: "Can you drink out of this?"

Cranking the Happy Birthday music box and listening to the tune:
    "Does this song have a name?" (n.b. not a foreigner!)

Holding our fireplace video: "How do I know the video is really in here?"
Us: "You're welcome to open up the package to make sure it's there."
Customer: "No, how do I know that the video is on the tape?"
Us: (no words)

(Phone call) "Oh good, you're open." Pause. "What do you sell?"

(Phone call) "Do you guys do repairs on saxophones?"

Youngish dreadlocked guy: "Can you hook me up with some weed?"

Walking past Breezy Singers (motion activated singing birds.) Robin
    tweets. "Has that ever done that before??"

The Tarzan clock goes off — loud Tarzan yodel. Woman asks me "Was
    that you?"

"Why can't everyone be joyful and content?"

*Compliments:*

From a young Chinese woman. "This is a very unique store. I'm very proud of you."

Twelve (?) year old boy to his mother on leaving store: "I bet people make pilgrimages to that store."

"It's like a visual Disneyland in here!"

Backhanded compliment from a customer buying something for himself: "This place is worse than a plant store!"

A new to us customer who had been looking around when asked if he had any questions. He said no — then added with a smile, "There are more surprises than questions."

*Random Opinions:*

Women to her two adult children who are looking at our kaleidoscopes: "That's the boring part of the store." (They continue looking.)

Cheapskate Woman: "It's easy to be nice in India because everything is cheap there — I could send my driver to the bakery and around to my friend's with pastries and it only cost me $4."

"I'll just go down (the block) to Paper Source and if I don't find something there, I'll come back here. I love this store."

"I'm getting this (a tin sheriff's badge) for my court hearing. She may be a meter maid and she says I tried to run her down, but I'm the Sheriff."

Looking at wind up pigeon toy: "That's not how a pigeon walks." Same person looking at small Pete Seeger finger puppet: "That's not what Pete Seeger looks like."

"It's very hard to buy things for people who have bad taste and are overweight to boot."

"This place is good for unusual gifts if you have friends that like that sort of thing."

*And...*

Probably my all-time favorite customer quote — which I heard many times over the years in many variations: It's 9:30 pm, the door is locked, the lights are mostly off, you're in there with a bucket of paint, the ladder opened up, one wall bare and things all over the floor. Someone knocks on the door. "Are you open?"

CHAPTER 23

# The Things We Do For Love — Customer Service

Customer service. Google it and you will find a billion results, though I suspect most are repetitive. I'll go with making sure the customer is happy. Or the support you offer your customers — both before and after they buy and use your products or services — to help them have an easy and enjoyable experience. Or following best practices, meaning valuing customers' time, having a pleasant attitude, providing knowledge and resources, and also taking things a step further to exceed — rather than just meet — expectations. Professionalism, patience, and a "people-first" attitude.

I'm not sure if we really fit the standard "professionalism" bill at Joie, being a rather casual bunch, but a large part of our customer service did fit, free gift wrapping probably at the top of the list. I had learned three basic gift-wrapping techniques back in my Village Gallery days, and they stood us in excellent stead. We "poofed" small toys in a few sheets of colored tissue cinched with a few ribbons, and flat-wrapped boxes and items compact enough to be almost a box. "Firecrackers" were made by rolling an item in tissue and tying off both ends. Double sided tape was one of our secret weapons, and our answer to "how are you doing that?" We learned that "Do you have a gift box?" is usually secret code for "I need this gift wrapped and can't imagine how I could possibly do it without a box." The vast majority of those who asked were delighted when we said, "Would you like us to wrap it?" and without a box, did.

Boxes were expensive. We tried to avoid using them when we could, though occasionally someone would insist on having a gift box for something that was already — in a box. Some larger or oddly shaped items could be challenging to wrap, but we almost always found a way, though staff could be reluctant to offer to wrap these. I considered it a personal victory when after much trial and error, I figured out how to quickly wrap a doormat.

Much as we wanted to provide gift wrapping all year long, we found we just couldn't do it in December. People bought too much, it was simply impossible. We tried to explain. "Sorry, but if we were gift wrapping, you'd have to come back to pick things up next week, we'd still be wrapping all the gifts bought yesterday." We did make exceptions, and I did have to explain to the staff more than once that you could not say you were "too busy" if there was only one customer in the store wanting only one thing wrapped. People did still have birthdays and non-holiday needs in December, and we tried to accommodate them. Some customers would come in the week before we stopped wrapping, to buy all their gifts while we still would. That made for some hectic days in late November!

But customer service was never onerous. If someone came in needing ten teacher gifts, it was fun to help them find the right thing for each teacher's subject. Or find every hedgehog in the store as a gift for a hedgehog fan. Significant birthdays were also something many customers struggled with. What was the perfect gift for someone turning thirty, forty, fifty, and up? I rarely bought anything that involved specific ages, but we did sell number sparklers for cakes and our "Whatever" clock, with all the numbers clustered at the bottom was very popular for "milestone" birthdays. So was our Emergency Affirmation button that said "You are awesome!" We tried to have one or two small silly things on hand for weddings too — a little Austrian plastic snow globe with a bride and a groom that said "Good Luck!" or a kissing bride and groom salt and pepper set. Some customers loved our somewhat unorthodox suggestions, others not so much, but it was fun trying to help people find the gift that felt "perfect!"

Of course sometimes it could also be a little trying, as in this entry from our blog, written by guest blogger and longtime Joie-ette: Julia Willwerth.

*Glum, sourpuss faced lady enters store. Walks up to counter. "I am looking for a joke." Me: "Oh, you came to the right store… let's see…" Lady, flatly: "What's this?" Me: "A bouncy glitter ball… hmm… we have this yodeling pickle? or an emergency clown nose — that's good if you need a quick funny fix." Lady, flatly: "What's this?' (it's an i-Top) I explain the top. She proceeds down the front desk — pointing at random things and asking "What's this?" (ignoring all my excellent Joie gift suggestions) She presses every button on the sound machine. Zero change in expression. "What's this?" "Ear clips." "What's this?" "It's a keychain with sparkles in it." "What's this?" "An Etch-a-Sketch." "Show me that red bird." I demonstrate and explain breezy singer — her comment, "That's not very exciting." By now I have ceased to care if she finds something she likes. (She does ultimately buy the sound machine.)*

Customer service also included placing custom and special orders for people or institutions, donating items for raffles and benefits, and occasionally delivering gifts. But I think the most important thing we did was making sure that what we sold actually did what it was supposed to do. For example: xylophones had to be in tune! There are lots of children's xylophones that are not, and a select few that are. It's not always price related, though that often figures in. But as a former musician of sorts, I was adamant. They had to be in tune. And I tried to explain that to more than one salesperson who looked at me blankly when I told them why I was not ordering their xylophones.

Adding batteries to toys and mechanical contraptions was not initially part of our service, but we soon added it, after a customer returned to complain about something she had purchased. It was a Bandit Box" —

a small black box with a slot in the top. You placed a coin in the slot and the box began to gently rock from side to side as a hand slowly emerged from inside, and grabbed the coin. Then the opening dramatically slammed shut. The batteries it needed to work were not included. That was not unusual and I didn't give it a second thought. I had gift-wrapped one for a customer, who gave it to someone at a birthday party. It was unwrapped, a coin put in the slot, and all waited for the hand to emerge. Of course, it never did and our customer was bitterly disappointed that her gift did not have the "wow!" effect she'd imagined. She was right. We should have at least told her before wrapping it up. I realized that some items were expected to make a slam-dunk first impression — and we would have to supply batteries to make sure they did. Removing battery protectors in items that did come with batteries was also important. Many people did not notice these clear plastic strips, in fact, they were sometimes hidden. And what fun is a yodeling pickle that doesn't yodel? Or a sound machine that's quiet as a mouse?

Adding batteries ourselves was also helpful with quality control — we instantly knew if something was working or not. We loved silly whimsical things but we did have standards — if it was a pencil sharpener, it had to actually sharpen the pencil. If it was a bottle opener, it had to open the bottle. Pens had to write, medieval weapon pushpins had to push paper into corkboard. Most of the time things worked as advertised, but not always and I'd find myself calling a company to report that ten of our twenty-four whistling mirrors were not whistling, only to find we were the only store reporting that problem. "That's because they don't come with batteries," I'd explain. "How would anyone know? We know because we put them in." I'm sure some companies thought of us as a pain, but I know others did appreciate the heads up.

We bought from one big company called Mr. Christmas. They made battery operated music boxes with lights and moving parts — very fun and popular. We would take each one and test it, and once found half our order wasn't working. They were very good about replacing them, but I realized at the time that most of their product was sold through much larger stores and there is no way a huge store is going to open and test each item. So a certain percentage of customers will buy them only to later find they don't work or are broken and then the burden of contacting the company and getting a replacement fell on the customer, not the store. Not if they bought them from us!

The unicorn pencil sharpener was an inspired and witty idea, a little unicorn with a small silver pencil in place of a horn. We opened one to use as a sample but no matter what we did, we could not sharpen that pencil to a point. We tried a different pencil, same result. We tried another unicorn, and a third. Ditto. I wrote the company to let them know their product didn't work. It had to be the plastic sharpener. We'd sold many $2 pencil sharpeners that worked just fine, so decent cheap sharpeners existed. This particular company didn't seem to care about the unicorns, so we never sold them. Another company with an even better idea — a beaver pencil sharpener — had the same problem and happily for us, recalled and remade them so they worked.

Another seemingly small thing we did for our customers that was often not easy for us was removing plastic packaging and labels from products. At one point in our existence, the powers that regulated the import/export world decided that each product sold in this country but produced elsewhere had to bear a label to that effect. That, plus the ascendancy of the bar code, led to a big increase in work for us. We wanted to present everything to its best advantage in the store and so removed any labels we assumed a customer would want to take off at home — for instance a large sticker with a bar code that said "Made in Thailand" on a small plastic toy. This was not always easy, as this blog excerpt will show:

*Last week we got in 200 small plastic kaleidoscopes to fill a special order for a department at U.Mass Boston. Each one arrived with a big label attached. We took them off — it was slow going — and the labels left a sticky residue that could only be banished through vigorous application of (commercial plug alert) Goo-Gone. This took us hours and hours. Strictly speaking, we didn't have to do it — but we can't imagine our customer would have been happy to have to do it themselves — and if they didn't do it, the items would have looked cheesy or felt sticky. This made us long for the good old days when this sort of labeling was not legally required. And another thought — we've been in business long enough to be able to say "in the good old days" — yikes!*

Another time a reorder of *Treehouse* books arrived, a handsome coffee table book filled with photographs of fantastic and inventive treehouses. It was $37.50, so more of a serious gift. To our surprise, this time the books arrived with a large sticker on the front cover that said "As Seen On Animal Planet!" That bothered us, it detracted from the beautiful cover photo and besides, it was an ad for a television show. Easily solved, right? Just peel off the sticker. We tried. And found the stickers impossible to remove without damaging the cover of the book. Easily removable stickers existed — we used them to price our goods. Why would anyone use one that wasn't?

For that matter, why would a company put a large sticky label on a pen covering a third of the pen's surface? A cute pen, a cow pen, the kind someone is going to purchase as a gift? Since so many of our customers are buying gifts, we try to take ugly labels off in advance of gift wrapping and in general, to make a nicer presentation. So we would start to take the labels off these pens. Fifteen minutes of concentrated effort and the three pens we tried all had lots of little pieces of label and sticky stuff still clinging to them. What about just leaving the labels on and letting the "end-user" deal with it? I can't say that thought didn't occur to us but it just didn't seem right. Another danger, leaving the label on could have led to one of our customers asking us to remove the label before wrapping and our having to admit that — we couldn't. We sometimes wound up returning items to companies for this reason but it was terribly annoying and drove us a little crazy.

Then there were the small paint by number kits I bought from a company, remembering how much I had loved them when I was young. When the order arrived we opened a few, thinking we would paint one and use it for display. It proved, to put it mildly, difficult. The little canvas was about the size of a greeting card, ridiculously over detailed and it kind of made my head hurt just looking at it, let alone imagining trying to paint it. When I called them about it, they were completely nonchalant, and claimed they had never had a complaint like ours. It seemed pointless to argue. But — would you give it to a six-year-old? A twelve-year-old? Rembrandt??

Our customer service was of course much easier to provide because we were such a small operation. If someone wanted just one rubber chicken, an item we sold for sixty cents, we could mail it to them. A very appreciative customer who lived an hour away actually mailed us a check for $1.10 — one rubber chicken and postage. We liked being the kind of store where one could do this and I should have kept that check as a memento, an illustration of the saying "Small is Good!" But it was true that being small gave us great flexibility — we could open early for someone, stay late, special order something or remember which earrings someone's wife particularly liked.

One more customer service we offered wouldn't really fit into the normal definition of same, our Playful Penguin Race. We kept this squeaky penguin perpetual motion toy on a low shelf across from the front desk and allowed kids to turn it on and watch the penguins climb the stairs, and slide down the slide. And climb the stairs and slide down the slide. And… so on. It captivated kids from one to five and allowed parents a little breathing space to look around the store. It also provided some entertainment for us as we watched the kids play. Some got so excited they could hardly contain their glee, and many loudly voiced the charming and incorrect notion that one penguin was "winning!" More than one kid could make for a little arguing, and more than one kid had to be physically torn away when their parent was ready to leave the store. But I think as customer service went, the Penguin Race was a smashing success!

CHAPTER 24

# Merrily We Rolled Along — The Middle Years

In three or four years Joie de Vivre was firmly established. We got some good publicity, (including being interviewed for a Japanese television show!) but we didn't have to advertise much; our customers spread the word. The things we sold, whether brand new or old school, silly or not, were unusual and the store atmosphere fun and very social. I was in my thirties, most everyone who worked for me was younger, and we got to know each other's friends and families. We went to hear our co-workers boyfriends' bands play out. We had art parties at night, drinking wine while making gift certificates with stickers and rubber-stamps and we were friends with almost everyone, UPS drivers, mailmen, (and occasional woman) and those who worked in nearby restaurants, hair salons, and other stores. We often met up for drinks after work.

The daily routine went something like this: One of us would arrive at the store, vacuum the floor, and turn on the various lights and contraptions, at least the ones we had remembered to turn off the night before. We would wipe the fingerprints and dust off the front door and clean the glass on our jewelry cases. Next was "the walk," a slow stroll around the store, checking all the displays for missing or errant items. It wasn't unusual to find a kaleidoscope upside down or the dancing ballerina's mirror in the basket of light covers. The windup toys needed to be placed "looking at" the customers, bins of small things like party poppers and finger monsters had to be replenished and the cards always needed straightening. Things got messy. Customers usually didn't remember exactly where they'd picked something up and just put it down wherever. I didn't blame them; sometimes the staff didn't remember either and I complicated things by doing constant, minute rearrangements. It was like playing a life size game of "what belongs where."

Next, turn on the music. This could be a subject of considerable disagreement but one where I really tried to use my "I'm the boss" powers. I had a pretty clear idea of what kind of music was right for the store and it was definitely not jarring jazz or loud rock and roll. Our reception was never good enough for most radio stations, so we relied first on cassette tapes and then compact discs. It was always a relief to find music that everyone liked, or at least, no one absolutely hated. But even when you love something, if you hear it over and over, your feelings will probably change. Later on, that was one technology that clearly made our lives better — the advent of Pandora and other music streaming services. We could have a hundred different stations and cut off a song by tapping a screen. Heaven!

There was no email to check, and for a long time we didn't even have an answering machine, so after finishing this routine, we just unlocked the door, and voila, we were open. If there was more than one person working, there would generally be a coffee run. In theory, we were all to arrive with breakfast eaten and coffee in hand, but in practice that didn't happen much. In any case, the first hour of the day wasn't usually too busy. Neighbors might stop by to buy a handful of cards or just to say hello. UPS would deliver our day's boxes. We'd catch up on who did what the night before, and make sure the bags, gift boxes and gift wrapping supplies up front were well stocked.

We had closing procedures as well, and really, there was almost always something that needed doing. *From Log book: "Believe it or not, I really care about things like whether the party poppers are filled up all the way and having a good variety of different pencils, etc."* There was usually an item in need of new batteries, something that needed gluing, flowers out front to be watered, trash to go out, dishes to wash.

Even when we were doing really well, it was hard to predict when the busy parts of a day would be. Once, I found myself talking about business with the guy who ran the gas station across the street as he filled my tank. The weather was awful, and I said something like "It must be pretty quiet here today." He smiled and told me what his Dad used to say about customers. "They're like thieves. You never know when they'll come." I had to agree. You could sit there for a half hour doing nothing much, and as soon as someone took a lunch break, five people would need something wrapped. It could be raining buckets and we'd be really busy, and a beautiful perfect day was no guarantee that we would. Except for major snowstorms and hurricanes, weather was not a good predictor of much.

Predictions. I remembered Mr. Fox saying it was a terrible neighborhood. He was still running a thriving business a block away. One day I was getting a haircut on the next block and discussing a potential new neighbor with the owner of the salon as he cut. "I don't know if they're going to make it in this neighborhood," I said, "I'm just not sure their idea is going to work." There was an unusual moment of silence. This guy loved to talk. Finally, he said, "I won't say anything about that." More silence, then, "Can I tell you something?" "Sure, of course," I said, curious. He put down his scissors "Well… when you opened your store, I told everyone you wouldn't make it. I didn't get what you were doing and didn't think you'd last more than a few months. And now you're a neighborhood institution. So now I never say that about any business."

Besides providing us with excellent coffee, roast potatoes, rotisserie chickens and pizzas, Mr. Fox continued to provide us with other amusements. One night I heard a knock on the door when I was working after hours, fixing some displays. I looked at the door, expecting to see a friend but it was Mr. Fox. Why was he knocking this late? When I opened the door, he asked me if I would like to meet him for a drink at a fancy bar in Harvard Square. Instantly, I had an inappropriately huge grin on my face, which I struggled to contain, lest he think it was a grin of delight. "No thank you," I said. "I have to meet my boyfriend." This was not strictly speaking true. Though the boyfriend did exist, he was then living in New York. My involuntary grin sprang from imagining telling the staff the next day, "Mr. Fox asked me out!!" Fuel for the teasing fire, but impossible to keep secret.

When it became clear that Joie de Vivre was something different and fun, I was approached multiple times by business types who wanted me to open another store, or a store in their mall, or franchise. Do the American business thing: expand, expand, expand. I listened, politely or not, depending on their approach, but always said a firm "No thanks!" It might have worked, but I was skeptical and I knew myself well enough to know I did not want to give up the daily operations of running a small business to incorporate, find and manage employees and keep track of inventory for a half dozen stores. Sometimes I berated myself for not being more of a risk taker. Sometimes I wondered if it was because I was a woman, or if I was just chicken, afraid to take a chance others might leap at.

But I had a little knowledge to back up my instincts. One of my favorite stores in New York, had tried to expand and failed, Mythology, the wonderful place on the Upper West Side directly behind the Museum of Natural History, on a notable block for retail. I don't remember my first time there but I was likely indulging in my favorite pastime, rambling around the city, checking out interesting places. It was small and crowded, packed with toys, jewelry, cards, vintage goods, posters, tiny original books drawn by Roz Chast, and much more. I bought my first rubber stamp there. You never knew what you might find on its shelves. I always went in with a sense of excited anticipation, and it was one of my inspirations when I began to think about going into retail myself.

I got to know its owners at the New York Gift Show because I had a crush on a French kaleidoscope maker I was buying scopes from. We had become quite friendly and I helped him at his busy booth whenever I could justify spending the time. I managed to justify it often enough, and became familiar with some of his other buyers, the couple that owned

Mythology among them. Their store had doubled in size since my first visit and that seemed to make sense — why wouldn't twice as big be twice as good? And it was still good, wonderful as ever, just a little less crowded. But a few years later they confessed that they regretted their decision to expand. They were not making double the money and starting to flounder financially. A short time after this conversation, they closed up and just disappeared. They stiffed some of their suppliers too. It was a shock for everyone but I remembered that confession. It reinforced my idea that I wanted to stay small enough to run the store alone for a week if I had to. A few times I did.

Still, it was nice to have employees. I could take vacations. Or visit my family, and when I did that, I often stopped in to see Lore and Vern at the Gallery. They rarely took even one day off and were always astonished to see me on a Saturday. "How can you not be in your store on the weekend?" was their inevitable greeting. I never said it, but always thought, it was watching you work every single day that made me decide I would not set my life up that way. I sometimes dreamed they were telling me how to run Joie de Vivre, and in the dream would eventually realize, to my great relief, no — I don't work for them anymore, this is mine, I can do what I want. But they remained incredibly important to me and when they decided to retire after thirty plus years, I went down and worked a few days with them for old time's sake. I learned so much about retail from Lore and I'm not sure Joie de Vivre would have come to be without my experience there. We kept in touch for the rest of their lives.

Besides employees, I had some charming volunteers, my three New York nieces. Once they reached the age of seven or eight, they took turns visiting for a week by themselves in the summer, and helping at the store was one of their favorite activities. I put them "to work" making gift certificates with stickers and rubber-stamps, and they sometimes helped with unpacking. Sitting at my desk in the back of the store one day, as Zoey helped someone unpack an order of nun snow globes, I heard her little voice. "It's a witch!" Pause. "She looks mad!" I realized she had probably never seen a nun in black habit. This same niece wanted to work at the front desk. She was nine, and when a customer signed her charge slip with the typical adult flourish, her name was completely unrecognizable to a kid with the painstaking handwriting of those with that newly acquired skill. She looked up at me panic stricken. "Is this okay??" I explained what happens to handwriting when you've signed your name a thousand times.

The store had its growing pains. We really didn't have enough room for overstock in the back, so I wound up renting a big room in the building's basement. To get there, you had to go out our rear door, into the back alley, down a dark flight of stairs, leaving both doors unlocked so you could get back in. Then you entered the big dark room that was our overflow stockroom. It was helpful to have it, but no one liked going down there, and often staff found it easier to say we were out of something than to take the somewhat scary journey; understandable, but not great for business. The landlord had a storage space adjacent to our store on the upper level. It was crammed with stuff, but no one used it, and I convinced them to let me rent it. We broke through a wall, put shelves on every possible surface and our storage problem was solved.

Sometimes Joie was quiet and peaceful. But even with just a few customers, it could be a rather noisy, you might even say chaotic space. There were the ambient background sounds; our music, the hammer crashing, someone playing the Pipe Dream, someone rifling through the basket of light covers to find another lizard or cow. You might hear "To me, that's an absolute disgrace!" in the British accent of the soccer sound machine. The yodeling of the pickle. The squeaking of a rubber duck. The animatronic singing plush goat, channeling Julie Andrews in the *Sound of Music*. *The Rites of Spring* (wind chime version), the oinking of the pig keychain, the crying baby on the Get Off The Phone Excuse Machine. Or the excited voices of teenage customers (three can seem like a dozen) or kids crying, "Mom/Dad!" The endless squeaking loop of the Playful Penguin Race. Sometimes all these sounds occurred in the same few minutes. It could be trying for the customer trying to choose a $150 music box. We got a little disoriented too, sometimes reaching for the calculator instead of adding up a sale slip ourselves. "Doesn't this drive you crazy?"

was a question we heard fairly often. Yet we really meant it when we said "that's okay," if someone apologized for pressing a button. I wanted people to explore, to think of Joie as a fun place to come with friends. Happily, a lot of them did.

TRUE CONFESSIONS #4

## *White Mouse*

Hi! I'm the white mouse puppet. Just like real mice, there are lots and lots of us, but they elected me to tell our story, and I was honored to accept. We first came to Joie de Vivre in 1997, not long after some company in California started making us. We quickly became very popular at Joie, although some of the less educated customers thought we were rats and said mean things about us. The staff always set them straight though, and pointed out our noses and tails were different. And our tags clearly said "White Mouse."

No matter what Devil Duckie says, we were in way more window displays than he ever was. He might have been in a few, but we were often the star. For one thing we were bigger, showed up better, and were definitely cuter. As soon as they started using us mice in the window, they realized we looked good in groups. People loved us.

One favorite was a Christmas window. We were on ladders, decorating a tree with fake swiss cheese. And some us were sitting on the floor eating cheese and drinking champagne. Then there was a winter window where we were ice skating on a mirrored pond, in a woods made from real trees. We had little ice-skates, and not only that, the owner of the store knitted little scarves for us to wear. We were also featured in a Valentine window — we got to hold up a very romantic poem.

I definitely would have fallen. It read:

*When you look at me, I love you more than brie,*
*And every time we kiss, I love you more than swiss,*
*Please be mine, oh please,*
*I love you more than cheese.*

Cheese. Sometimes people ate cheese in the backroom of the store. Sometimes they didn't remember to put it back in the fridge. That's how we wound up meeting a very different kind of mouse. The kind that breathe air and have actual fur. People call them "real" mice and we noticed they kind of scare some people, but we found them easy to get along with. They'd tell us about their life, we'd tell them about ours. Very different lifestyles for sure. Some of those real mice had serious hard luck stories to tell. People chasing them with brooms, relatives caught in mousetraps, sobering stuff. Made us appreciate our "plush" existence, and that most people thought we were really cute.

There was one dark time which lasted a few years when we weren't so cute though. The company that made us had to find a different factory, and the new people couldn't get our ears right. When we were unpacked, we could hear people saying, "What's wrong with their ears?" and they would pull and rub them sometimes for almost half an hour until they looked a little better. That really hurt!! We were glad when the ear problem finally got figured out and we could just go right from box to shelf. I don't mind saying we were more than a little worried they might stop ordering us because our ears took so much work.

The people who worked at the store played with us a lot. They liked to pick us up and make us wave at customers, sometimes we even "talked" to them. It wasn't our real voices of course, just the voices of the people holding us. One woman, the owner I think, liked to make us seem very shy, hiding our heads in her arms. She'd ask us if we wanted to leave the store and make us nod our heads as if we might consider it. Or she'd ask if we liked cheese and have us nod yes, yes, yes. It was this little act of hers. We're not really shy but it was fun to help make the customers laugh. Sometimes we wished we could scare them, like the real mice did, but we were just too cute for that.

One customer, I think her name was Karin, would always talk about us whenever she came in. She had bought one of us for her kid, and years later, she brought that mouse back in for a visit. We hardly recognized him — he had turned completely grey. We'd heard that could happen when you are loved soooo much, but seeing it up and close and personal was amazing and a little scary. Another time the owner of the company that made us came to visit the store. Someone took a picture of him and the owner standing together, one of us in each hand. It was a great picture!

That company that made us? It was called Folkmanis and we found out that they began right here in Cambridge, MA. Pretty cool. They moved to California long before we were made, and we wound up back at the origin, so to speak. They made a lot of puppets and we were one of their best sellers, in their top ten for many years. Then we started to slip some, and I recently heard someone say we're not even in the top fifty anymore. But then, I heard the store owner say that we would always be the number one puppet at Joie de Vivre. That made us feel good.

Some of us live at her house now. She didn't want to run out of us at the end so she placed a big order and those of us that didn't sell got to go home with her. One or two live downstairs, but most of us are up on the third floor. There's a lot of stuffed animals up there, and a couple devil ducks, and three very old Folkmanis bear puppets. Those guys are big, but they've been very nice, and they told us all about the old days at some store called The Village Gallery. That's where they came from, long before Joie de Vivre opened. It sounds like a pretty cool place. We wish we could have seen it.

This woman I've been calling the owner, her real name is Linda. She said she'd give some of us away eventually, but we don't want to go. We're hoping she keeps us all. It's comfortable living here and sometimes kids visit and play with us. We also heard that sometimes real mice live here too. It would be nice to meet up with some of that kind of mouse again. Maybe we can find some cheese...

# CHAPTER 25

# Happy Everything!

I knew Christmas would be big; I'd worked in retail on and off since I was seventeen. It wasn't that big the first year because the store was so new that most people were still discovering us and we didn't come to mind when they panicked the week before the big day. From then on, the stretch of time between Thanksgiving and Christmas was crazy. I had clear memories of being behind the counter at the Village Gallery the day after Thanksgiving, looking out at a sea of faces and hands, hands holding things those imploring faces wanted to buy, and it was just like that.

So, being busy at Christmas didn't surprise me. What did surprise me was just how "big" other holidays were. Valentine's Day, Easter, Mother's Day, Halloween, and even the two least commercial, the 4th of July and Thanksgiving, all brought in people looking for something special to buy for their celebrations. People wanted merchandise specific to each holiday and we also needed to do a window display for many of them.

Valentine's Day was easy, mostly cards and hearts. I ordered new Valentine cards every year, and made sure to add some special and new themed items to what we already had. Snow globes with floating hearts instead of snow, picture frames, kissing couple salt and pepper shakers, heart stickers, glass paperweights, earrings and necklaces with a heart motif, heart-shaped hanging crystals, sometimes a heart themed kaleidoscope, and more. Love and heart themed things were easy to find and if they were silly too — so much the better. We had a catapult that launched tiny plastic cupids, a love gun that shot a big pair of foam lips, glass candy kisses, heart-shaped eyeglasses, long-stemmed chocolate roses, a heart-shaped hot water bottle, and any number of takes on the classic conversation hearts. Another great thing about Valentine's gifts — unless they specifically referenced the day itself, we could sell them all year, for weddings, anniversaries, whatever.

It was fun helping customers choose Valentines. Their aims varied as much as our cards. Long time couples, hopeful early daters, moms and dads buying something for their kids, and always a few kind souls buying something for a Valentineless friend. We put out bowls of candy kisses a few weeks before, and ordered a lot of red and pink tissue and ribbon — Valentine's Day was very gift-wrapping intensive. Another thing we quickly noticed about the holiday. Though the majority of shoppers at Joie were women, the day or two before Valentine's Day the store was filled with men. They didn't shop as far in advance, and this was a Christmas time Joie joke as well. Sometimes on December 24th, we would realize that the store was filled with — only men. This changed some over the years, but was noticeable to the end.

I think the demand for gifts on most holidays surprised me in part because I grew up in the 1950s and 60s. We usually made our own Valentine cards, and got some chocolate from Mom and Dad. We made our own Halloween costumes too — the only things we bought were pumpkins to carve and candy to give out. Those lit-up pumpkins and maybe some spider webs were all that was needed for decorations. On Easter, we dyed and hid eggs and got an Easter bonnet, and a basket filled with jelly beans and chocolate. Chenille chicks made an appearance. We made cards or wrote poems for Mother's and Father's Day, (and asked why there wasn't a Children's Day, receiving the inevitable "Every day is Children's Day" response.) Sparklers on July 4th. Christmas was different though still relatively modest. We got to choose an ornament at Woolworths, "Santa" left us each an unwrapped gift, we had stockings and gave each other presents, but we didn't go crazy the way some of my customers and their families did.

Easter was trickier. I loved the spring solstice parts of it, rabbits and eggs and chocolate and flowers, but as I was not religious myself, and knew that there were lots of non-Christians living in the area who might be walking around looking for something to do that day, we didn't close for the first ten years or so. Still, as it turned out, Easter was always a really slow day. It was odd, but being open on Easter just began to feel wrong, and then one beautiful Easter Sunday afternoon, the person I was working with asked if she could leave to go to the park with her friends. After letting her go, I impulsively decided to close the store, went home to hang out in the garden, and we never opened on Easter again. It's interesting too, that all the big stores that open on New Year's Day, the 4th of July, Memorial Day — days we would never be open — were closed on Easter. Still are. In retail it's something that just isn't done!

I was very firm about closing on those other holidays. New Year's Day, Memorial Day, Labor Day, the 4th of July, Thanksgiving and of course, Christmas; these were sacrosanct, and it seemed insulting to use them as nothing more than another day to shop. All of my friends who had small stores closed them. It was fine to keep a drugstore, a grocery, or a liquor store open, you might need bandaids or ketchup or beer, but who really needed a rapping hamster on Memorial Day? If someone did, and complained the next day, I felt bad. But never bad enough to consider opening.

"Holiday creep" was another phenomenon that took hold as the economy became more and more dependent on consumerism. Over the years, I watched as neighborhood chain stores began to put out Valentines on January 2nd, Halloween appeared in early September and Christmas items were never far behind. One year someone asked us for Christmas cards in August. We tried to hold the line. I had read a short story by Doris Lessing about a woman whose life revolved around Christmas and her summer holidays. As soon as one had ended, she found herself depressed, until she immediately started planning for the other. It made a big impression on me.

From the logbook: *The Monday* Boston Globe *had a front page story about desperate retailers putting out their Christmas merchandise in September. They think this maximizes their chances of getting every possible dollar out of their customers. Maybe they're right. I don't know. The article certainly made me think — yikes, I have to do our Halloween display. After all, it's almost October 1st — Halloween is just... four... weeks away. I have an issue with holiday creep. Pumpkins and witches in August leave me cold. Reading the article, it seems many shoppers agree that holidays are more special when they truly come once a year — not hang around for months and months. Call me old-fashioned, but you won't see much Christmas here at Joie de Vivre until right around one of our less retail-oriented holidays — my favorite — Thanksgiving.*

Of course this made it necessary for me to work on Thanksgiving. I'd round up available help, sister, husband, whoever was around and free, and we'd do the window display and get the holiday merchandise out. One year I cooked a turkey at home while doing this, rushing home from the store to baste it once or twice, but realized this was perhaps a little dangerous, and didn't do it again. We went out for dinner, relied on the kindness of friends, and later, after I was married, family took over, and I'd come home exhausted, to find wine, turkey and trimmings at the ready. My husband and I tried, but were not able to have children, and I was well aware that if we had, life would have been different. But I never had to figure out a way to work less, and my husband was a bit of a workaholic himself, though he did say to me wistfully one year, "You never have time to do anything Christmasy at Christmas, like go to the Messiah."

He was right. If there was a real emergency, I found a way, but otherwise I worked every day from the week before Thanksgiving until December 25th. We didn't have a big sale on "Black Friday," and I hated the way the media began to report on that day as though it was a sporting event: how many cars in the mall parking lots, how long the lines, how many fights over the last big screen TV. But that was the day our busy season began. For us though, it just kept getting busier and busier right through Christmas Eve with the last weekend before the 24th generally being the busiest. It was both exhilarating and exhausting, and we often made as much in a single December day as we made in a January, March, or September week. A single December sales slip could total more than an entire January day's total. The season was almost athletic. One year Peter, whose job was then mostly restocking, wore a pedometer on an eight-hour shift — by the end of the day he had logged over six miles!

In the early years, we took in a lot of cash at Christmas, and felt we should hide it during the day in case we were held up. We'd put it in a box of string lights marked "defective" in the back, and once we stored — and almost forgot it — in the vacuum cleaner bag. I'd take it home with me at night and count it out on the kitchen table so I could deposit it the next morning on my way in. "I've never seen so much cash before," said the then sixteen-year-old Peter, down from Maine to help out for a week. It was kind of crazy but it became much less of an issue as people began to use credit cards more and more.

By then we were keeping a very anxious eye on the weather. A big snowstorm could ruin a day or two of business at a time when every day counted. Before internet shopping, it wasn't as much of a problem because it would just be busier the days after a storm, but once it was easy to sit home in your pajamas and shop, with tea or a drink at your side, snow was not our friend. It was beautiful yes, and made the season "seasonal," but we could no longer easily make up the lost sales. They were truly lost.

There were other things about the season that never got easier to deal with. The extra staff we needed for one. It was hard to find people who could learn everything quickly and be willing to work for six weeks, making me even more grateful for my perpetually happy-to-return regulars. Even harder was estimating how many of any particular item we'd sell. We might sell ten or twenty times as much of something as we would in normal times, and I couldn't always predict what. I also had a hard time believing how much we sold in December, even after years and years. Would we really sell a hundred Food Face plates? Six dozen nesting snowmen? Fifty *Pretty Good Joke Books*? Or we'd have a beautiful item I'd ordered six of in the summer, and by November we'd sold only one. Didn't seem like it would be something to order a lot of — and then people would come in and want them. "I want three of them, maybe four." Who knew? We always tried to order more for customers, but it wasn't always possible at the very last minute, especially after rush shipping got more expensive. Still, I often over ordered in a panic. "We can't run out of that!" I felt that way about too many things.

Once up and running, our website complicated inventory. I'd get a request from someone in Texas, wanting a dozen Daily Mood calendars to give as office gifts. He was thrilled we had them. (All orders with us were ultimately placed by phone, so we got to talk to these online customers.) It was a good sale, but suddenly we had little stock for our local shoppers. Even if I tried to predict how many we were going to need, our customers were now competing with internet shoppers from everywhere. I certainly didn't want to say no to anyone calling us to order, but I felt bad disappointing those who supported us all year round.

I hated disappointing anyone, and it happened more at Christmas. We couldn't provide our usual free gift-wrapping — people would have had to wait hours or days, and we didn't have space to do it either. We ran out of things people wanted. And because some years we had great new items, the first thing many people asked was "What's new? What's the must have this season?" Some years I dreaded that question. I wanted us to have the must have item, the thing you'd show one customer and suddenly everyone around bought two or three. But some years, we just didn't have one.

Even after years of experience, I began to get anxious by early November. I'd try to explain to a friend or my husband. "I don't have enough people to work! I'm not sure how many hamsters to order! I haven't figured out the window display! There's no must have item!" "Come on, you say this every year," was the usual response. "It always turns out alright." That was more or less true. Some seasons were much better than others but we never had a true disaster. And once the season started there was nothing to do but give in to it and go with whatever was happening, another zen lesson in letting go.

So many people told us that we made their Christmas special. Some came just once a year, saying we were the only thing they looked forward to about the season. One couple bought multiple silly singing animals and Santas for a yearly holiday party, one woman always ordered several dozen surprise balls, people came specifically for our glass ornaments, others bought wind-up toys for everyone in the family. I know we helped create a lot of family traditions. And people came for stocking stuffers though their varying definitions of what exactly those were never ceased to amaze me. One person's stocking stuffer is another's major gift.

We made it festive. We strung little colored lights all around the store and wore reindeer antlers and silly Santa hats. We put little Santa hat stickers on the people and animals in our black and white postcards, and always had a bowl of candy kisses on the front desk. We stayed open late weeknights all December, and had a neighborhood weekend "Midnight Madness Shopping Party," serving cookies, snacks and wine, which of course we partook of liberally ourselves. That made for a fifteen-hour day, and a somewhat bleary-eyed Sunday staff, but we survived and it was always fun.

And then it would be December 24th, the last day before Christmas. There was a sense of relief; no matter how busy it got, we were done. Following the lead of my neighbor/friend/mentor Barbara, I decided early on to close at 4 pm that day. One of us would stand at the door, quizzing the 3:59 arrivals. "We're about to close, do you know exactly what you want?" We all had families to visit, some had drives to make, and really, if people hadn't bought their gifts by then… they'd just have to buy them somewhere else, while we all sat on the floor, had champagne, cheese and cake and exchanged not only gifts but the best stories of that year's season. After the first year or two we realized we should paper over the door so last-minute customers couldn't see us and desperately pound on the door.

By five or so, we picked up the giftwrap, washed out the glasses, vacuumed the cookie crumbs and went our separate ways.

I put all the Christmas merchandise on sale the week after, and many people kept holiday shopping, buying last minute gifts or spending money they'd received on gifts for themselves. It was still a busy week. Then we closed early again on New Year's Eve, and while we were closed on the 1st, I worked all day "taking Christmas away." January 2nd, we opened up, sat there and marveled at the crazy difference in sales. And soon after that, I started thinking about the Valentine's window. The winter gift shows were coming up. And when was Easter this year, early or late? The holiday cycle began anew.

CHAPTER 26

# Design and Display

"Designing" seems a rather lofty word for my process when I first picked up a pencil and sketched out a floor plan for the store. I didn't have much money to spend. What I did have: some fixtures left over from our Vermont woodworking days, an almost ex-boyfriend who was good with a hammer and had lots of tools, an electrician friend, and another acquaintance who agreed to make the displays that had to be custom built. I tried to imagine the space. What would people see first when they walked in? Where should the main counter and register be? What type of merchandise would go best where? My instincts were not bad. Thirty-six and a half years later when I closed the store, the basic floor plan was still in place.

The store was smallish, rectangular in shape. When you entered, you looked to the far end and saw wall mounted card racks. I chose not to use the kind where the cards overlapped. Instead, you would see each image complete. It made for fewer cards, but I liked the way it looked and we sold a lot of cards, so no regrets. We did have an unforeseen "danger zone" though. Our birthday card section was right next to the stockroom door. If you came out too quickly and someone was looking at those cards, it was easy to bump into them and though we never had a serious injury, we must have apologized to hundreds of customers over the years.

The front desk was on your right as you came in, about a third of the way down the space. Anyone working behind it could see the entire store, and was immediately visible to entering customers. I felt we were captains of a ship — that people needed to see someone visibly in command of the space. The only place you really couldn't see from the desk was the aforementioned danger zone, and over the years, we occasionally suspected a customer or two of taking advantage of that one blind spot to pocket something.

I put the more expensive merchandise up toward the front, so we could talk about it with customers easily. Then there was a narrower space between the desk and the opposite wall, a bottleneck when things got busy. It featured our plastic wind-up toys, small treasures, and the tin toys you wound up with keys. To the right of the desk was a table of tiny things; party poppers, water marbles, nose flutes, double dice, fortune fish, and other items good for party bags or a tiny gift. It was also the "you can choose one thing from here" go to for parents with small children. Nothing was more than a few dollars, and for years, there were plenty of choices that cost even less. We kept all the little things neat and well organized. "Display with Dignity" was our motto, no matter how seemingly inconsequential the item.

The corner display in the back opposite the danger corner doubled as a seasonal area. Christmas things at Christmas, rabbits, chicks, flowers and other spring-like items at Easter, black cats, owls and skeletons at Halloween. And as years went by, mini sections began to evolve here and there — the science shelf, the birthday area, the cat and dog shelf, the Paris shelf. Some came and went, others became as immovable as the card racks on the wall. There was definitely a benefit to moving things around. People thought they'd seen everything, but they never really did. And yet it turned out there were some things you just couldn't move. Kaleidoscopes had to be to the right of the desk, wind-up toys directly across. We'd experiment, but they'd always wind up back in their "rightful" place. Some kind of intuitive Feng Shui perhaps.

We displayed items way up high, hanging from the ceiling, and way down low, close to the floor. Of course for adults there was an optimal height; items displayed waist to head high were the most easily noticed. It was always interesting to move something that wasn't selling and see what happened. It often improved its sales. (There's a reason why companies pay for "product placement," i.e. having their products get prime display spots in grocery stores.) I used to fantasize about redoing the store — one eye level shelf running around the entire perimeter. It would have been fun visually, but of course we would have had a lot less merchandise on view.

Some things sold better if there was a little group of them. Some did better if we showed just one. Should a Solar Queen be alone on a shelf? Or should we display one, and show another in a box so people would know she came packaged? Would ten different sets of marble coasters be too many? Should all the lava lights be together, or should we spread them throughout? Should we take the plastic shrink wrap off the touchable bubbles and poppers? Would people know the crown wearing frog was a bottle opener, or did it need a sign? And what should we display in the front window? Many decisions to make.

We didn't have formal displays in the front window at first. I had a pretty stained-glass lamp I'd brought from Vermont that hung in the center, and underneath, there were a few shelves and pedestals to display a bit of what we were selling. We'd occasionally try something simple like a color themed window, but didn't go much further until I started dating Gerry. He became my boyfriend, then husband, and luckily for me and for the store, he was very good at creating window displays. We found that a really good one would stop passers-by in their tracks, and those who stopped to look would almost always come in and check us out.

The first one we did together, Joie's first real window "display," was meant to showcase Frozen Moments, a line of surreal food sculptures: a carton supported by a ribbon of "milk" pouring down into a cereal bowl, a cracked egg hovering above a mixing bowl, an ice-cream sundae with chocolate sauce pouring from its airborne jar, the precursors to all the simpler coffee and ice-cream spills we sold years later. We planned to have two bear puppets eating breakfast, one of the cereal bowl sculptures on the table, real toast popping out of a toaster and suspended in mid-air, cornflakes all over the floor, a crazy kitchen theme. It took a few hours to do it all, and just one task remained — to hang a swirl of plastic forks and knives around that stained glass light. That was when we discovered we had very different styles of working. I thought, just hang a few randomly, he thought hang some exact number meticulously. By 2 am, we were having our first fight. He won, and I had to admit he was right, details did count and the window was a smashing success. A few months later he made a wonderful Christmas window. Directly under that glass lamp, he built a cardboard cathedral, painted grey, with a stained-glass window made from theatre gels. There were real branches in the background, with glass bird ornaments clipped on, and a circle of handmade dolls dancing in the snow. It took him hours and hours, and was completely magical.

The lamp came out after that. It didn't lend itself to most displays. Others we did included two snowmen playing chess, a "Would you like to swing on a star?" theme — handmade starlights (that are still in my basement) with Georgia Landau dolls on their swings, and flying fuzzy winged pigs. We made a rainstorm of Koosh balls the better to show off our world map umbrella, a chef barbecuing wind-up toys on skewers (that one actually brought some complaints of cruelty!), a fantastical Easter window with chicken puppets laying colored eggs, a winter scene — mouse puppets with paper clip skates on a frozen mirror/pond surrounded by real trees. One Halloween display had a handmade cat/woman doll sitting on a crescent moon which hung over a field of real pumpkins. (We found out that real pumpkins in a hot sunny window rot quicker than you'd think.) Of course not every display worked out as planned. The giant Christmas stockings looked awkward and lumpy. And one Easter, stuffing a giant white rabbit costume with enough newspaper to make it stand up was way more difficult than we thought and once done, it looked vaguely threatening.

But there were so many fun and wonderful windows. Besides holidays, we had store anniversary displays for years one, five, ten, fifteen and every five years thereafter. I was a creative consultant, but most of the ideas were Gerry's, and when he later decided to quit his job as a picture framer and go back to school to become an architect, photos of his window designs were a prominent feature of the portfolio that got him accepted to more than one program. When he left to go to school, Danielle, another talented artist/ designer started working for me and was able to keep our creative window tradition going, with enthusiastic help from our crew. After she left, my boyfriend, now husband, was back and continued to help when he could. Since he now also had his own architectural projects going, working on the windows could be stressful for us, though it's not what broke up our marriage. And when we divorced, I got to "keep" his family, and his brother Peter did some great displays for us too. Happily, over the years, we almost always had someone with either a good idea or the talent to help me with mine.

One Valentine's window featured five life-size cardboard policemen, one holding a stop sign emblazoned "Stop! In the Name of Love." People climbed into the window to take their photo with Obama and Romney in a Halloween window — Obama dressed as Superman, and Romney as Dracula. Four years later we superimposed Hilary's Face onto a Glinda the Good Witch stand-up and Trump's onto Bozo the clown. That one got several write ups and quite a bit of attention, and happily, only one complaint. Sometimes it felt onerous to have to constantly think of new displays, but once you had your idea, it was fun.

The Christmas windows were the most stressful as those were the ones the most people would see and it was always a big relief when I got an idea a few months in advance. That first cathedral window set a high bar, and my second favorite was as different as it could have been — Gerry filled the window with zig-zag strings of different sized Christmas bulb lights, completely abstract and glorious. Another favorite was a Christmas tree, its top half covered in ornaments. There were none on the lower branches, but lots of broken ones on the floor, surrounded by a lot of our very lifelike cat doorstops. Interestingly, the comments ran 50/50 between "Ha! that's great!" and serious versions of "What happened to the ornaments?"

I thought of our bags, cards, website, and general "branding" as an extension of display, though I guess it would more properly be called design. We were extremely low tech at first, using rubber stamps on both our gift boxes and bags, decorating each one slightly differently in our spare time at the front desk. The first business cards also featured my own calligraphy and a rubber-stamp image of a grown man in a tie, riding a polka dot rocking horse. A few years in, I hired a fancy design team that had an office on the corner of our block, and we worked together to create a design image for the store, new door graphics, bags, printed embossed gift boxes and eventually, a new business card and a big new sign for the storefront.

I wonder if any store or business that sticks around for thirty-six years keeps the same exact designs and color schemes on their walls, cards and graphics. My guess is no. It's funny — we would be thrilled with a design and then over a period of time, gradually come to feel that it wasn't quite right, that we needed a change. Not counting our first, extremely short lived "Toys for Adults" business card, we went through four major design changes over the years. The bags changed, the stickers changed, the business card, the sign, the color of the walls, the background of the website. An element of the old was always included in the new — the typeface used for "Joie de Vivre" or the yellow rubber duck that appeared on our last two business cards.

Companies would often provide displays with our orders, but we almost never used them. They took up too much space, looked too commercial, displayed too many of the same thing. And while the computer brought changes to all aspects of retail, one I particularly noticed was the advent of "computer graphics." With some notable exceptions, this often resulted in a sad blandness of design. Walt Disney bought Winnie the Pooh and E.H. Shepard must have rolled over in his grave. Those beloved characters began to look fatuous and drunk to me and eventually they were no longer hand drawn.

Of course a good designer will use a computer to do wonderful things, and many of our best posters and flyers were done just that way by our talented in-house designer, my sister Nancy. Still, I made our door signs myself, the ones announcing "Closed for New Year's Day" and etc., using postcards and stickers and my ancient calligraphy pen. Inside, I mostly hand-wrote our smaller signs with that same trusty (and leaky!) pen. I had been in charge of writing signs for the Village Gallery long ago and on my visits there years later, spotted some of them still in use. They showed their age, but it was fun to recognize my own handwriting, and to marvel at how long they'd lasted. And every once in awhile, I'd come across something at Joie that a long-gone employee had written or drawn years ago. I'd recognize their handwriting, think of them, and smile.

In a sense advertising is also a form of display. You put something on a page and send it out into the world, hoping it will convey something of what you're about. We didn't do a lot of it. To be truly effective, you needed to do it a fair amount, consistently, and it was expensive. Besides, for the first ten years we really didn't need to, we had plenty of business without it. We would take out small ads in programs for organizations we believed in/wanted to support. The Christmas Revels, the American Repertory Theatre, auctions and events to raise money for music or specialty schools, or the homeless, or abused women. But by the time we could have used new customers, advertising was changing. People were doing most of their newspaper and magazine reading online now and as someone who found most online advertising intrusive and annoying, I recoiled at the idea.

I've rarely if ever deliberately clicked an online ad. Plus, unlike print, with online ads, you couldn't even be sure where they'd be placed. They jumped around like loose cannons, intruding into articles. I didn't want Joie to annoy people. Maybe my distaste for some of the new ways held us back. But for better or worse, I took some pride in being old school. For the most part, we let our windows, our store, and our loyal customers do the talking.

CHAPTER 27

# Joie de Vivre Icons

Some of our items took on a life of their own, but it wasn't predictable. Which of the many things we sold would be elevated to icon status was a mystery; we just got fonder and fonder of something over time and began to use its image to represent us. Two, the white mouse puppet and the devil duck, have had their say in these pages. The cat paw has its chapter too.

Some reigns were brief — the plastic vegetable goddess, hated by some, loved by others, and some lasted long after they were no longer made and we just had one left, like La Luciole, the tiny French Firefly Fairy. These items had to photograph well, as they appeared on flyers, sale posters, our website, postcards and much of the limited publicity/advertising we did. Singing Hamsters, incredibly popular, did not make the cut in part because of that, besides, there were too many styles and they were available only for a year or two. In the end, the mouse puppet, the devil duck, the French fairy, and the enigmatic cat paw were our go-tos. They all had that inimitable *je ne sais quoi*.

To achieve iconic status, personality was needed, but other items became strongly associated with the store as well: the Yodeling Pickle, the Stylish Mustaches, the solar powered Rainbow Maker, the Pin Screen, the Pipedream gamelan, the magnetic Dancing Ballerina, the rubber finger monsters, the Penguin Race, snowglobes, the Buddha Board, and Rudy, the Tiki head tissue holder. We sold all of these for well over twenty years, some the entire thirty-six. They were our classics.

Many more things certainly would have achieved this status had we been able to sell them longer but tragically, they were discontinued. The tiki drummer, toilet paper man (a wooden cyclist who pedaled atop a roll,) the neon moon clock, the Singing Hamsters, the lady in a bathtub bank, the motion activated Breezy Singer birds, Chicken-in-a-Blanket, the Teacup Fairy, the large Folkmanis bear puppets, the microcopter that could fly the length of the store, the mirrors that whistled, screamed or laughed, and the crashing hammer. Customers came in asking for them years later, right through our very last months. These inquiries always began with "I'm looking for something I bought from you a long time ago..." We hated disappointing these hopeful people, but were grateful for all the products that remained available for years. And to this day I have a French fairy, two devil ducks, multiple mouse puppets, cat paws, and more than a few of our other classics at home. Essential parts of Joie history!

CHAPTER 28

# My Three Signs

My first sign was painted by a woman named Grace who lived about ten blocks from the store. I don't remember how I found her. Simple and elegant, it spelled out Joie de Vivre in silvery capital letters, on a dark blue background with pink, a lighter blue, and silver flourishes in each corner. She delivered it right on time, and we hung it a few days before our official opening. It was perfect, and stayed up for five years. I paid $500.

My second sign was a lot more elaborate. There was a hip design firm with offices on the end of our block and their designers all shopped at the store. I can't remember if I asked or they suggested we try their services, but a year or two after we opened, they designed the graphics for our front door and window, printed bags, and stickers for our gift boxes. When I decided it might be time to design a larger, jazzier sign, I asked them and they jumped at the chance. They proposed lots of different things, spinning letters above the roofline among them, (nixed by the city's building code.) We finally settled on a multilayered sign, with silver hand cut letters pinned to float slightly above its surface, over a pink neon wave that topped a blue sea. Images taken from our rubber stamp lines were added too, a star, a heart, a cow, a banana peel and more. (A cherished line I spotted in some meeting minutes I still have: "Clifford relayed to Robin a discussion with Linda where it was decided that the upside-down bunny should be changed to a heart.") An old school pointing hand hovered above the door, and there was a blue neon line running across the very top. It was spectacular, sophisticated and eye catching. I paid $5000.

Once the sign was up there, hanging above our window and door, that was that. I didn't think about it much, except when the overhead light bulbs hanging over it burned out, making it hard to see at night. I'd call JoeD, he'd climb onto the roof and replace them. After ten years, we started having a little trouble with the neon, but I found a neon guy named Carmen in Boston who'd drive out to Cambridge and fix it. Watching him work one day, I realized that the blue and black background paint had faded. How had I not seen that before? We repainted. Then the day came when Carmen returned yet again to fix the neon wave. He looked at me sadly. "There's really nothing I can do," he explained. "And I can't replace it, the wood it's screwed into is rotting." This was a blow. That pink wave of neon was sweet and distinctive.

Money had become more of an issue and I convinced myself that even without the neon, the sign looked pretty good. A few years passed, and then one morning I found a largish piece of splintered wood on the sidewalk outside the store. It was painted yellow on one side, rotting, and seemed — a bit familiar. I glanced up at the sign. The star on the top right-hand corner was gone. I was holding part of a star in my hand. I looked around and spotted the other pieces, picked them up and brought them to the back of the store. Maybe it was time? I went back out and inspected the sign more closely. The painted strawberry was gone. When had that fallen off? And why hadn't anyone noticed? Now I saw that the whole bottom part of the sign was buckling. Alarmingly. What if it fell off as someone was going through the door? I did a quick calculation. That sign had been up there for twenty-seven years. It was time.

My third sign felt urgent, we needed it designed and up there fast. The second had become the last remaining link to an older graphic identity. Our business cards and bags had evolved, now designed by my sister and we needed something more in line with our new look. But there was a new problem, our bank account. I couldn't afford the equivalent of a sign that had cost $5000 twenty-seven years ago. Neither Joie de Vivre, or my personal bank account had any extra money at all, so this would have to be a much simpler project. My sister saved the day, coming up with a simple design that still, by way of a daisy and an upside-down duck, managed to convey the spirit of the store, while being relatively easy to execute. I got in touch with a local sign shop I knew had made many of the other signs on our block. I scraped up the cash and they did a great job. We scared a few passersby who saw them taking down the old one and thought we were closing, but an hour later the new sign was up, and I breathed a sigh of relief. Then I went out and took a good long look at it and breathed another. I liked it. It looked right. Success! That sign was up for our last six years and it was strange taking it down. I don't know what I'll do with it, but it's living in my basement. The guys who brought it home for me put it down the wrong way, righting the upside-down duck. But no one really sees it there, so I left it that way. For now.

CHAPTER 29

# Wired! or, Jane Snowball Bites an Apple

In 1984, a 72-year-old grandmother in Gateshead, England with the wonderful name of Jane Snowball sat down in her armchair and used her television remote to place an order for margarine, cornflakes and eggs. This mundane event was part of a local council initiative to help the elderly, and was in fact, monumental, cited by many as the first time something was ordered "online." A piece of computer technology called Videotex sent the order from her phone line to the local Tesco store where the goods were packed and delivered to her door. Mrs. Snowball never saw a computer, her television linked her to the shop. But 1984 was the start of something big. That same year, Apple released its first personal computer. Other events of note: Clara Peller first asked "Where's the Beef," Bruce Springsteen released *Born in the USA*, and a gift store called Joie de Vivre opened up in Cambridge, MA.

I was completely unfamiliar with the internet in 1984 and it was quite a few years before I had reason to think much about it. It wasn't until 1994 that Amazon sold its first book, and eBay began in 1995. (Note of interest: its first sale was a broken laser pointer, sold to someone who actually collected — broken laser pointers!) Then, in August of 1994, the *New York Times* printed an article titled "Attention Shoppers, the Internet is Open." It began: "At noon yesterday, Phil Brandenberger of Philadelphia went shopping for a compact audio disk, paid for it with his credit card and made history. Moments later, the champagne corks were popping in a small two-story frame house in Nashua, N.H. There, a team of young cyberspace entrepreneurs celebrated what was apparently the first retail transaction on the Internet using a readily available version of powerful data encryption software designed to guarantee privacy." History says that the first regular internet users were affluent males over thirty, ordering wine, chocolate and flowers. At Joie, we did not notice any effects on sales.

My husband bought a tiny grey Apple computer for our home. I didn't use it much though I remember watching with him as a photo sent by his brother who was working overseas downloaded line by line by line by line. It took a good hour before we saw the entire picture and if that seems laughable now, we were wowed at the time. For me, the computer was basically a better typewriter. No carbon paper! No White-Out! Even when I got one for the store and we started using email, I had not the least suspicion how the machine on my desk would eventually change the retail world. I was more concerned about stores like Target and Walmart — the bigger is better problem. I instinctively disliked Amazon because I loved our plentiful local bookstores, and did not want to see them suffer, but it didn't feel like a threat to Joie. Of course I was wrong. Amazon proved to be the single most destructive force both small and even much larger businesses had ever faced.

But that was still down the road in the mid 1990s. It would take awhile for Amazon to start selling anything and everything, using dishonest and sleazy tactics to squash its opposition as well as its own employees. In the meantime, as computers became ubiquitous and essential for most businesses, there were other issues at hand. A big one was, should we have a domain name, so we could send email directly from the store? This was a subject for much discussion with my peers at the Gift Show. Did you get your name.com? Do you think this matters? When I finally decided, yes, we do need a domain name and probably even an actual website, joiedevivre. com was already taken, by a hotel chain, owned by Hyatt, which advertised their hotels as "a community for the spirited, the light-hearted, the young at heart." I was mad at myself for dragging my feet, but we were able to snag joiedevivre.net (just ahead of the Joie de Vivre French food catalog who had to settle for something else.) This was 1999, and putting up a website didn't seem that pressing. Our customers knew where to find us.

And did I mention — we had email? It's a little hard to remember, all these years later, but email was kind of exciting. So easy to get in touch with people! Ask questions at weird times, even the middle of the night if you wanted to! Easily communicate with more than one person at a time! I also bought a fax machine for sending orders, orders that I had either mailed, or called in. Previously I'd often called our rubber-stamp vendors to place our orders: two angels A515, two surprised cats, A 640, four beating hearts; and on and on. I could be on the phone with them for a long time but there was a good side to that. I got to know the people at the companies I called regularly, and if we needed a favor, say, something shipped extra quickly, or a tiny below minimum special order, they were likely to say sure.

The dark side of email began to dawn on me a few years later. It was harder to resolve things, easy to go back and forth with no one coming to a decision. And we started to get way too many emails from businesses. Back when they had to call, or print something up and mail it through the post office, a company might send you something once every few months, but with email programs, they could send as many times as they wanted, and they did. It drove me crazy. If it was a company we did buy from, I felt I should read it in case it was important and it almost never was. The Gift Shows, which had automatically preregistered you and mailed your badge if you had attended the previous show, started requiring everyone to register online or via email every single time. And then they sent floods of emails before the show. It was total overkill and I didn't always read them. And of course, if you didn't read them, you could miss something that actually was important, like the "Night on Broadway" email I didn't read with information on discounted tickets for the event they held each NY show. I missed Hamilton tickets. That was a tragedy!

Email quickly lent itself to the fine art of the scam. Some of the early ones were easy to spot. How likely was it really, that your friend's daughter (unnamed of course) was being held hostage and needed money wired immediately? Or that an African prince had lost his fortune and chosen you, among all the people in the world, to assist him in regaining it? Or that Mrs. Linah Mohohlo — the governor of the Bank of Botswana would like to give you the 10.5 million dollars currently languishing in her account? Not very likely, but all of them landed in my inbox. (Luckily, I was contacted by U.S. Chief Judge Susan Gertrude Braden, whose email was, oddly, tonymore558@gmail.com, to offer her assistance with these scams.) Scammers are now generally more sophisticated. Who amongst us has not felt at least a moment of panic when reading the official looking email that says your account was used to buy something expensive you never would have bought and would you please verify all your information? That is, before you check the senders' address and see there's no way that it came from Apple or whoever.

A lot of our scam emails were disguised as business inquiries. I wrote up a little something on our blog for fun:

A Little Advice for Etherington

*This advice is for all would be scam artists in foreign countries. I know you're not likely to be reading this blog... but, I have just a bit of advice for you nonetheless. First, when you make up a name — choose something a little less "unusual" than say... Etherington Parton. Second, don't ask if we take credit cards. All store websites with things to sell take credit cards. And 99.9% of legitimate customers know this — or figure it out by actually reading our website policies. And last, do not end your inquiry with this phrase: "I await your urgent response so we can proceed." I have never received a legitimate order inquiry that ended that way, and I have received a lot of order inquiries. I have also received a number of inquiries where my "urgent" response is requested. None has ever turned out to be legit — so it just screams "I am a scam artist." Etherington, if you are an actual would-be buyer, you will already have received my polite but no-nonsense response to your inquiry. I haven't heard back from you though, so I guess the whole matter turned out to be rather less urgent than you led me to believe!*

Sometimes we didn't spot scams until we were well into them. The dancing ballerina by Magneto was probably our most ordered web item — they were hard to find. We sent them all over the world and had many delightful interactions with people who remembered them from their childhood, and at one point, people who had seen her twirling at the beginning of the movie Doubt. To end this chapter, here are our emails back and forth about a ballerina sale, back in the summer of 2016. I call it: A Strange Interaction, or Two Ballerinas to Mexico Por Favor!

*6/18/2016 – Edgar Aviles to Joie de Vivre (sent by someone else "Decarlo")*
Question: I've been looking for the ballerina for a long time a lot of stores have an ad for it but they don't have it in stock — do you have it?

*6/18/16 – Joie de Vivre to Edgar Aviles*
We do have these in stock, both in the blond/blue dress and the brunette/red dress. Shipping/handling in the U.S. is 4.50, $5 for two. You can call us or email us your address and call with credit card info — thanks for asking!

*6/18/16 – Edgar Aviles to Joie de Vivre*
Hi — yeah, I would like two ballerinas. VERY IMPORTANT it has to be insured it doesn't matter which service do you use, here in Mexico they steal things that come from US if they are not insured. It has happened to me several times. It doesn't matter if it is FedEx, DHL, etc., just let me know how much it would be for the insurance, my address is: (redacted!) And the cellphone service is very bad where I live cannot get a signal and here in Mexico using a payphone it's very insecure, can I give you my CC info by email?

*6/18/16 – Joie de Vivre to Edgar Aviles*
Hi, the shipping and insurance to Mexico would be 13.50 — so your total would be 24.00 for the two ballerinas and 1350 — $37.50.
It's fine to send your card information by email. And let us know what color ballerinas you want, blond or brunette.
Sincerely, Linda/Joie de Vivre

*6/29/16 – Edgar Avila to Joie de Vivre*
Hi, I would place an order. I hope you and your family are well and with good health, I got a message from you that the insurance would be 13.50 and the total 37.50. I would please like the 2 ballerinas insured, here is my info. (censored!)

*6/29/2016 – Joie to Edgar Avila*
Hi — thank you very much, we will send this out to you today.

*7/11/2016 – Decarlo wrote:*
I called USPS two times and told them I have not received my package. I also told them that my package is insured which they told me both times that is not insured and they don't know where it is, can you please give me the insurance # so I can call them back again thanks.

*7/11/2016 – Joie wrote:*
Hi — I just tracked the package and the site said it is "in transit" from Mexico City — that it left on July 5th — so I would give it a few more days and then let me know if it has not arrived — I will keep tracking it too. And it is insured through us — if you do not receive it, we will resend the order — don't worry.

*7/11/2016 – Decarlo wrote:*
Thanks Linda have a great day.

*7/13/2016 – Joie wrote:*
Okay, I will resend it tomorrow.

*7/13/2016 – Decarlo wrote:*
Yeah, don't send it, I'll wait 5 more days, then wait for my email, thanks.

*7/14/2016 – Joie wrote:*
Okay, just keep us posted. I will be away next week but my sister will be reading the email and I will tell her about the situation. She can also mail the new ones if you don't receive the first ones.

*7/15/2016 – Decarlo wrote:*
Linda, a lot of people has taken advantage of me in several times, I have not been able to recuperate my losses, it gets sometimes to the point that I don't know what to do, I'll give you an example, I ordered the same figurines through a German company, I never got them but I used eBay. I sent a message to the sender, he never answered me, I send another message to eBay customer service well you believe it they never answer my message, eBay, I did not comment negative, I know that if that person keeps doing the same thing it's going to flunk. Have a great day Linda.

*7/21/2016 – Decarlo wrote:*
Hi Linda, you put my other email as spam maybe by mistake, I have not received the ballerinas, but I was thinking, I joined a company that sells basically anything from any brand over the internet, they provide you with a free website, they do all the delivery, they charge the people, they take care of complaints, all you have to do is advertise, there is no charge whatsoever for you to join or any fees at all, so I was thinking you already sell things over the internet, why not sell everything? For example tell your friends and family about the new store and tell them instead of purchasing in

Walmart, Safeway, etc., but it in my store, anytime they purchase
anything you get paid. My site name is allpalace.com now this
is my site but explains you how the company works, the site of
the company is very big so people get confuse, in my site I talk
about the most important stuff about the company. So here is the
deal, if you join my business I won't make you send me the items
(ballerinas) again, you will send them again but I would pay for
them again, I want them sent via DHL, and insured by DHL, here
where I live there is only DHL and if you send them via FedEx is
a mess, they lose the packages, etc. so why don't you think about it
but don't answer me today answer me the 23rd so you'll give it a
good thought, thanks.

*7/21/2016 – Joie wrote:*
Sorry, but we are not interested in your company. As we cannot
guarantee when your package will arrive, with or without insurance,
we will refund your credit card for $37.50

*7/21/2016 – Decarlo wrote:*
Okay, thanks Linda, yeah, it's pretty bad the situation in Mexico
when Mr. Trump gets the seat, he will fix some things here in
Mexico, I really feel bad for your loss. But you are more than
welcome to see Ivanka Trump present her Dad as a Republican
Nominee on my official Spanish site (presidentedonaldtrump.com)
the speech would be in English look for the link Ivanka LIVE, hoy
aqua a las 6:00 pm (it would be 7:00 pm Cleveland time) I wish to
you the best of everything.

*7/22/2016 – Joie wrote:*
Attached is a copy of your refund slip.

*7/22/2016 – Decarlo wrote:*
Linda, I hope your business grow as you never imagine, but most
important that you always be happy. Brandon Decarlo.

Happily, we never heard from Brandon/Edgar again. But you can see how this kind of thing took up time and psychic energy we could have used better another way. At least in this particular case we wound up with a good story.

CHAPTER 30

# www.joiedevivre.net

Today, if your store has no website, most people assume you're not a legit business. You can't even register for many trade shows without one, at least without special dispensation. I knew we needed one, but found the design process challenging. How to communicate the feeling of the store online? I registered our domain name in 1999, but put off getting serious for quite awhile and our website was not designed and "up" until 2007. (We failed to note the exact date at the time, not realizing one day there would be a need to remember this momentous occasion!)

There were plenty of commercial/make your own website templates available, but they tended to be bland and generic looking. A designer friend tried her hand, and I hired some professionals to submit proposals, but it was tricky. Their designs invariably had at least part of the feeling I couldn't quite define but knew I wanted, and some of their ideas were really fun, but none felt like an accurate reflection of the store to me. Yes, we were silly and zany, and maybe even a little hip, but that wasn't all. I began to despair of ever finding someone who would be able to come up with a concept I liked.

Then my sister, who has an art background and was working for me at the time, emailed one Sunday night. "I was fooling around with an idea for the website this weekend. Here's a link, see what you think." I took a look. And I felt a tremendous sense of excitement. In just one weekend she had come up with something I instantly felt was perfect. There were plenty of details to work out, but the look and feel of it seemed exactly right. A few months later we were up and running. We had a website! We decided to keep it old fashioned in one way though; we didn't have a shopping cart. Customers had to email or call us to place orders. That no doubt lost us business, but it helped us keep our personal customer service, and we always enjoyed talking to those who found us randomly and lived in different parts of the country, or sometimes, the world.

Some of our local customers began to pre-shop on our website. One day two different people came in, walked up to the desk and asked for something they'd seen there. One said it made it easier for her because we had so many things in the physical store she sometimes found it distracting. This made me slightly uneasy. If people just came in and bought the thing they'd seen online and left, weren't they maybe missing something? Was our website making us — the people behind the desk — superfluous? And we had so many things that weren't on the website, how would they know about them? We wanted the website to be an accessory to the store, not the main event. But would some people rather browse our website than the store? And who was I to object if this way of shopping made their lives easier? They were still our customers.

There were at least two things about the internet that did make me happy. One was the ease of communicating with suppliers in Europe and abroad. Before we had email I once called a Danish company about a xylophone of theirs we were selling. We wound up having a lovely conversation for about twenty minutes. When my next phone bill arrived, it was more than twice its usual amount. I looked it over and found that phone call to Denmark had cost $85! Whoops! Had to sell more than a few xylophones to make up for that. I could have written them for the price of an airmail stamp, but that back and forth would have taken at least two weeks. International email was very much appreciated.

The other happy thing was not xylophone related, but it was musical. With just an iPod and our wifi, we could stream music, and (commercial plug) for a mere $3.99 a month, create 100 different ad-free stations on Pandora radio, each one themed around a specific artist or song. After years of music wars (with more than one person working, there will never be complete agreement on what music should be playing) we made relative peace, with the huge bonus of not having to hear the few CDs we all liked a million times a day. If a song came on we didn't like, it could disappear with the touch of a finger. It's true the stations could get a little weird with Aretha Franklin or James Brown suddenly belting out the next song on a Joni Mitchell station. Nonetheless, music streaming was a very big improvement in the quality of daily life at Joie de Vivre.

The internet did serious damage to advertising via print media; it gradually eroded its primacy as papers and magazines started to struggle to keep their readers. Not that I could ever afford to advertise that much. For years, I didn't feel the need to, although we would take out an ad for a worthy cause benefit, or in a program for something particularly festive we wanted to support. By the time Joie needed new customers, the constant and annoying presence of ads chasing people all over the web made the idea of advertising that way seem useless to me.

When you bought a space in a magazine or paper, you knew where your ad would be, and that it would remain there. Of course it was more expensive to have better placement or a whole page, but you knew what you were paying for. Internet ads jumped around all over the place, and I didn't believe the Google, Yahoo, and other reps assuring me that my ad would be at the top of a page if I paid more. What would happen to the advertiser who'd signed up before me and paid the same rate? Would my ad bump theirs off? Well, in most cases, yes.

YELP offered "Enhanced Business Profile with competitor's ad removal." Call me old-fashioned, but that sounded sleazy and unethical. If a store in my neighborhood was paying less to YELP, my ad would appear and theirs wouldn't? And of course the opposite — if we didn't go for the more expensive advertising, whose ad would be removed? Cheap little us! Or did "at the top of the page" mean it would be there once or twice for twenty seconds? I must have gotten several thousand calls from these companies about advertising over the years, but I stuck to my no thank you guns.

We also entered the age of discounts, discounts, discounts. Groupon was a company that let its users purchase at steep discounts by buying as a group. It aimed first at restaurants and "experiences," but soon added retail, and we were harassed almost daily by them for a long time. Their plan made absolutely no sense for small companies — you had to agree to sell merchandise at a 50% discount, breaking even at best — except that they took a 50% commission on everything you sold. Theoretically you would get new customers, but practically, you would lose money on every sale you made. No thanks!

Still, Groupon was a huge success for awhile, garnering much talk, praise and press, and "inspiring" many other would-be entrepreneurs to try the same model. Soon we were besieged with calls from similar start-ups that wanted us to offer their customers special discounts. We kept refusing, but it was annoying and though we tried not to be rude, I can't say the same for some of the callers who weren't particularly inclined to take our "not interested" for what it was. Then a new type of discount crept in, the good cause discounts.

Discourage people from driving — give discounts to bike riders! Encourage people to shop local — give discounts to members of Shop Local groups! The more traditional too — discounts for students! Discounts for seniors! Discounts for anyone who belonged to your business association! We did give some discounts. People who worked in the other stores on our block or close by got a discount, our staff got a huge discount, and we gave a courtesy discount to their household members too. But if we had given discounts to everyone that asked, it would have in effect been the same as permanently lowering our prices by 10 or 15% and that made no sense to me. We rarely even had sales, reserving them for special celebrations or to get rid of things that were discontinued or damaged. I thought our prices were fair.

"Fair" became an outmoded concept as Amazon revved up its game. Without storefronts to maintain, they could sell things for less than we could, and for years, they willingly lost millions in their quest to dominate the market by shipping for free and undercutting others' prices. Some companies had minimum retail prices for their goods. You couldn't sell for less than that price. But many didn't enforce their own rules. And going after Amazon was not the easiest thing in the world, as many who tried and failed will attest.

So we were no fans of Amazon at Joie. No one who owns a small business is. Some customers began "show-rooming," going to stores to check out prices, then ordering what they wanted for less online. And brick and mortar stores from hardware to clothing to shoes began to struggle. Many went out of business. This wasn't solely due to Amazon — there were other large chains that made survival difficult. For us, it was a bit easier because most of our customers were not looking for anything specific when they came in. They didn't know that a snoozy lamb, a remote-control unicorn or a picture book on the language of clothes even existed until they saw them on our shelves. We may have lost some repeat sales though because once you do know something exists, you can usually find it online. We were of course happy to ship things, but we couldn't afford to ship for free.

Here's a blogpost I wrote some years ago, when I could still be shocked at Amazon's tactics:

> *This article I read in the* New York Times *today kind of blew my little shopkeeper's mind. I couldn't decide how to title this post — "Amazon Goes Completely to the Dark Side," or "Will They Stop at Nothing?" Evidently the answer to that question is "They will stop at nothing." Read this and judge for yourselves:*
>
> *"Amazon's effort to pay shoppers to scorn physical stores is prompting a bit of a backlash. The retailer is offering a bounty for those who venture to the mall or Main Street on Saturday and compare the price of items against Amazon's price. Customers who use a special price check app on their smartphone will get up to $5 off on up to three qualifying products from Amazon in eligible categories (electronics, toys, sports, music and DVDs). This is not sitting well with physical retailers and their fans.*

*The American Independent Business Alliance said it was "jolting" to see the company "overtly encouraging people to spy on local stores while turning those businesses into showrooms for Amazon's profit." The alliance also noted that while Amazon said it was doing this to lower prices, the comparative data might also encourage it to raise prices on some items to a level just marginally below the physical stores' prices. Oren Teicher, chief executive of the American Booksellers Association, wrote in an open letter to Amazon's chief executive, Jeff Bezos, that this was "the latest in a series of steps to expand your market at the expense of cities and towns nationwide, stripping them of their unique character and the financial wherewithal to pay for essential needs like schools, fire and police departments, and libraries." And it goes on, I won't include the entire piece — but I do agree with its final statement: "Even if it doesn't work fiscally, it sure is giving them a lot of free publicity. But on a more philosophical level, I just think it is mean." I would add unethical and greedy. They DO want to take over the world — watch out!*

We couldn't blame Amazon for everything though. There were other problems caused by the wide availability of information once companies got their own websites up and running. We "cherry picked" items from various lines, choosing the ones we thought would fit our theme the best. And even if we had wanted to carry every single item a given vendor made, our small physical space would have made that impossible. But now customers could visit a vendor site and see every single thing that vendor made. They wanted us to have it all. We were happy to special order things when possible, but often items had to be ordered in dozens, so if a customer only wanted one or two, we'd have to refuse. Luckily not all vendors did direct sales to the public, but the ones that didn't created a different kind of problem.

The phone would ring. "Hi, you carry products by Department 56, right?" an eager voice would inquire. "Yes, we do, " I'd begin, while realizing it was inevitable I was about to disappoint them. "Do you have the Snowbabies First Haircut? or Puppies with Pocketbooks? Oh, and what about Christmas Village New England — Coleman's Trading Post?" "I'm sorry," I'd reply, "we actually only sell one Department 56 item these days — the Twinkle Brite Tree." This was a wonderful item we'd been selling for years. "Oh," the voice would say flatly, "well... thanks anyway." I hated this. Department 56 was a huge company, with over 3000 items. We sold a few of them, but they listed us as a supplier on their website leading to constant disappointment for the people who called. The only people who ever called about the Twinkle Brite Tree were customers who had either seen it in our store, or those who'd been told to call us by a friend who'd purchased one from us.

Another "feature" of the internet, not so common in the earliest days but soon unavoidable: Targeted Advertising, or as we not so fondly refer to it — Product Stalking. Everyone who uses the internet to look up anything is familiar with this supposedly helpful but incredibly annoying technique. It's particularly obvious if you google something like rubber ducks, which for professional reasons, I sometimes had reason to do. Rubber ducks would then appear everywhere, every time I went online. A *New York Times* article about famine in North Africa? Blanketed with bright yellow rubber ducks. An op-ed on voting rights, an article on child abuse? Rubber ducks for sale. A recipe for bulgur pilaf? Rubber ducks! I made a point of never ever double-clicking online ads, but it wasn't hard to imagine that a customer short on time might.

Targeted advertising is relentless. But experiencing it myself helped me understand why people ordered things online. They might have preferred to return to a brick-and-mortar store but maybe it was raining, or their kid was sick, or it was the holidays and they were just crazy busy and every time they looked at their computer — there it was — the item they wanted, popping up everyplace. What could be easier than just placing that order? I realized this was one of the reasons customers who said they'd be back for something often didn't return. Of course, maybe they just changed their mind; I'm not completely paranoid. But seeing the web work its insidious magic was both fascinating and sobering.

Still, I mostly felt confident that the value of being in our store, in the real world, with other humans, would keep our customers faithful, though some days I felt more confident than others. One day a woman was looking through a book on the front counter. "Are these available online?" she asked. It had been a quiet day, and I was both bored and discouraged. I didn't talk to her about the importance of supporting small business or shopping local. I didn't mention that we were always happy to ship. I just said, "I think pretty much everything is," and left it at that.

CHAPTER 31

# Phones, Phones, Phones

The thing that changed life at the store the most was hands down, the cellphone. It made a huge change in the dynamics of our interactions with customers. In the early days, it was often humorous. Phones would ring, and their owners would desperately try to find them. (These desperate owners were usually women; men simply carried them in their pockets.) People set their ring tones to top volume and some were quite outlandish, others seriously dramatic, and some just silly. Chickens squawking, dogs barking, bumble bees, carousel music, electronic versions of the New World Symphony and the Wedding March, frogs croaking, disco, beeps, jazz, and some that sounded exactly like the standard 1950s ring. And at least at first, people didn't appear to realize that you could speak on your phone quietly. From logbook: *Why do people feel the need to BELLOW into their cell phones? I think the technology is probably to the point where you can speak in a normal tone...*

It surprised me that our older customers were the worst offenders. I'm not sure why, but they seemed the least likely to realize other people could listen to their conversations and thus they needed to use a little discretion. Once, a very nice regular customer stood in the front of the store talking on his phone, loudly, for twenty minutes to someone about someone else he had interviewed for a job and was considering hiring. Halfway through, a woman approached me at the front desk. She motioned pointedly toward the man speaking. "I know," I said. "I'm afraid he doesn't really get the etiquette of this yet." "That's not it," she said in a bit of a whisper. "I know the person he's talking about. It's a breach of privacy to discuss someone in public like this." I promised to mention this to the offender. When I did, he was horrified. The thought that someone might overhear sensitive information had simply not occurred to him. To his credit, he was a quick study and it never happened again.

We listened to customers discussing intimate medical problems, cancer, divorce, all kinds of things we did not want to hear. Cell phones brought people's private conversations front and center. When there were a few of us working, we were often talking about something behind the desk, but I always stressed to staff that it was a public space, and that any conversations we had should be open to the customers in the store, particularly if there was only one or two of them. Just a simple "We're just chatting, so please feel free to interrupt us if you have a question." Or, if we were talking about some current issue, "Feel free to jump into this debate." I didn't want anyone to feel there was a party going on they weren't invited to attend.

Now I was sorely tempted to jump into more than a few conversations myself. "So, sounds like you're really having trouble with your taxes." Or, "If I were you, I'd leave that man in two seconds, he sounds horrible!" Sometimes, listening to someone talk was so annoying that I wanted to turn the volume up on our music just to interfere with the phone conversation, but I think I only did that once, pushed to my limit by a younger woman who was the sole customer one morning. She took her time looking around, chatting about nothing the entire time she was in the store. Loudly. I did turn up the volume more, and then more, but it seemed to have no effect.

And of course that wouldn't have worked if there had been other customers shopping.

*******

Related logbook entries:

*There is only one customer in the store and she is breaking up with her boy-friend on her cell phone while she shops! Very odd. I feel like an eavesdropper but I can't help it — go outside!*

*There was a customer in here — spent about $100 – who's on his cell phone to no less than three different parties at any given time, barking orders to one, describing the enormity of his house on Avon Hill to another, and griping about his ex-wife to another. Straight out of a sitcom or movie. He was still on the phone when he left.*

*Woman comes in who says she hasn't been here in years and is so happy to see we're still here — then spends almost the entire time she's in talking to someone on her cellphone.*

*Isn't it a little tacky and/or ill-mannered to discuss — in a public place on a cell phone — whether or not someone's death was suicide?*

*Customer asks if she can use her cell phone in here. I say, (friendly), oh, of course, go ahead. She goes on about how she doesn't want to be obnoxious, etc., etc. I assure her, no, really, you were polite to ask, yada yada. (Thinking, wow, a polite cellphone user!) So she calls whoever and proceeds to ask him LOUDLY AND AT LENGTH about his "pathology reports." At one point, "So, you have pancreatic cancer," then whether he's a candidate for surgery, etc. At one point she turns the volume up so loud I can hear the guy on the other end too. This seems like a fairly fraught and personal conversation, one you'd want to have IN PRIVATE!!! Good Lord! And not while browsing the wind-up toys. Update — Medical conversation still going on. The guy is her brother and yes, he's certain that he not only has pancreatic cancer but it's metastasized. It all sounds very serious and sad. AND INAPPROPRIATE FOR A LOUD*

*PUBLIC CELL PHONE CONVERSATION!!! She hangs up and leaves. I feel like I should have consoled her. I hate cell phones.*

*Words we don't hear enough at Joie: "Sorry to be on my phone."*

*******

There was a huge Catch 22 to letting customers know that we thought they were being rude. We needed their business. Some stores posted "no cellphone" signs on their door, but I didn't want to do that. It felt slightly hostile and might keep people out, and cellphones were clearly here to stay. But it was difficult to interact with anyone who was on one. Even saying hello, you were interrupting them. One customer we were already not too fond of, stood right at the desk talking on his phone. He covered it for a second, looked at me and said smugly, "My phone allows me to be rude to two people at once." "Yes it does," I thought, "and now I like you even less."

I noticed that husbands would come in with their wives and just stand at the front of the store on their phone, not even looking around. It was frustrating not to have a chance to engage with them. The store wasn't to everyone's taste, but I'd found there were usually at least a few things anyone would get a kick out of, and I loved making that connection with people. People began to walk in looking down at their phones. They looked at me blankly when I said hello. I watched others walk by the store, heads down, looking at their phones. They didn't look at our window display and notice we were here. I began to hate that head down look. And I knew from my own experience that they were rarely talking about anything important. (I loved being behind people on airplanes who narrated the end of their flight. "We're here!" That I understood. But then I'd hear, "We're waiting to get off the plane. Still on line. Now we're almost off the plane." The eternal narration of the mundane, the unremarkable.)

I watched phones affect the interactions of many a parent and child and it wasn't kids who were on the phone the most. So many kids tried to show their parents things they liked. They were excited and engaged but the parent on a phone often ignored their curious child. One girl, maybe eight, was in with her father, and tried to get him to play with things, really pay attention to them, but he just wanted to take pictures of her looking at things. She became annoyed and they did not seem to be having a good time.

My main problem with phones was that just like some of the kids I observed, I felt upstaged by my customer's phones. Normally, if I saw someone pick something up and I could tell they didn't quite know what it was, or that they really liked it, I would talk to them, it would be a conversation opener. Not if they were on the phone. And where people had typically asked me for advice, some now preferred to shop by committee, get everyone's opinion via their phone. If they could reach them, which often they couldn't. People became noticeably less able to make decisions for themselves. This wasn't everyone. But it was a big change.

Eventually phones became quieter. Those annoying but often funny rings were not heard as often and oddly, I almost missed them. Everyone was silently texting, and while I guess it was an improvement, it still meant their attention was at minimum, divided. Then cameras became an essential part of most phones, capable of taking excellent photographs. In our early years, we bristled if we spotted a customer was taking photos in the store, suspecting they were trying to source products for various nefarious purposes. I would go talk to them, and ask what they were doing, explaining that it's just polite to ask permission if you want to take a photo. Even in later years, although most didn't, some customers still asked for our permission to snap. We always said yes.

But sometimes the follow-up then went like this. "Oh thank you, I want to take a picture of this magnet/card/postcard to send to my sister/mother/friend in California. She'll think it's hilarious!" And I would smile, while the phrase I often uttered when talking about business with my peers flashed across my mind. Texting photos of cards is the new sending them. Nothing really could be done about this. It was not a good move to make people who were having fun feel badly. Phones were here to stay and I knew things would not turn back to how they used to be, that I couldn't make texters buy and send cards. We still sold a lot of cards, just not as many.

Customers could also use their phones to "remember" something they were interested in buying later. This was certainly fair, but as years went on it began to feel like a photograph to "remember" was pretty much a lost sale. It was certainly true that if you were out for a walk, stopped into the store, and saw a set of bowls you liked, you wouldn't want to carry them around for the rest of the afternoon. In the "olden days" you would probably return and buy them later, or if you lived farther away, call us and ask us to ship. But with that image on your phone — and one of the handy "find that product" apps available via Google, Amazon, Apple and more, you could find and buy it with a click from your couch. It was hard to compete with that kind of technology. We knew people had good intentions, and wanted to support small business and real stores, but we were also well aware of the seductiveness of convenience. The cell phone was not our friend.

One day there was a mother and daughter in the store — just the two of them and me. We exchanged hellos and they looked around a bit. After maybe ten minutes they were both standing near the front desk, working their cell phones. To try to get attention back to the here and now, I said "like mother, like daughter!" They did look up, and the daughter said to me, "I'm trying to find where the next place we're going is." I asked the name of the place — thinking it was probably off in another part of town, and she said "WardMaps." Which was two and a half blocks away. It struck me how much things had changed. They didn't even think to ask me if I knew where it was, though of course I told her. But it felt to me, eerily like the new normal was becoming — why talk to someone if you could consult your phone? Maybe they were being considerate and thinking they wouldn't bother me but I didn't really think so. They were just more focused on those phones than they were on the person right in front of them and that made me feel more than a bit superfluous and also sad. I wasn't busy, and I was right there. I like to think I would have been nicer to engage with than a phone, and could have mentioned what a nice place WardMaps was. I doubt it was a conscious choice on their part and they were happy when I told them how close they were. And I felt I'd done a good thing by getting them into a conversation. But the implications were troubling. I liked talking to people, it was a big part of why I did what I did. I didn't want to be replaced by a phone!

CHAPTER 32

# Some Seemingly Small But Very Frustrating Events

Some of the little things that drove us crazy — as chronicled at various times in our blog.

## ARRRGH!

*No, I'm not practicing for International Talk Like a Pirate Day. My ARRRGH is about something else entirely. My telephone rang at 8 am this morning. I was drinking coffee and reading the Sunday papers and thought who can that be? Family emergency? Someone with really good news? An invitation to a delicious brunch? Nope — it was Earthlink's financial office, calling to find out why they had not received Joie de Vivre's check for $40 that was due on Friday. Calling me at home. Sunday morning. As it happens, that check had been mailed. But even if it hadn't — Joie de Vivre has had an Earthlink account for over five years. Our account has once or twice been more than a few days — that's days — not months late and our monthly bill is never more than $40. I could not believe they would call me at my house at 8 am on Sunday about this. And Earthlink is one of those companies that if you are having a problem with their service, you can spend hours and hours and hours just trying to get through to a human being who can actually help you. Perhaps they should take the money they spend hiring people to harass customers in good standing in their homes, and switch those funds and people to their customer service account. Just saying…*

183

## Google

*I was looking at the* New York Times *this morning and saw an article about Google listing businesses as closed that were in fact, still open. The main point of the article was how difficult it was for the owners of these businesses to correct this information on Google. I read with an increasing sense of solidarity, and reaching the end, was moved to add my own comment which I will just duplicate below. But — come on, Google — it should NOT be this difficult to contact you and it should NOT be difficult to change incorrect information. And after spending hours and hours trying to deal with this online, it should also be possible to access a live, breathing, accountable human being!! Live up to your own motto – Don't be Evil!! (author's note — I believe they have actually dropped this motto.)*

## My NYTimes comment:

*I own a retail store in Cambridge, MA. We have been open for twenty-seven years and have always had the exact same hours. For some reason, Google recently posted incorrect hours on our listing, and customers have been showing up expecting us to be open later than we really are. We have spent at least one full business week attempting to fix this — to simply, as the owners of the business, get them to change our listed hours to our actual hours — and have been unable to do so. It's outright Kafka-esque and we really are at a loss as to what the next step should be.*

Postscript:

*Miracle of Miracles!! Joy in Joieville! We received an email from an actual person at Google today, (and are cynically wondering if the bad press in the* New York Times *prompted them to start dealing with these issues.) Whatever the case, "Bryan" said that they were aware of the incorrect listing and would fix it. His exact words: "You should see the information appearing correctly within four weeks' time. If, in four weeks, you are still experiencing this problem, please respond to this email." Okay, I am happy that finally we got a response from an actual person. But it boggles my mind that it could take Google up to 4 weeks to fix two lines of text. Isn't the computer age supposed to make things... you know... happen fast?*

## Joie a la Kafka Take Two

*At the end of every day we close out our charge machine and Eleavon, our processor, then sends the money to our bank. The settling process is easy — you punch in "settle" — it gives you the amount in the machine; you say "yes" for correct and that's it. It's the simplest system we've used and we've had it for about five years with not a single problem. Until last night. The machine gave me the total as usual — and when I hit "yes," it hesitated, then said it did not agree. I recounted the slips — the total was correct. I tried it again a few times as I'm optimistic that way but always got the same message. I then called their customer service line, anticipating an easy resolution. An hour and a half — an hour and a half — later, I hung up, after talking my way through various increasingly high-level supervisors who could not tell me why they had no record of a $300 charge on their end. I pointed out (many times) that they had given us an authorization number for that amount and that I had the slip to prove it. At one point someone said "an authorization number is not a guarantee that a sale will go through." And sadly, at that point, I did use just one curse word, inquiring why the F we bothered to authorize anything in that case. At the end of the hour and a half they were admitting that this "virtually never" happens and agreeing to credit us the amount we were due. Though I don't think I'm permanently damaged, I left the store with a little less sanity than I had when I entered that morning.*

## Advance notice please?

*The Joie blogger was reading the* Boston's Globe's *last minute gift guide over coffee this morning. She approached it with a bit of apprehension, not having been contacted by anyone there to see if Joie had possible products to include, and felt she would see other, newer, stores listed and remember the days when Joie was likely to be there. Preparing to feel ill-used and yes, slightly jealous, she began to look through — of course there were items from Etsy, and various websites — and then, something we were selling caught her eye, the Field Guide to Famous Felines poster. And, lo and behold, there was our name and information, listed right above it. So — yay! Someone is still using us as a resource. But — not yay — they didn't even tell us. So now, I'm wondering, how many of the posters do we actually have in stock? How fast can I get some more? After thirty years in business, I feel entitled to say, "back in the old days" so I'm saying it now — back in the old days the writer would have let us know so we could be prepared. On the other hand, happy to be included, and thank you for the shout-out, anonymous Globe source!*

## Really?

*Recently, looking through a Toy catalogue I don't order a lot from because it's mostly aimed at kids, I was taken aback to see their science kits divided into separate sections for boys and girls. In the girls section: Snowflake Factory, Lip Balm Lab, Bath Bomb Factory, Luxury Soap Science Lab, Beautiful Blob Slime Lab, Perfect Perfume Factory and Magic Crystal Oasis. For boys: Volcano Crater Lab, Spooky Ice Planet Lab, Weird Slime Lab, Hyperlauncher Rocket Ball, Practical Joke Soap Laboratory, and Wild Physics and Cool Chemistry. Pictures of girly girls on the girl's boxes and intent young male scientists on the boys. Really? After all we've been through? I thought we'd come a long way! To be fair, the girls kits did advertise "learn about the structure and changes of properties of matter, mixtures and solutions and chemical reactions." They are not entirely fluff. And I believe that most boys are probably not interested in making the perfect perfume or luxury soap. But why exclude girls from Wild Physics and Cool Chemistry? And what kid wouldn't be intrigued by a Spooky Ice Planet Lab? Is it 2012 or 1952 here? I don't think that boys and girls are exactly the same, but these divisions are just plain silly. And definitely bad news for girls.*

## Really? take two

*Fred Food Face 10-inch china dinner plate — with a large choking hazard sticker on box? How does a child fit a 10-inch plate into their mouth? Inquiring minds want to know!*

## No Need for Batteries?

*We briefly sold a crazy top last year — it had laser lights that radiated circles of light and it played a wacky version of the "Beverly Hills Cop" theme. It was oddly compelling and very popular, but we stopped selling it because the batteries were not replaceable — once they wore down, it was basically a throwaway. This made us sad because we kind of loved the crazy thing. But yay, at the August Gift Show I found a similar top with replaceable batteries. They arrived and we decided to include the happy news in our October newsletter. Went to the company's web site to get a picture, and read a description of said top that ended: "All that spinning generates energy that powers the music and lights, without the need for batteries." I went back to look at one in its box. It said the same thing. Really? It plays music and lights up without batteries? I knew there were batteries in the top so I emailed the company to find out why they advertised it this way. "If there is no need for batteries — why did ours come with batteries?" Their answer — which I present to you word for word: "Yes, the statement is correct. Technically, NO BATTERIES are required because they are included and sealed in at the factory." I don't know about you, blog readers, but I call this — let's just say — misleading at best! (But regardless of their silly claim, the top is great!)*

Hmmm — Should We Really Be Selling These?
*The text on the small piece of paper that comes with each of our $2 rubber half ball poppers: Warning: Use extreme caution. Do not place your head above activated or jumping popper. If "activated" popper does not jump, reach to it — from the side — and "deactivate."!!!*

Unacceptable!
*We have an email list and on the first of every month we mail out a link with our monthly news. Each time a few bounce back, old email addresses, or undeliverable for some reason but this month we had a first — this return message: "Returned because the message contains inappropriate language that violates the Boston Public Schools Acceptable Use Policy (AUP) for Computer Networks. If you believe there is no inappropriate language AND the message is AUP compliant, please REPLY to this email and request that the message be released, and your request will be considered." I didn't even think twice*

*— I wrote the text and I was 100% positive that there was no unacceptable language in our email. So I sent it again. It came back with the same message. I then decided to take a closer look at what I had written. Here it is — the preamble to our actual newsletter: "Dear Joie de Vivre mailing list, We wanted to let you all know that because it's been a hard winter and we needed a little cash, we have sold our mailing list to QVC.com — we hope you don't mind. APRIL FOOL! (We of course will never ever ever give your names to anyone.) Happy Spring! We're loving looking out our window at pussy willows instead of Xmas greens buried under dirty, icy, snow. And loving seeing more of you come in the door... it's much more fun here when we have customers!" And when I took a closer look, I realized what must have happened. Their scan must have picked out the X in Xmas, the dirty in dirty, icy, snow — and of course, the pussy in pussy willow, maybe the word come, and decided that our email was inappropriate. It's the only thing that makes any sense... and it reinforces my belief that machines with all their artificial intelligence will never be able to do what we lowly humans can do with our brain.*

CHAPTER 33

# Minor Problems, and The Mysterious Case of the Disappearing Rabbits

Over our thirty-six years in business we had one (very amateur) break in, one brick thrown through our front window, one would-be thief enter through our back door in broad daylight, one band of thieves sweep through the store removing an amazing amount of large items quickly, one group of aspiring young thugs, a handful of bad checks, a couple counterfeit bills, and one stolen dumpster. This last was the strangest. I went outside with a bag of trash and — our dumpster was gone. Assuming the company must be replacing it for some reason, I called them, but nope! They had nothing to do with it, and that was how I learned that people actually steal big heavy dumpsters, usually to take to construction sites.

The more common problem was garden variety shoplifting, as defined by the dictionary: stealing goods from a store while pretending to be a customer. We would add, or actually being one. People shoplift for many different reasons. Some need food, some are drug addicts, but our merchandise was not the kind of thing you could turn around for quick cash. Hey — wanna buy a kaleidoscope — cheap? Some people just like the thrill of taking a risk. Some younger ones see it as rebelling against the rules, or do it for fun with their friends, seeing who can get away with the most. And a few are genuine kleptomaniacs, unable to fight their compulsion to steal things they don't want or need.

I know we must have lost little items to casual theft from time to time though if someone took a few postcards, or a squeeze toy or a high bounce ball, we would never have known, we couldn't keep track of that kind of thing. But when something larger disappeared, we noticed. The little robot clock that was on the display case at the front desk? It's gone. I see a kaleidoscope stand… but where's the kaleidoscope? Weren't there three ring watches on display? A search ensues. Often the missing object is found. Sometimes not. Then we try to think — who could have taken it?

Some of our shoplifters were kids, though I'm not sure I'd really use that term for the youngest. It was hard to be mad at them. A little kid would be looking at all the fun things in our "smalls" section, but of course they never had any money. If their parent said no to their impassioned request for a pink unicorn eraser, squeeze frog, or alligator clicker, sometimes they would just help themselves. Usually their parents discovered this before they left the store; I'd hear "What's that in your hand?" and the item would be returned to its place. Sometimes a kid would be brought back in a day or two after their visit, and stand silently in front of us at the desk. "What do you want to tell the lady?" the parent would prompt. A small hand might reach out holding a finger monster and we'd hear a tiny voice, "I took this and I'm sorry." A short conversation about right and wrong would follow, but I always reassured these kids that it was very brave of them to tell the truth, and that I was happy for them to come back to the store anytime.

We never got apologies from our adult shoplifters, but then we didn't catch many of them. Thefts always seemed to happen on quiet days, when everyone working would swear that no one at all suspicious had been in. Which in itself was unsettling. A regular customer had taken that paperweight? That clock? That nice wooden box? I did know appearances could be deceiving. Years before when I'd worked at the Gallery, a rather down and out looking couple had come in to look around. I was happy to let them but I was astounded, and embarrassed when they decided to buy a $350 glass vase. They didn't look like they had any money. Wrong.

And nicely dressed middle class customers didn't look like they'd steal. Also wrong. At Joie, I was forced to conclude that most frequently the customers who took things were middle class types who aroused no suspicion. After noticing something missing, I would wrack my brain trying to think of a possible suspect, almost always unsuccessfully. Of course there were exceptions — the wild-eyed drug addict, the woman reeking of alcohol, or that band of thieves, who got so much we had to admire their technique. There was an occasional couple working as a team, one to distract with a question in one part of the store while the other helped themselves to something in another.

We did catch a few. Some very quick thinking by Emily Winston saved a kaleidoscope one day. She'd seen a woman put it in her bag, but when she came to pay for her goods, the kaleidoscope was not among them. When she headed for the door, Emily ran after her, a second bag in hand. "I think I gave you the wrong bag!" she said. "Let me make sure that one is yours." She grabbed the bag and the customer grabbed it back. A tussle ensued but Emily won, and in the bag about to leave the premises — our kaleidoscope. And Deb suspected one customer, who did appear to be on some sort of drug, of taking another scope. She followed him out of the store and down the block, saying "Put down the bag. Put down the bag," while wondering if she was crazy to be doing so. Luckily, he did put it down, but I urged her not to do that again. I wanted no injuries in the line of duty.

We had a few serial thieves. The same item would disappear time and time again. The little wooden clock whose face showed the phases of the moon. The ring watches. The pocket compasses. The robot clock. That tiny robot clock was stolen every other Tuesday for months. We kept it right by the front desk to keep a close eye on it and it still disappeared. We thought about tying it to the counter with fishing wire so that it would jerk when picked up but realized that the wire would probably pull a lot of other things with it, breaking them. Despite our best efforts, we never caught the thief, but they did lose interest — or maybe just finally had the number of robot clocks they wanted.

When we discovered a theft, it felt like a betrayal. It was hard to realize that some person you'd just been nice to had turned around and stolen something. Even harder was convincing some of the staff not to treat the customers who came in the rest of the day with suspicion. "Don't bad vibe them, they didn't do anything!" I'd insist, but it was a tall order when something had just been taken. Hardest of all was finding out that we did in fact know a thief.

"Who sold the rabbits?" I asked as I entered the store one afternoon. I was excited. Those porcelain figurines, made by Paris Bottman, were among the most expensive things we sold. Buying them was a risk I had taken hoping that customers would appreciate their quality and find the price worth it. I knew we wouldn't sell many and had instantly noticed that two rabbits were not on the shelf where I had displayed them; I had a photographic memory of what I put where and though it might not have looked like it, nothing at Joie was randomly displayed. The staff working the desk queried each other. "I didn't sell them, did you?" "No — definitely not." Okay, not sold. Had someone picked them up and put them down in the wrong place? That wouldn't be unusual, but a careful look around revealed no wandering rabbits. We knew and cherished each one of these little animals, the pig with printed flowers on her dress, the cat holding a tiny bowl of fish, the sheep wearing a blue wool sweater. When the two rabbits disappeared we were upset, shocked and indignant. But as usual, we had no suspects.

A case of special small things sat right next to our cash register, the case where the Bottman animals were usually displayed. One afternoon, a few months after the theft, two adolescent girls were hanging around. We knew one, she lived across the street and often came in alone or with her parents. Two animals were displayed on the little case that day. "I have two of these!" the girl we knew told her friend. This caught the attention of Deb, who was sitting behind the desk. She began to draw the story out. "You have some of those? Just like these?" she asked. "I'm jealous! They are so amazing!" Craftily she added, "What do yours look like?" The description matched the missing rabbits. "How did you get them?"

was her next question. The answer, "My Dad gave them to me." "Wow, what a really special present. You must have a great Dad," said Deb. As soon as they were out the door, she ran to tell me.

I knew the family. Both parents were customers. They bought nice presents for their daughter and occasionally something expensive. But those rabbits had not been sold. No one would have forgotten selling them; the sale would have been over $500. No one would forget that, our average sale was closer to $25. Either the daughter had taken them or her father had. Though both seemed unlikely thieves, part one of the crime had been solved. Our missing rabbits were living right across the street.

I decided to write the father, reasoning that if his daughter had stolen them, he would want to know. I also entertained the hope that if that were the case, they would be returned or paid for. I knew it was possible the father himself was the thief and if so, at least my asking about it would let him know that I knew, and might prevent future theft. I was careful to be tactful and non-confrontational in my letter. Or so I thought.

A few days later, the father stormed into the store. "You're accusing me of stealing from you?!" he said loudly, turning quite a few heads. Whoops! This was not behavior I had anticipated. I quickly ushered him into the back room. "How dare you — how dare you accuse me or my daughter of stealing?" he continued. "I bought those rabbits for her. I paid for them in cash." "That's just not possible," I said. "We don't have any sales receipts for them and no one would make such a large sale without writing a receipt." It was true that we sometimes sold cards or a small toy without a formal written receipt, but even in the very unlikely event that no receipt had been written, it was impossible that any of us would forget such a large sale.

His face flushed and began to turn a dark alarming red. His voice got even louder. "How dare you," he began again. He moved much closer to me. I was totally unprepared for the ferocity of his response. My carefully thought-out plan was blowing up in my face. My courage deserted me, and instinctively, I started trying to defuse the situation. I took a little time, saying I don't remember what as I tried to calm him down, and eventually said "Well... we do have a few new employees being trained for Christmas. I guess it's possible that one of them sold them to you without writing up a receipt. It can take awhile for new people to get used to doing things right."

There was a slight release of tension in the room. "That must be what happened," he snapped, "but I won't forget that you accused me of stealing." Feeling craven and cowardly, I attempted to placate him further. "Yes, that must have been what happened," I said. "I'm going to have to speak to them about procedure." Somewhat mollified, he took his leave but I was shaking. My heart was pounding and my face was aflame. He had scared me and though I knew I was in the right, I'd completely backed down.

As I watched him walk out the door I felt an awful mixture of anger and relief. Maybe he was protecting his daughter. More likely he had taken them himself. His wife and daughter continued to be customers. I know that eventually there was a divorce. All these years later I can still see his face as plain as day, but he never came into the store again.

I did a little research after this incident and discovered that if no one actually sees a suspect handling the merchandise they are thought to have stolen, it's very hard to make a case. If I was suspicious of someone from then on, I just approached them in the store and asked if they wanted me to hold the item in question at the desk, or if they'd like it wrapped. It let them know that we were paying attention, which is in fact the best way to prevent theft, and really, over thirty-six years, we had an astoundingly small amount of it. But from then on, we held to this policy: if you didn't see it happen with your own eyes, it didn't happen.

TRUE CONFESSIONS #5

## *Careless*

I've always been kind of careless. Just ask my ex-husband. I'd get going too fast and pull out one of his beloved plants while weeding. I'd pull the knife toward me when cutting a box and cut myself badly. I'd pick up the cat when it clearly didn't want me to and it fought back, scratching my face. My car had dents. I never thought I'd get paint on my clothes when I impulsively decided to paint something. I always got paint on my clothes.

If I found a small thing on the floor at the store, and couldn't figure out what it was, I'd often throw it away. Then it would turn out to be the important missing piece of something, that everyone was searching for. Sometimes I'd admit I'd tossed it, other times, trying to protect my reputation, I'd remain quiet. I'm also a fan of the quick easy fix. The bungee cords I wound around the legs of the chair behind the desk held it together just fine. Another bad habit? Letting things go too long. Waiting to replace the ladder in the store until it fell apart with someone on it. Who was miraculously unhurt. I bought a sturdy new ladder the next day.

But I had another problem with ladders, overconfidence. I climbed too fast, stood too high up, in fact, got a secret thrill about being what I thought of as quick and fearless. One morning I was in the store alone, early. We had just gotten new fixtures for our track lights. I wanted to get them installed before we opened that day but the tracks themselves were old and it was hard to get the new lights securely in place. I was down to the last five or six but to finish, I needed to reach a track that ran above a display I couldn't move. Even standing as high on the ladder as possible, I couldn't quite get to it.

I solved this problem by balancing one foot on a shelf, leaving the other on the ladder, and in this precarious position, began to try getting those new lights in. When the ladder started to wobble, my arms were up in the air, and there was nothing to grab onto. It swayed and rocked and I lost my balance and fell, hitting a display table in the middle of the store on my way to the floor. They say time stands still when you're ~~having fun~~ in an accident, and it seemed I had enough time to wonder if I would hit my head and pass out, or be able to get up. But I did get up. Feeling something wet on my face that turned out to be blood. There was a gash under my eye. Frighteningly close to my eye. My forehead was a mess too. Still, I felt lucky. I was standing, and I could see. I held a cold wet towel to my face and waited for the ~~calvary~~ the morning crew to show up.

Within a day my face had turned all kinds of colors. Then the bruises continued to bloom and that's when I realized I looked like someone had hit me. And that no one was asking "what happened?" a question I thought everybody would. I realized they were too polite and didn't want to ask. "I fell off a ladder," I started immediately telling people. It broke the ice, I could tell they were relieved. For all they knew I had a crazy boyfriend or a drinking problem leading to a car accident. It took another two weeks for my face to get back to normal. And I made a video about it. Wrote a blog. Public service announcements, you know, to help others. I called both "Ladders Can Be Dangerous." I hope the public was grateful.

*The Joiedeblog scribe has a confession to make. Said scribe is not the most careful person in the world, and often does things too quickly and somewhat recklessly. Said scribe probably breaks more things at the store than all the customers and other staff combined, simply by "virtue" of her impatience and foolhardiness. So far, she has never broken herself, but her luck almost changed the other morning. There is nothing quite like the sensation of being high up on a ladder — with one foot off the ladder balancing a bit precariously on a shelf, and feeling the ladder start to wobble. Sometimes you are lucky and can get down before it collapses. Research has actually proved that luck is just about the only thing that can help you in a situation like this, and sometimes your luck runs out, and you crash to the ground, scraping your face on the ladder as you go, ending up looking like — well, we won't go there. Then just a little bit of luck kicks in — you stand up and realize that although your face is a mess, you can walk and move all parts of your body. So, as a public service, the Joie scribe would like to alert readers to the fact that, ladders, improperly used, can be dangerous. Please use them correctly, as we will be trying to do from this point forward. And… if you're here in the next few days to a week, now you know — "we" haven't been in a bar room brawl or arguing with a difficult customer. As one of our magnets puts it, If I can't be a good example, I'll just have to serve as a horrible warning. So — happy to be of service!*

Author's note: I treated ladders with much more respect after this incident. For at least a few months!

CHAPTER 34

# Joie Esoterica

Inevitably, when you inhabit a place for years and years, and run our kind of business, you find yourself saying or writing things in the logbook that would sound crazy or at best baffling to the uninitiated. Or you might come across things in the back of the store, like… a candy corn hanging in a small plastic bag labeled "frog." Here, from our logbook and elsewhere, some Joie de Vivre esoterica!

*"The voice changer is now displayed in a black cone — I think it suits it better than the bottom half of the mushroom."*

*"I inflated another iguana."*

*"If 'dreamy' bears seem sticky, they are not leaking — but a water wiggle worm did leak in that box. And dreamy update — the dreamy guy has basically no idea why some harden but he'll take them back — if you find them that way, put in 'defective dreamy' box on broken things shelf."*

*"Buddha wallet keeps going off on its own — was it doing that yesterday?"*

*"Where are the fizzy unicorns stocked?"*

*"I'm concerned about the water marbles."*

*"Tiny Eel lady came in and paid for her order — 140 tiny eels!"*

*"Aliens are stocked with squeak pigs and a few with cats. Small Peekaboos — there's an extra box stuck up by little hands and etc."*

*"Linda — there are seahorses in the sand again."*

From Checklist for Display:
*"Is there a necklace hanging on the black hand? Good variety of frogs?"*

Sign on Cash Register (that remained there for three years, until we closed):
*"Don't Move the Candy Canes taped to the Register!!"* (Our antique register suddenly started locking when we pushed in the cash drawer, and Jenn devised a clever way of preventing it from ever closing using two candy cane ballpoint pens we were selling that year.)

Missing Anything?
*In most job situations, if an employee said "I found an arm" it would be cause for horror, fainting, calls to the police. Here at Joie de Vivre, such statements are received with a laugh and "Oh, I think I know where that came from" — e.g. the Marilyn Monroe magnetic paperdoll, the wind-up frog, the light up Santa Claus... the possibilities go on and on.*

Peep Show Water
*So, say you were cleaning up at the front desk and you had only worked at Joie de Vivre for a few months. And you came across a small bottle of water with a taped-on label — pink with black magic marker letters spelling out "Peep Show Water." You would most likely think "what the heck is this??" You probably wouldn't think what I thought when it was shown to me. My thought was "oh... I remember those shot glasses!" We sold these cool shot glasses — with no liquid in them they looked like plain clear glasses — but when you*

*added water, or more likely vodka or gin, a cheesecakey girl or beefcakey boy appeared at the bottom of the glass. A very cool optical illusion… leading to a perplexingly labeled bottle of leftover water.*

Candy Corn "frog"
*A day or two ago I noticed a plastic bag push-pinned to the back of a jewelry display. Inside it was a candy corn and a note scribbled on a post-it that said "I am the Mirage Frog — currently replaced by a jelly bean." ?? It took me a minute or two to figure this out — but when I did, I realized how completely unfigureoutable it would be to anyone but the staff of Joie. Jellybean? A candy corn that calls itself a mirage frog? Explanation — we have an item called the Mirage which has a reflecting mirror — it comes with a little plastic frog. We must have replaced the frog with a jellybean way back at Easter, then put the frog back, then replaced it with a candy corn at Halloween and for some reason saved said candy corn when Halloween was over. I kind of cherish these odd little moments.*

CHAPTER 35

# Ch– Ch– Ch– Changes

Everything changes, nothing stays the same. You hear it in love songs, read it in philosophy texts, see it on inspirational posters. Children grow up, people get old, accidents alter lives, and science tells us that a single butterfly flapping its wings can affect the weather on the opposite side of the globe. Those of us who like stability will inevitably be disappointed.

When I opened the store, the area was rent controlled and we had a lively mix of students, artists, professionals, and old time Cantabrigians. They had unpredictable schedules and many were around during the day, stopping in to buy a card, or just say hello and see what was new. When rent control ended in 1996, many of those people were priced out and moved away. The newer, wealthier residents worked more, usually out of the area. It was quieter on the street. By the time we had to learn to teach ourselves not to begin every date with the number '19," and were wondering if we would say "two thousand and ten" or "twenty-ten," things were really changing. Post 9/11 in 2001, our President urged people to show their patriotism by going out and shopping, and for a while, they did, but as time passed, smaller businesses began to have a harder time. You could see the results of this all around our neighborhood.

Many of the small businesses were struggling. The office supply store, the chocolate shop, the bakery, the sporting goods store, a children's clothing

THE BOOK OF JOIE

store, the antique shops, a candy store, two small health food stores and more all moved or closed. Previously, there had always been someone ready to take a chance with something new, but now they were replaced mostly by banks, chain drugstores, hair salons, and restaurants. There were empty storefronts, "For Rent" signs fading after a year or so with no takers. The UPS Store on the corner did a brisk business though, with Amazon pick-ups and returns.

Some changes happened earlier. Mr. Fox and Marcella's were gone. My days of resenting him were long over, and eventually, so was our endless teasing about one of us dating him. I still went there almost every morning for coffee and noticed he kept a glass of wine by the register as early as 9 am. He passed by Joie sometimes en route to the bank and we noticed he had difficulty walking. Then he disappeared and we heard he'd had a heart transplant. When he returned a few months later, he seemed to have mellowed and we joked that he must have received the heart of a seven-year-old girl, unsure how else to explain the change. But running a restaurant proved too much for him afterwards and he sold it to two men who had no idea how to keep up his standards. The business suffered and Marcella's closed. He had driven us all crazy but we found we missed him. A bona fide "character," he'd provided many outrageous stories, and such good food.

The windows of Mr. Fox's lair were quickly papered over and we heard a new store was moving in — a paper and art supply store. One day two unfamiliar women came into Joie and asked if the owner was in. I was, and they introduced themselves as the owner and manager of the Paper Source, a Chicago store. They were about to open their second location where Marcella's had been. We chatted and I asked what they sold. They listed invitations, paper goods, a few gifts and rubber stamps. We had a wall of rubber stamps at the time, and this disturbed me. "But, we sell stamps here," I said, wondering if they hadn't realized, "and you're only a block away." I waited for some apology, for them to say, oh no, we didn't realize, some acknowledgment that they were infringing on my territory. "Oh, that's okay, the more the merrier," the woman introduced as the store manager said.

I kept silent but I strongly disagreed. We weren't in Manhattan with throngs of people walking by every minute. Their customers would be ours, and for the most part, a rubber stamp or gift bought at Paper Source would be one less thing sold at Joie. They turned out to have more than a few items I was already selling. Some were lines I'd sold well for years. I spoke to vendors and many had no idea their work was being sold down the street; all the ordering was done in Chicago. We had good working relationships and most of them offered to require that their products be sold only in the Chicago store. This seemed like a reasonable compromise.

As it turned out, Paper Source did whatever it wanted. I frequently saw items they had supposedly promised not to sell in Cambridge in their windows. They also had big ambitions, wanted to grow, and did. The Cambridge store turned out to be the second of 135 across the country, each store pretty much the same. Their motto appeared to be — all's fair in retail — may the strongest survive. This was the opposite of how I thought about business, but there was nothing to do but shrug my shoulders and ignore them. I never went in because I didn't want to be influenced in any way by what they were doing, or upset at what I saw there, and for the most part that worked. When I wanted fancy white tissue for my own wedding invitations or paper for a display, I sent an employee. Still, it was hard when customers came in to Joie with the distinctive striped bags of our neighbor and we could clearly see those bags held many things they could have bought from us.

We never said a word about this to our customers. Those who had shopped at Joie from the beginning knew the difference, but new customers had no way of knowing who sold what first. I wanted us to make it on our merits alone, not by badmouthing the competition, much as I would have liked to. Besides, there was now competition coming from a lot of unexpected places. It was getting harder to survive and businesses did whatever they thought would help.

In the "olden days," drugstores did not sell English muffins and toys and everything under the sun. Hardware stores did not sell pretty night lights and candles, or light-up pig keychains and jigsaw puzzles. Bookstores did not sell funny kitchen accessories, or candy and coffee mugs. Before Whole Foods got ambitious, grocery stores did have those machines where for a quarter you could get a surprise plastic toy, but did not sell puppets, cards, rubber ducks, calendars, yoga clothes, etc. This was the new way, but it wasn't realistic for Joie de Vivre to start selling Stephen King novels, or garbage bags or potato chips or hammers and nails (although we did once sell a line of hammers decorated with sequins and marabou.) They could add what we were selling but it didn't work both ways.

Location became more important as well. When I first thought of opening a store, I never considered the mall a few blocks away, it seemed too bland. I wanted to be among the smaller, funkier stores that lined the main drag. But a lot more of our customers were driving to the store, and street parking was not easy. I was surprised when both a long-established local toy store and our nearby Natural Foods store, now calling themselves a "Wellness" store to better describe their wider range of products, decided to move to the mall but on reflection it made sense. People were already there shopping and there was a big parking lot. I used the stores and services there too and understood how convenient the location was. If you were there for milk, lightbulbs or exercise, why not pick up your vitamins, baby toy or gift too? And no problems parking.

Despite all this, the store was still doing pretty well. People were also shopping online and that didn't feel like too serious a threat yet either. They still came to Joie de Vivre to find what they didn't know they wanted. Why wouldn't they prefer a store where they could pick something up, play with it, joke around with the staff, come in for a lark with family or friends? The "busy disease" everyone now seems to suffer from was only beginning, leaving people time to wander the streets, to browse, to play. We celebrated our 20th anniversary in 2004 with a big sale and a glorious party, one in the store for our customers and friends, and one for the staff at a beloved local restaurant. I paid for an open bar, and was later told that our smallish group came in second only to a feisty bachelorette event in terms of drinks consumed. Of course some of us drank much more than others, but this time, I wasn't one. Having learned my limits, I felt fine the next morning. I don't think everyone present was able to say the same!

In preparation for the 20th festivities, I decided to close for a week of painting, plastering, and general sprucing up. We somehow crammed all the merchandise into the back stockroom so we could work with abandon, and put up big signs on our window and door, saying we were closed to renovate, but we still got some panicky phone calls and knocks on the door. "I drove by last night and the store is empty!! You're not closing, are you?" We'd tried to get the word out via word of mouth, but we didn't have a real mailing list, or website yet, and Facebook wouldn't be available to the public for another two years. It would be ten more before we finally succumbed and put up a Facebook page, but only a small group of our customers would really follow us there.

It was interesting to see the store empty again, and as we rushed to get everything back on the shelves, I felt a pang of regret that I had not allowed a little more time to think and possibly change a few things around. But it's hard to close, even for a week and a half. You lose money, there's no really good time, and Easter was coming soon. I was soon so involved in simply getting everything back on the shelves that I stopped thinking about my lost chance to redesign. After all, everything worked. And the customers wanted back in. Maybe another time. It seemed then that things would go on and on. It felt like Joie could be there forever.

Actually, every time we had an anniversary I was amazed. We had a party on the first birthday in 1985, and after that, a party and sale every five years. I never had children, not for lack of trying, but the store felt like my child in some ways, and marveling over its age was one. How could it be five already? Ten? Fifteen? Thirty? How old did that make me? As time passed and new customers asked "How long has this store been here?" my answer seemed to stun them, and it had the same effect on me. Really? That long? Was I going to be one of those people who tottered off to tend to her store at 90, like a woman I had recently read about? I found that hard to imagine. But I found it equally difficult to imagine how I would ever walk away.

CHAPTER 36

# The Best of Joiedeblog

Our blog began in 2009, as usual, a bit late to the game. It lasted for six years, until I reluctantly started a Facebook page for the store. I enjoyed writing the blog but Facebook was ascending and we felt we "should" have a page, its shorter form seeming to fit the times. Inevitably the blog was neglected. It's now just an archive, with six years of stories, thoughts and reflections. Some favorites, lightly edited.

Platitudes into Practice.
*A customer this week was very excited to see that we had a paperweight by Goldenflow Designs — a glass apple filled with gold leaf floating in a water-glycerine combination. She was excited because her (former?) boyfriend had deliberately broken hers during an argument and she had been trying to replace it for awhile. At the same time that she was standing at the desk buying the apple, a young boy was falling in love with our $4 ray gun keychain. He counted his money but came up short and asked if we would put it aside for him until he could come back the next day. As we began the process of filling out a "Hold" form for him, the apple customer grabbed it, said "Random Act of Kindness!" and bought it for him. He was thrilled, and everyone else felt pretty darn good as well. And I thought of how we often make fun of sayings like "Practice Random Acts of Kindness." They can get a bit tedious after*

*you see them on mugs, bumper stickers, posters, etc. — but they are definitely*
*wonderful when brought to real life. Thanks, Golden Apple Lady!*

## What is that guy doing?

*This week a man stood in our store holding a lenticular dog cup, one of a set of*
*four, each printed with a different dog. He was well dressed, and he held the*
*cup from many different angles, scrutinizing it closely. He put it down and*
*picked it up again. he rotated it in his hand. He held it closer, staring at it.*
*At least ten minutes passed. Now, there was nothing particularly strange about*
*this cup to the casual observer. Anyone who saw this man inspecting a plastic*
*puppy cup at such length might have thought — that guy must be a little crazy.*
*I know if I saw a person staring at anything that intensely for that long,*
*I would be wondering. But I was not alarmed because I knew this customer.*
*He is a regular shopper and a theoretical physicist. When he stares at something*
*for that long there is always a reason. And this time it turned out that he had*
*never seen a lenticular image on a curved surface. He was trying to figure*
*it out, and how it could be done just a little bit better. Another customer got*
*involved in the discussion. This sort of thing is one of the things I love about*
*standing behind the Joie de Vivre desk!*

## Got a Little Spare Time?

*We received a sales email from a Taiwanese lighting company today. I had*
*seen and liked one of their products at a show but as they did not have a U.S.*
*importer yet, had forgotten about them. I read through the sales pitch on their*
*color changing jellyfish lamp and stopped dead in my tracks at "The lamp is a*
*decoration with 16,000,000 color moods. Flowing color or choice the color you*
*like to display your room." Not the best translation but wow. Sixteen million*
*colors. I went straight to Google to find out how many colors there are in the*
*world. An infinite amount was the answer, so I could not dismiss their claim*
*out of hand. I wondered. How long would it take to cycle through that many*
*colors? Sixty seconds in a minute, sixty minutes in an hour... there are 86,400*
*seconds in a day. Not even close to sixteen million. How many seconds in a*
*year? 31,556,926. So, if the color changed once a second, and you looked at the*

*lamp without sleeping or otherwise taking your eyes off it, you could determine the choice of color you preferred to display after a mere six months. That is IF you could remember any of them once you got past the first thirty or forty. I have a feeling that if they bring this lamp to the U.S. market, they just might be revising that copy…*

## A Singing Sheep goes from Joie to Cuba!

*A customer came in today asking for the rooster alarm clock we sold years ago. They're no longer available, which she was sad to hear, (but, at least I remembered what it was; sometimes no matter how hard I try, I just can't remember the item they're asking for. I thought I would never forget anything but twenty-five years of items is a lot to remember.) She was consoled and excited when she saw the plush sheep who sings "Thank God I'm a Country Boy." She will be taking it to Cuba to give to a retired priest who lives "in the middle of nowhere" and runs a farm museum showing children the way farms used to be in Cuba. And, he really enjoys battery operated singing animals. Hmmm… I bet they didn't have battery operated singing sheep back in the old days. And I love knowing that Joie de Vivre can brighten the day of a retired Cuban priest.*

## Annoying Comment of the Day

*Yesterday a customer was looking at a little dish of level and compass rings we have displayed on the front desk. They are plastic but they work and have been very popular over the years — especially after people see the sterling silver handmade level and compass rings we sell for quite a bit more — (plastic level rings are $8 — silver, $60) This customer was well dressed and carrying a bag stuffed with socks and tights from a neighboring store. She picked up a plastic level ring and turned it over in her hand. "If this was $2, I'd buy it," she announced to me and all within earshot. And I'm sorry, but that comment is just plain annoying. It's fine to think that to yourself, it's rude to announce it to me. Exceptions: you are under ten years old or you are truly destitute — neither of which was the case. We do sell some expensive items here at Joie, and if a customer looks at a $150 kaleidoscope, loves it, and says they would definitely* *buy it if it was $50, it doesn't offend us at all, we understand. And over the years we have always allowed people to buy an expensive thing that they loved on the installment plan. Which makes me think — too bad I didn't offer that option to the compass ring customer — $1 a week, 8 weeks, and it's yours!*

## Guess Who's Coming to Dinner?

*A friend came shopping for a hard to please woman. "She likes flashy and over the top" was one of the things I had to go on. That doesn't really describe much of our merchandise but I started to wander around the store, looking for inspiration. My eye landed on the Koi Toy, the floating, color-changing light up goldfish from our friends at Fred. "Do they have a pool?" I asked. "Yes" came the answer, and a Koi Toy was wrapped up to go. A few days later I got a report. It was a success, she really liked it. She liked it so much that she brought it to dinner at the Red Inn in Provincetown, and asked for a bowl of water. Many patrons stopped by to admire or covet as it floated on her table, serenely changing colors and lighting up the rather traditional Inn. I wonder if it's the first Koi Toy to go out on a dinner date with its owner?*

## Various Tiny Things

*The other morning freshening and straightening the front desk displays, I saw something that gave me pause. For years, we've had a little container of "various tiny things" at the desk. It's always been an odd little collection — tiny devil ducks, ninjas, nuns, brides and grooms, snakes, rubber chickens, Japanese creatures of indeterminate species, tiny frogs, cats, cows, etc. Then about five years ago there was a big shake up in the toy world when a few companies were found to be importing things from China that might not be 100% safe for children. This led to industry wide testing and stringent new testing requirements. Every individual item had to be tested — so if you paid $2500 to have your tiny rubber frogs tested, and your tiny rubber snakes were made of identical material — you still had to pay $2500 to separately submit proof for the snakes. (My $2500 figure is arbitrary, but various companies have assured me it was in that range.) Needless to say, many smaller companies dropped their tiniest items, rather than pay these fees. This is why we no longer* *have tiny devil ducks and ninjas — a Joie tragedy. Anyway, our available "various tiny things" pool has shrunk considerably and when I looked at it the other day I noticed something unsettling. The collection consisted of rubber chickens (evidently popular enough to justify the testing expense), a group of very realistic tiny animals from a major toy company — and a bunch of black men. Weird, but I knew why. Of the various races of tiny brides and grooms we once had (white, brown, black) the black men were always last to sell. When they were scattered in with the other brides and grooms, it was fine, and I guess because I knew this I didn't really think about it. But that morning, I suddenly thought — what would a black man think if he came in and glanced down at this? It really does look strange. I will be removing the mini black men from our display!*

## It Never Hurts to Ask

*A woman was shopping today, and asked if we could ship her purchases back to the west coast so she wouldn't have to lug them around town for the rest of her stay. Of course we could, and I asked her to write down her name and address on a piece of paper — actually, it was a bag as all our shipping forms had mysteriously disappeared. I looked to see where she lived — Corvallis, Oregon. I hesitated. One of my best friends from high school lives there. What were the chances? But I decided to ask — do you know ? Her face lit up. "Yes, I do!" she said. "I've known her for a long time — and my husband teaches with her at the University of Oregon." This woman comes to Cambridge every year or so and always stops at Joie — she says it's one of her favorite things about the trip. And all these years we had a friend in common and didn't know. So, as my mom and grandmother taught me… it never hurts to ask!*

## A Rather Unusual Request

*First thing in the morning the phone rings. It's a woman who saw on our website that we sell jewelry and wants to know if we offer a particular service. Do we take stuck rings off people's fingers? Specifically, off the finger of her mother-in-law. (Please note that the date of this call was not April 1st!) We suggest the classic remedies — did she try water? soap? a little oil?*

*The woman tells us that her mother-in-law's whole hand is badly swollen and she also has arthritis in her knuckles. We suggest that maybe she would want to see a doctor — but she doesn't like that idea. We apologize that we can't be more helpful — but wonder — what planet does this particular caller live on?*

## Shop Local

*What does shopping local mean to me? It means I'm always running into my customers. Sometimes they know they know me, but aren't sure where from. It's the same for me — the older you get, the more worlds you've lived in — someone could be familiar from anywhere. Contra dancing thirty years ago? Montreal? Vermont? The craft world, back when I was a woodworker? Or maybe just their occasional visit to Joie de Vivre? Yesterday I was at the gym, washing my hands post exercise when a woman stopped me to tell me that what she had bought a month earlier had been a big success. "It was the jeweled pretzel necklace," she reminded me. "I was going to give it away but I decided to keep it. It's so great, thank you so much for finding it. I just love it!" I was smiling as I opened my locker and took out my street clothes. Partly because a $15 necklace could bring someone so much pleasure. And partly because I was thinking — this is what shopping local means to me — meeting a customer in the locker room at the gym.*

## Pickle versus Kaleidoscope

*A kid and her Mom are browsing the store. They're pretty independent of each other, but when the kid sees something she likes she brings it over to show her Mom. It's clear she's been told she can probably have "one thing." Her item of choice seems to be the yodeling pickle which she brings over while it yodels. Mom doesn't seem too enthusiastic and on hearing the price — $16 — says it's probably not going to happen. A bit later, the daughter picks up the ribbon kaleidoscope called "Slow Yo-Yo," made by the talented Tom and Carol Paretti. It's a wonderful object, you throw down three feet of ribbon which become the scope's object case, and you look through as you slowly wind the ribbon back up. Our girl was enchanted. She wandered over to find her mother. "Mom, I don't think I want the pickle. I found something I really like a lot more." Just as her*

*Mom is beginning to ask how much it costs, I interrupt. "I'm afraid I have bad news; it's more than the pickle." I say it this way because I don't want to say the actual price — over $300. A moment of silence as the sad news is digested. "I guess it must cost $50, it's so awesome" says the daughter. She said it without resentment. She understood that it was clearly in a different league than the pickle. She brought her Mom to see it, unrolled it and rolled it up while Mom looked through and agreed it was indeed a wondrous thing. They stayed awhile longer while Mom picked out a card and small present. Then her daughter chose a pickle-pult — a toy that catapults miniature pickles — $6 — and they left.*

Accoutrements Catalog

*My sister Sue's husband works at a sporting goods store and for some reason they received a catalogue from Accoutrements, one of our star purveyors of fun. She brought it to our family summer vacation to show me, in case I didn't know about it. (Though of course I did.) It was discovered by her daughter and the other two kids in the house. They were very impressed by the contents. Reading through the pages has become a daily activity and it's funny to listen to them shriek with horror at the bacon jelly beans and hear them try to puzzle out why anyone would want some of these things. Of course some of the things (say, apple flavored gummy maggots) make me react pretty much the same way. But their timeless chicken chuckers, finger monsters, devil ducks and singing pickles — Joie de Vivre could never be its silly self without them. A funny intrusion of work into vacation! And for the record… I asked each kid what their favorite item in the catalogue was. They did not go for the disturbing or gross. One picked the cupcake mints. One picked the toothpick bird. The last one could not decide.*

Happiness is

*Things that make us happy — when someone comes rushing in first thing in the morning and says "I need a xylophone and a magic wand!" and we can say "Okay, let us show you our selection."*

******

We switched to Facebook on Joie de Vivre's 30th anniversary. What made me finally decide to do this was a conversation I had with my dear friend Stuart. I had asked him if he thought Joie should be on Facebook, and he said absolutely! He told me that he thought of a blog as a dinner party with good friends — thoughtful conversation on a range of subjects — and described Facebook as more of a cocktail party — where you're chatting with friends and acquaintances — or making new ones. Suddenly I decided — I want to have a cocktail party *and* a dinner party! But it didn't really work out that way. I soon abandoned the blog, and eventually felt I had to write this entry on our page: "We have become the kind of blogger we never wanted to be — the kind who has a 'read our blog' button on our website but the newest post is months old." From then on, I occasionally posted a long piece on an anniversary, but the blog effectively ended. It became an archive of sorts and I appreciate the memories those longer stories bring back.

CHAPTER 37

# Odds and Ends

You never knew who would like what. Jabber balls were cute soft plastic Japanese cartoony animals that made silly sounds when squeezed, sticking out their tongues. I gave one to a friend who worked as an event planner, and was setting up an MIT Graduation, a job that turned out to be much more demanding than she'd imagined. She needed stress relief. Job done, before leaving town, she came in and told me her pink jabber ball bunny was gone. "What happened to it?" I asked. She explained. She had lost it somewhere on the site, and when she went to the construction manager's office to say goodbye, she spotted her bunny on a desk. Relieved, she went to grab it. "You're taking it??" said the big burly guy of the little pink bunny. He looked alarmed. "It's yours?" "No, that's okay, it's yours!" she said and made her exit. After hearing this story, I gave her another one and wound up with a great story to tell. "If I suggested you give a pink jabber bunny to a construction worker, you'd look at me like I was crazy, right? Well, let me tell you what happened last year..."

\*\*\*\*\*\*

I'm completely against taking videos of anyone without their knowledge but we had a product that made me want to. It was called the Woodland

Diorama and it sat on our front desk for several years, an illustrated box with a scene of woods and trees, and five or six animals who, thanks to a motion sensor, quickly disappeared into the woods when someone passed by. It made a little click and stopped people in their tracks. "What just happened?" they would ask, and we'd tell them to watch the box, but "don't move a muscle." The animals would slowly, slowly emerge again only to disappear as soon as anyone moved, and I would have loved to film both adults and children while they watched this happen. Their faces were as delightful as the box itself. This was a beloved item, the kind people came in specifically to show their friends and kids loved to visit. We were terribly sad when it was discontinued. (And yes, it was the old "we didn't sell enough of them" story. As usual, not the case at Joie!)

*******

For many years, we sold little movie viewers. They were about an inch by three inches, and used actual tiny rolls of interchangeable film, including Disney excerpts, Fred Astaire and Ginger Rogers, Science Marvels, all kinds of thirty second clips. They were a sensation but we always wondered, keychains? They were kind of bulky. Why were they keychains? And so I asked the supplier and found out — as a keychain, they were deemed a useful object, not a toy, fell into a different customs category, and were cheaper to import. Which of course made sense and of course we would never have guessed.

*******

We always wrote our sales slips out by hand, never got a computerized register. We added them up using our elementary school math skills — in our heads, no calculators. This actually made some customers nervous and they would scan the slip, even ask for a calculator so they could check our work. We almost never made mistakes, though if we had a big sale and it ran on for a few pages, I would take it to the back and run a tape. We also "counted up" when giving a customer change for cash. This terrified some of my younger employees at first, but almost to a person they later thanked me for teaching them math. Interestingly, it turned out to be the ones who relied on calculators who didn't realize when they'd made an error. If you're constantly adding things up, you develop a sense of what it's going to be before you even start. If you're $40 off one way or another, the math voice inside your head says, "that can't be right." That voice appeared to be silenced when the calculator came out, but I could glance at what someone was adding up, hear the total when they told the customer, and quietly suggest they try it again. Many of us became super fast at addition and that seemed to unnerve customers too. Whereas I become unnerved when I hand someone a twenty and a one for an eleven-dollar sale and they look at me confused!

*******

In a related note, for years our sales tax in Massachusetts was 5%. That was easy — you just took 10% of the sale and divided it in two. When in doubt — say a 50-cent sale — the government got the extra penny — 2.5 cents became 3. But in 2009, the tax rose to 6.25%. Not so easy, but after a few years, we basically had memorized the amount on most sales. Again unnerving customers who thought we were figuring it out in our heads.

*******

Storing holiday merchandise for the next season: A few days after Easter, we would look at our Easter stock section to see what was left over. Of course wind-up rabbits and chicks and a great deal of spring and chicken related merchandise just went right back into our year-round stock, because we sell chicken bags and rabbit puppets all year long, same for egg shaped ice cube molds and pinwheels and butterfly bubbles. However, if something says "Happy Easter" or is too overtly Easter related, we'd pack it up and put it away until next year. (Sad thing about that Easter chocolate that wouldn't last a year without going bad — we were forced to eat it!) The fifty cent chenille chicks were among the items packed away, put in a place as far out of the way as we could, because we knew we wouldn't need them until next year. And then someone would come in and ask for — chenille chicks. They really needed a few. A basic law of the retail universe — pack something up and put it in a hard to access place — and someone will really really want it!

\*\*\*\*\*\*

One of our employees, Julia Willwerth, (then Julia Pafumi) was the inventor of "National Embarrassmints." The Unemployed Philosopher's Guild had come up with some witty tins of mints including Atonemints, Enlightenmints, and Empowermints. Julia, working alone one slow Thursday evening was inspired and took a Dan Quayle postcard we were selling, cut out his head, glued it to a tin and labeled it "National Embarrassmints." I thought it was genius and sent it off the UPG folks and they agreed. They substituted George W. for Dan, and soon we were selling tons of them. I asked for a couple free cases for Julia, and later regretted not asking for more, although it was an idea that probably would have occurred to them sooner or later as they wound up producing many variations on the mint theme including RBG Judgmints, Mr. Roger's Encouragemints and Alice's Enchantmints. Still, that particular honor goes to Julia!

\*\*\*\*\*\*

The Cat versus Dog phenomenon. It's true I love cats, and will plead guilty to tending more toward cat items than dog — but in my defense, cats are definitely funnier than dogs. Their apparent inscrutability leads to a wealth of attitude interpretation where dogs are much more straightforward. But the biggest thing relating to retail is that cat owners tend to like almost all cat things. They may want a black cat, but they almost never request the dreaded specific breed. "But do you have this in a dachshund? a bulldog? a poodle? a golden retriever?" and on and on and on — it was impossible to stock all the hundred plus dog breeds people would request. So sometimes it was easier not to carry a dog item at all, and let the pet stores, and those truly devoted to dogs do it. When we considered adding a "cats" page to our website, we quickly came up with a good seventy-five items — could never have done that with dogs. That said, our best-selling doormat ever was "Ask Not for Whom the Dog Barks — the Dog Barks for Thee."

\*\*\*\*\*\*

You know you've been in business awhile when a customer tells you they know the baby who was the model for the cardboard "Instant Infant" you've sold for years. And he is a recent college graduate.

\*\*\*\*\*\*

The experience of shopping at Joie de Vivre could vary wildly. A customer could come in and the store could be a madhouse… especially around Christmas, Valentine's Day, or a busy weekend. But during the week, we could go for an hour or two some days without one person walking in. And when one did, they'd often say "I've never been in here before when there was no one else here." I think they were partly amazed, but it seemed clear that some felt a little odd or anxious being the only customer. I often felt the need to reassure them — telling them how normal it was for it to be quiet on a weekday morning when no holiday was looming. I also intuited that what they also wanted to hear was — this is not unusual, and we're not going out of business anytime soon. And over the years I noticed that some customers preferred to shop when it was relatively quiet; if it got too noisy or hectic, they'd walk right out. Others loved it when the sound machines were beeping, the singing goat was yodeling, someone was trying out a kazoo, and all the clocks were going off.

218

# CHAPTER 38

# The Show Must Go On?

Years down the road, I still loved the things I'd loved about running a store from the start: going to shows, getting to know my suppliers, finding unexpected things to sell, introducing my finds to customers, doing displays and most of the day-to-day things we did at the store, from the somewhat mundane straightening and restocking of the card racks, to discussing life with whoever wandered in. And when I started our blog in 2007, I found I really enjoyed writing little stories about it all.

I did not love what I saw happening to the Trade Shows I attended every year. They really began to struggle to stay exciting and relevant in the age of huge chain stores, Amazon and the internet. The New York Gift Show which at its glorious height filled the gigantic Jacob Javits Center on the West Side of Manhattan, as well as three nearby Hudson River piers, and had a lengthy exhibitor waiting list, started to falter as smaller stores struggled to hang on to their traditional business. Those buyers were the ones who had filled the aisles, making the first days of a show something of a genteel, or not so genteel, contact sport. The shows had a buzz, and you could feel as well as hear it.

Trade shows were where you saw the actual products you might sell, there or in one of the showrooms that were also found in most larger cities. Besides my trips to the Javits Center, I often spent time walking the halls of the "225" building on lower 5th Avenue, going from showroom to showroom. The Toy Building, across the street on Broadway, open to small buyers only during the Toy Fair, was a resource too. Boston had its own smaller gift show and collection of wholesale showrooms. But small stores and small shows were beginning to go out of business.

Showrooms started to close. And with fewer buyers to come to the shows, some vendors decided the expense was no longer worth it. At the same time, there were more shows, promoters having looked at the biggest thinking, we can do this too, make that happen here. New York lost its storied "first big show of the year" position to the rising Atlanta Show, and by the time buyers got to New York, they had seen most of the new at least a month earlier. Or seen it online, as companies started to release their new work on the internet. New York began to lose its "must attend" status. Some older wholesalers decided to retire. By the mid to late 2000's, the Boston Show was tiny, and the New York visibly on the decline.

Walking the New York show from about 2010 on, I watched as it shrank drastically. It no longer filled the whole Javits Center and here and there, spaces within the show were empty, turned into "lounge areas" consisting largely of chairs and tables, occasionally filled by someone the likes of me eating their peanut butter sandwich lunch. By 2017, there were far too many lounges. Even worse, for a few years show management rented booths to "businesses" hawking on the spot eye lifts, massages and personal make-up. I don't use the word hawking lightly here. You'd walk down the aisle and hear "Hey, you look so tired, we can help you fix that," the absolute last thing I, a tired buyer, wanted to hear when I was trying to work. Nothing like a total stranger criticizing my appearance to put me in a good mood. I complained bitterly to management, and I wasn't alone. After a slew of complaints from irritated buyers, these booths disappeared.

Desperate to stay in business, the show, which had trendily renamed itself NYNOW, although most people still called it the Gift Show, tried other strategies too. Whole sections of the show would be leased to merchants from China. I inquired a few times about their products, only to find that they were looking for distributors and wanted a minimum order of thousands of units. After that, I stopped walking those aisles. I'm sure most other buyers did too, and I felt bad for these exhibitors who had traveled so far, having been promised pie in the sky and winding up with empty plates. Of course, they just needed to make a few connections, but it never appeared to me that this happened.

As more exhibitors pulled out, show management responded by raising booth prices, making it even more difficult for the exhibitors that remained to cover their costs, resulting in more questioning if the show was really worth it. The last few years I attended, "Will we do this show again?" was a constant topic of conversation, even with companies that were successful and had been exhibiting for years. Exhibitors who had done the show forever were attached to it, and most loved an excuse to come to New York. Still, breaking even was one thing, losing money another. I still loved going, and no matter how small a show got, always managed to find enough new merchandise to make it worth it. And I liked seeing the vendors I'd gotten to know over the years. Some I saw three times a year or so, more than I saw some of my friends. But I had a free place to stay, and didn't have to travel far. And I was a small store. An order from me would not make someone's show. I felt terrible for some of the new exhibitors. They had been lured in, promised lots of buyers who just weren't there and most were clearly very small if not one person businesses. Doing the show was a big financial risk.

You could see the desperation in their eyes as you walked by their booths. By this time, I could often tell at a glance if a booth looked like it might hold something of interest for us, and I didn't walk into those where that was clearly not the case. But now people were trying to pull me in, asking "Have you seen this product? Tell me about your store," outstretched hands holding brochures or little product samples. Sometimes the work was good, sometimes ghastly. And sometimes I stopped and explained that what they had just wasn't right for my store, but I couldn't do that at every single booth. Back when the show was crowded with buyers, I felt no obligation to stop, knowing some other more interested buyer was likely to come along. Now I felt terrible as I walked right by. I knew these exhibitors had been schooled in how important it was to be personal, helpful and assertive. But clearly no one had explained that you usually waited until someone had shown at least a shred of interest.

At this point many of the buyers weren't legitimate businesses. Management wanted to make their numbers look good so they eased up on the credentials required to attend and a lot more personal shoppers with "design businesses" began to fill the aisles. It was easy to spot these people. They were the ones arguing about minimum orders, walking the aisles talking with their friends about where to go for lunch or drinks, unlike actual buyers who worked the show all day. The show started selling space to importers of expensive linens and beds, who rented huge booths, and I'm sure did many personal sales. There were multiple booths featuring wall sized "art" that in no way could be considered giftware. Who gives someone a 20 by 20 foot painting or print? I rarely saw anyone in these peculiar booths. They were almost funny, but I couldn't help but remember the rows of smaller businesses each one replaced, booths that might have had something that would work for me.

Email and the internet made the trade shows more annoying. Constant emails about nothing much, and constant requests to fill out surveys immediately after the show. You know a show is not doing well when they ask for instant feedback/affirmation. And frustratingly, like most internet surveys, they never allowed for any kind of meaningful or nuanced response, just the inevitable "choose one, on a scale of one to ten" ratings. I once read an article titled "Onslaught of customer satisfaction surveys is fraying customer patience," and after being requested to rate my experience buying something as small as a box of envelopes at Staples, I wholeheartedly agreed. And yet I usually at least started to fill these show surveys out, hoping there might some chance of actually being helpful.

The American Crafts movement still had its own shows. The first one I went to, back in the 1970s, when I was working for Lore at the Gallery, was in Rhinebeck, NY, in the Hudson River Valley, and from my first step inside, I was transfixed by an amazing variety of handmade American goods. I had seen individual pieces of handblown glass, wood, or ceramics at the Gallery, but the abundance and variety of artists and media on view at this show was overwhelming. It was glory days for handmade American goods. I wasn't a buyer yet but I spent every cent I had with me on jewelry and handmade coffee mugs and gifts for friends. Soon, Lore sent me to buy for her Craft Gallery, which I did for a few years. Then, when I lived with Bill in Vermont, I was back with him as an exhibitor, the woodworker's girlfriend who could not have made a single thing in the booth by herself. After I opened Joie de Vivre, I returned as a buyer again. By this time, the fairs were held twice a year, in different cities, and soon a third big wholesale craft fair was added to the mix. But now, thirty years after they'd begun, these fairs were having their own problems.

This was in part because those who began the American Craft Renaissance were getting older. Many were in their 60s, 70s or 80s and wanted to retire. Some no longer wanted the pressure of traveling to shows anymore, or of producing work for wholesale. And the market wasn't the same. The buyers who crowded booths vying to buy glass bowls and goblets or quilted wall hangings, cherry side tables, shawls and scarves and seaglass jewelry, now had customers with crowded homes who were paring down, no longer collecting. And "one of a kind" work had gotten really expensive. When I walked the illustrious winter craft show in Baltimore I only wrote a few orders now. Much of the work on exhibit was out of our price range. Another show, more production oriented, was better for my purposes, but that got smaller too. Younger people were not going into craft, or if they were, often preferred to sell direct to the public on Etsy and other websites. The Craft Shows still showcased some beautiful work, but felt a little dated. Many exhibitors had grey hair.

The storied New York Stationery Show, that had filled the Javits center with cards, stationary and related gifts, ceased to be in 2018, after shrinking to a shadow of its former self. Only the International Toy Fair, held every February in New York, remained a fairly lively and fun show. It was smaller than it had been, but toys were one of the things that still really sold, especially as baby boomers became grandparents. They didn't want to buy much for themselves anymore, but they enjoyed buying for their grandchildren, many of our customers included. And though there were serious men in suits, and a big business aspect to Toy Fair, it remained fun. Giant animals and characters still wandered the floor, the Lego booth always made a few amazing life-size creations in the entrance hall, and adorable kids flounced down the Ty runway holding fuzzy animal bags and backpacks. As a bonus, I could relive my youth in the Breyers, Steiff or Madame Alexander booths. We didn't sell plastic horses, dolls, or much plush, but I loved them, if not quite as much as I had at age ten.

Still, things were changing there too. The Toy world was cut-throat and the biggest companies spied on each other's creations, sending undercover agents to check out the little booths in case there was something promising to imitate. The show was divided into two very different sections, the first upstairs and the second, down. When I first started to attend, all the booths were open, but now, on the main floor, larger companies began to build fortresses, erecting high walls so it was impossible to look inside. Instead of looking at product, you'd see a blank wall with a huge logo — Mattel, Tomy, Innovation First International, Melissa and Doug. The entrances were defended by staff with clipboards, asking if you had an appointment, and it was often impossible to talk your way in without one. "I'm a small store, I just want to take a quick look through," I'd plead. "I really don't need a salesperson to go with me." I knew that person would try to sell me everything when all I wanted might be one special item. I didn't want to waste their time, or mine. Sometimes a clipboard holder would look at me, judge me harmless and relent, but many did not. And it was a strange feeling walking those aisles — like being in a gated community. Weren't we here to buy? How could we even consider it without seeing the products?

Downstairs, things were open and more chaotic — still lots of little booths. Smaller inventors took their chances there, and smaller companies as well, even some bigger names that weren't afraid to let buyers get an open look at what they sold. Magicians and more costumed animals roamed the aisles, you might get hit on the head by a remote-controlled shark balloon, and many buyers had little helium filled chickens, dogs, and ponies attached to their bags, courtesy of a smart and generous balloon company. (I once brought a chicken balloon uptown on the subway, causing lots of stares, laughs and many inquiries.) Balls flew through the air, hired teenagers demonstrated skateboard tricks, and I could have watched the giant bubble ring produce its magic for hours. European toy companies preferred the downstairs to show their goods, and there was a section reserved for small inventors who had tiny companies, or just one product. Downstairs at Toy Fair remained fun.

But things had changed in the trade show world. The once essential shows now spurred debate over whether it was worth it to go when you could sit home and look at things online. I tried that, and found although it was fine to reorder things once you had seen them in person, ordering things without seeing them first didn't always work out. Something could look good in a catalog or on a website, but that didn't mean it would be. And looking through catalogs and websites takes a whole lot longer than looking at physical objects in a booth or showroom. I wound up returning things I thought would be wonderful because — they weren't. And that was tedious and time consuming. Of course, I made mistakes even when I saw something in person, maybe too tired, or too distracted, or even too desperate to find something new. All buyers make mistakes. But I didn't mind blaming myself. If I had seen a product, ordered it, and it didn't work, that was on me. Sometimes it was even funny; what could I have been thinking? But if I saw a product in a catalog or online only, and it disappointed, that was a different story. So I made a decision. I would be a holdout, the old-fashioned buyer, the one who always checked the survey box that said the most important thing about a show is seeing product in person. I would be the person who still went to the shows, who would not give them up, no matter how small they got.

CHAPTER 39

# Surviving Is The New Good

As trade shows got smaller, the question "How's business?" the standard show greeting that had been our version of "how are you?" forever, became more serious. People really wanted to know. Were you really okay? Would you be placing your usual orders for Christmas or were you considering closing? We all threw around quips like "okay is the new good" and "surviving is the new success." Back home, when my friend Barbara asked how our weekend had been, I often found myself saying "passable," or "barely mediocre." We laughed, but it was a little sobering. I "lent" the store money that was never paid back, its credit cards were always at their limit, and I began to take a pre-Christmas advance every year from the bank. In January, I'd pay it all off and start again. I didn't like carrying debt through the year, it was stressful but — I had to.

I wanted to know how other businesses were doing, across the country and in my own neighborhood. Interpreting the reports could bring mixed feelings. You don't want to think that everyone else is doing much better than you, but at the same time, if that's true, you're quite likely doing something wrong, something you might be able to fix. If everyone is doing badly, it's a more serious problem. What do you do then? I started noticing tip jars in all kinds of unlikely places including — the specialty seafood store? And I began to hear the classic "add on" questions at many checkout points. "Is that all?" "Did you find everything you want? "Can I get you anything else?" You knew they'd been instructed to ask, but it always irritated me. I was waiting in line to check out, not to buy more. We never asked those questions at Joie.

Faceless corporations started replacing local companies. We had had two dumpsters out back, one for trash another for cardboard and recyclables. For the first twenty years we used two different companies, both local. I switched to the second after finding out my neighbor was paying a different company much less for the same service. When I called up to cancel so I could switch, the first people promptly offered to match the lower price. "No thanks," I said, infuriated to think that they'd only been charging me more because they thought they could get away with it. But soon both local companies were out of business, replaced by a giant company whose main offices were down south somewhere. If you called their customer service line, they had no idea who or where you were.

Not that it was easy to get them on the phone. It was increasingly difficult to get anyone on the phone. This had been true for awhile in my personal life — good luck talking to someone at Verizon, or Comcast. By the time I reached a human I was inevitably frustrated and angry. Now this was becoming the norm in the business world as well. I liked talking to people and one year, I made a New Year's resolution. I would start calling companies again instead of emailing with questions. This proved more difficult than I'd imagined. You'd call a company and instead of a human with a friendly "Hello, how can I help you?" you'd have to listen to a long program of choices before you hopefully got to the right person. And the constant taped reassurance that "we really care about our customers," was no consolation, especially when the obvious way to prove that would have been paying someone decent money to answer the phones. Companies didn't put their phone numbers on their websites anymore either. You could usually find one eventually, but it took some detective work and too much time.

There were lovely, refreshing exceptions to this reluctance to answer phones. Some were big companies too. I always made a point of thanking them, of letting them know that human contact was still appreciated. We might chat about the weather, or an upcoming holiday for a minute, and next time I called, they might even remember me.

We were already dealing with a lot of scam emails, and now we started receiving scam calls as well. Someone would call from the "Electric Company" and warn us that our electricity would be cut off in twenty minutes if we didn't pay our overdue bill. We never paid a bill more than a week late, and I knew we would receive plenty of warning if something had somehow gone wrong, maybe a check lost in the mail, so we quickly cut these scammers off, but it was annoying to say the least, and you knew people, probably older people, must sometimes fall for this, or why would we get so many of these calls?

As bad or worse were the robo-calls. Some began "Don't hang up!" and I took great satisfaction in immediately doing just that. But they got better over the years, to the point where for a minute you might be tricked into thinking you were talking to a human being. They had even been programmed to answer brief questions. It drove us crazy, and I have no idea why robocalls are legal. Everyone hates them, yet they are allowed. We can't legally light a beautiful sparkler in Massachusetts, but robots are allowed to harass us day and night. There's something very wrong with that! And customers looked at our website for directions and information now instead of calling. I missed the ringing phone with a human on the line.

I still picked up our phone thinking it would be a real person, the same way I opened my mailbox each night at home, thinking there might be a letter, or something personal inside. Old habits die hard. That phone had rung constantly for years. Before the reign of cellphones one of our more popular employees sometimes got twenty calls a day. "Emily! It's for you." (*Again*, I would think.) And then there was: what are your hours, do you sell clocks, do you have twelve mood rings in stock and can you wrap them, do you sell puppets, how do we get there? Of course giving directions while trying to gift wrap a lava lamp could be a bother, but — it was interaction.

Strangely, the myriad ways of communicating wound up making communication more difficult. If I needed to reach a customer should I email? Text? Call? Message on Facebook? Customers had become reluctant to answer their own ringing phones, sounding deeply suspicious if not hostile when they picked up at all. I understood they were expecting a robot, or a scammer, or someone asking for money to fight any of the many evils in the world, but it was unsettling to be on the receiving end. I identified myself as quickly as possible and generally got a relieved apology.

It was quieter without a constantly ringing phone, and we no longer had the same customer flow. The neighborhood residents were working, and there wasn't much foot traffic. It had also become incredibly difficult to park. Cambridge was trying hard to discourage driving — a not unreasonable position at least environmentally, but they eliminated parking spaces left and right, and instead of rewarding small size cars, made the remaining spaces really large, losing several on every block. Less space and higher prices — now a quarter got you only twelve minutes. Spaces in our neighborhood that had been metered were inexplicably eliminated. It was extremely frustrating for us to have customers tell us they'd tried to find a space for an hour and given up. Many came from out of town, and there was not a realistic public transportation alternative for them. Every meeting I ever went to with city officials where they asked what they could do to help small business, the response from all of us, retailers, restaurateurs, various other services, was — we need more parking. But it only got worse.

It was also quieter because customers had mostly stopped talking on their phones. They weren't talking to us though, now they were silently texting. We felt like we were interrupting them when we said hello because, we were. Log entry — *"First customer in — wearing headset — looks at me blankly when I say hello. One minute later she's texting — and then she's gone."* If a customer walks into a store and it's got a few people in it, laughing and looking around, they feel at ease, but if there's just one person, sitting behind a desk doing a crossword puzzle and that person says hello, for some, that seemed to be annoying. *Me to customer walking in: "Hi." Customer: "Just looking!!!"* I found that response discouraging. We never tried to sell people things just to sell them, but I could tell some customers feared we were going to try to do just that. Though the ones on their phones might be oblivious to us in any case.

Or people on cellphones might be checking prices. That had become quite easy to do, and we couldn't offer the better prices they might find online. For one thing, we had a physical store with all its related expenses. For another, we were small. No one was going to give us a break on wholesale prices. One day a woman picked something up and brought it to the desk. She asked me if I would match the Amazon price. I didn't even try to educate her on just how rude a question that was; asking a small business to match the price of an evil behemoth. I don't think I even said "sorry," just "no."

The ease of finding things online had become a bigger problem for us, and two different items illustrate why. We had started carrying some funny t-shirts, "It's All Fun and Games Until Someone Ends up in a Cone," "Dance Like Russia isn't Watching," and one of our most popular ever in the Trump years, "Sorry About Our President" printed in 18 different languages. We loved them, customers loved them, but — they came in so many sizes! Four different women's sizes, extra small to large, and five choices for men, small to extra extra large. My respect for people who owned clothing stores instantly increased. How could you possibly know what sizes to order?

The short answer is — you couldn't. If you had six mediums in stock when you reordered the sizes you were out of, you were sure to have run out by the time the order came. And, you couldn't order just a few shirts, there was a wholesale minimum of $250. And, they shipped out of California so they took awhile to arrive. But if a customer wanted one now, there was of course no minimum for retail purchasers. They could order it, most likely receive a retail discount because the company made more when selling direct, and the shirt would be there in a couple of days. It was frustrating and every time a customer asked for a certain size, we went to the stockroom with trepidation — would we have that size in stock? It got to be funny — we felt like we'd hit the jackpot if we did, and for awhile we rang a little silver bell to let each other know that — score! A t-shirt miracle had occurred.

We had the same problem with a wonderful poster company. They sold highly detailed and visually compelling "infographic" posters — The Very Many Varieties of Beer, The Chart of Cheese Wheel, A Visual Compendium of Cameras, The Grand Taxonomy of Rap Names and the like. They came rolled up so we printed and laminated a small sample of each, but they made many different styles — some thirty or forty. There was no way to keep them all in stock, and again, we couldn't order one or two. If someone wanted one right away, they were easy to order direct, and we couldn't blame people for doing it either — why wait three weeks if you need it now? We never used the silver bell for these, but felt the same sense of great good luck when we actually had the one a customer wanted.

People thought nothing of talking right in front of us about how they'd bought something online that we were selling in the store. They didn't seem to make the obvious connection — that they could have tried us first. One day a woman asked if we had an item we were out of. "We'd be happy to order you one," I said. "Oh, no thanks, that's okay," she replied. "I can just order it from Amazon." It amazed me that she appeared to have no sense of how this sounded to a shopkeeper trying to survive. Very occasionally I would attempt to respond, but it was tricky. One Sunday, a woman and her husband were shopping. It had been a very slow day. She took a photo of a card, and I impulsively made a comment along the lines of "In the old days, people used to buy cards." She then said, "Sometimes you can't afford them," and I instantly felt bad. Cards were expensive now. Add a stamp and it could easily cost you $5. But then she and her husband decided to buy themselves a $25 print. As they were paying, I felt like asking, "Are you sure you can afford this?" but managed to refrain. If you make someone feel guilty, they get defensive. They might not return. You might lose a much needed customer.

Back when we were doing great, I didn't mind losing a customer or two. Now I was acutely aware that fewer people were walking in the door. It made our days less interesting too. Far better to make $800 because forty people come in and spend $20 each than to have two people spend $50 and have one other big sale. More people to talk with. It was boring to sit there alone. Those larger sales had previously been the icing on the cake, making a good day into a very good day. Now they often were the only thing between a day that looked okay, and a disaster. Saturdays and Sundays had always been our busiest days, but except during holidays, that wasn't the case anymore. Sometimes they were slower than the weekdays. It was very unpredictable, but I never quite stopped expecting a weekend rush. I've always had trouble adjusting to change, happy to try to ignore it. But it was getting harder not to see how much things were changing.

Some of our best customers had always been employees of other stores and businesses in the neighborhood. Hyperlocal shopping. But I began to realize that was no longer really the case. One time I was shopping in a neighboring clothing store, chatting with one of the young employees. She had worked there almost five years and never once been in my store, just halfway down the block. Then I thought about my own employees. They didn't really leave the store during the day much either, and if they did, it was usually to buy their lunch, or supplies. But they weren't too busy working to spend time in other stores, especially now. Was it all the fault of cell phones? The internet?

The young people who staffed the incredibly popular (and delicious) bagel shop next door? Most of them had never even come in to look around. And most of their customers, who waited patiently in line (right in front of the store) for a half hour to snag a bagel, didn't come in either, preferring to chat with each other or look at their phones as they inched toward the door. Was the store no longer interesting? Those who came in seemed to enjoy it. It puzzled me.

Around this time I had an unsettling experience while on my annual fall trip to Vermont. There was a craft gallery in Brattleboro I liked to stop into on my drive home. We shared some artists, and I often spent some time talking about business and art with their staff. This time I got to talking with an older man who was sitting behind the desk. He told me he was one of the owners, and that things had been slow. He wondered if maybe he was too old to be sitting there, if he was out of touch, if seeing an older man at the counter made people less likely to come in. I'd defended him. After all, he knew a lot about the artists and their work. And he was an owner and had interesting stories. I said of course you're not too old to be here.

But back home, I started thinking about it — a lot. What about me? Did people look into Joie, see me and decide not to come in? Older people had always come in when my staff and I were all young, but were young people doing the same now that we were all, to be charitable, a little older? We did have customers in their twenties and thirties who loved the store, and I felt like we had plenty to talk about. But we needed more customers.

I knew we were not cutting edge, whatever that was now. I didn't care about that, never had. I had always just bought what I thought was fun, engaging, interesting or beautiful. I wasn't trying to be trendy, though we occasionally almost accidentally were. And I still believed, even as the world seemed to be going in the opposite direction, in the power of the small, the personal, and of limited selection. Or the limitless variety of a handheld kaleidoscope. I still believed in the book and the wind-up mouse and the postcard. I still believed in bubbles, though some customers would look at me like I was crazy if I suggested a simple tube of bubbles as a present for a child. I wasn't crazy, they had just forgotten how magical bubbles could be. Still, a seed of doubt had been planted. Had my time passed?

CHAPTER 40

# Almost Ready

"So when are you going to close the store?" I was at a family Labor Day get together, eating lunch. My brother-in-law, who'd posed the question, looked at me seriously. "You've been talking about it for a while now. Are you making any plans?" I was annoyed. It was hardly a secret that I'd been thinking about closing. But I had made no real plans. And my sister who worked for me was sitting there looking uncomfortable. She was my bookkeeper, so well aware of our situation, but she didn't talk about it much, just listened to me complain. This was supposed to be a relaxing weekend. I felt put on the spot, but he persisted.

"You really should close it on your own terms, before you're forced to," he observed. "I'm thinking about it," I finally replied. And that was true. I had been thinking about it a lot. But this was what I always said. In truth, I just couldn't seem to come to a decision. It never felt like the right time, and I was good at concentrating on the small picture, ignoring the big one. I had been raiding my own small savings account for years. And there was more on the store's two credit cards than I could keep up with. In theory, and as far as the IRS was concerned, we were making money. I paid taxes every year, and supported two full time employees. But somehow, in practice there was never quite enough money. I couldn't pay those two employees as much as I wanted to, and I barely paid myself.

And there was that ongoing list of things I knew I should be keeping up with but wasn't able to.

After thirty some years, lots of things at the store needed maintenance. Busy with more immediate projects, I often didn't see them, and I hoped the customers didn't either, but I knew that our carpet was frayed and stained, the counters needed refinishing, a couple of our card racks were cracked and held in place with packing tape, and the whole place needed a paint job. I hoped our merchandise and general joie de vivre would prevent others from noticing all this, the same way I always hoped my sparkling personality would win out over the holes in or paint on my sweaters and jeans. Still, a general sense of shabbiness was certainly felt by me and in my heart of hearts, I knew I probably wasn't alone.

When I really let myself look at how much I needed to do, I would sometimes remember visiting Lore and Vern at the Gallery during their last years in business. I was always struck by the holes in the ceiling, and how run down everything was. They still sold a lot of beautiful things, but a few of those things I recognized from thirty years earlier. They had less staff and fewer customers, and though I still felt some of the magic of the past, the place felt a little forlorn. Now sometimes I wondered if my store felt that way too. I'd then immediately think of the ways it was different. Their ceilings were much lower for one, no wonder I'd noticed the holes and empty hooks.

When the store had turned twenty, we'd closed for a week, replaced the carpet, and repainted everything. It looked great, but the years went by and the maintenance we did from then on was generally out of absolute necessity. Our elderly track light fixtures started acting up, sizzling occasionally, and once, a very hot light bulb fell out, burning a little hole in the rug. That terrified me. What if it had fallen on a customer? I replaced every last one of the old light fixtures. I'd had to replace our beautiful, crumbling, second sign too.

Our original customers were getting older now. Some disappeared. They may have moved, or become ill, but some undoubtedly had died. Those who were fifty or sixty when we opened would now be eighty or ninety. Some we saw only once or twice a year, yet after twenty-five years in business, we knew them pretty well. I would worry when I didn't see them anymore. One couple came in faithfully once a year in late November to do their Christmas shopping. Armed with a list of everyone in their family, they'd ask for suggestions and usually manage to find something for each. Then they'd go for lunch at the Thai restaurant next door while we wrapped their gifts. Over the years I noticed as they got a little shaky, and the husband, who had always been a bit adversarial but fun, became downright crotchety, the way people do when they have physical problems. Then one year I realized they hadn't come. It was strange to think I would never see them again.

A lot of our long-time customers no longer bought anything for themselves. Some would come in, look around, and announce their bona-fides, saying, "I already have everything in this store." Of course this was never true, just their way of telling me what others said a different way. "I have no room," I don't need anything," "I love this, but at this point in my life, I'm trying to get rid of things." They did like to talk, sometimes at length, about what they had bought from us years ago, and on a slow day, that could be dispiriting. I know part of the reason some didn't buy was they didn't have the income they once did. Taking care of yourself when you're older in America is expensive.

Others were happy to spend money, they just wanted to spend it on their grandchildren. We had plenty of things that kids loved, but it was neither our specialty nor my aim. I didn't want to go "deeper" into kid stuff. There were two excellent children's stores nearby for one thing. And I liked our merchandise mix. Still, I found we were selling more and more gifts intended for grandchildren. Customers were also happy to spend money at Christmas. We had a lot of shoppers that came in once a year to do holiday shopping. After seeing them for years and years, they were true regulars. This didn't really surprise me. I had doctors that I'd seen just once a year for various check-ups, and after twenty years, felt I had a genuine connection with. I felt the same way about our seasonal shoppers. Still, it was a little hard to hear their cheery "You always make our holiday special

— see you next year!" when they left with their bags full of gifts. "Why not come back sooner?" was what I wanted to say. "Thanks so much, and okay!" was what I did.

Our merchandise mix was getting harder to maintain. It was still interesting but it was wasn't as easy to find new things. Shows were smaller, craftspeople were retiring or selling direct at shows or on Etsy, and the quirkier items like dancing flowers and Singing Hamsters were few and far between. When long-time shoppers came in and asked "What's new?" that's what they wanted; the wind-up dog that turned into a truck, the framed Mona Lisa that stuck out her tongue when you walked by, the mysterious fuzzy cat paw, anything that did something silly, unexpected or crazy. With so many brick and mortar stores closing, and so many stringent regulations on imports, and a general rise in the cost of everything, companies didn't take as many chances with new products.

Shipping within the United States had also gotten much more expensive. In the early days, if we ran out of mustaches or bacon band-aids, I would pay to have them flown across the country by two or three-day air and it would add some, but not a mind-blowing amount to their cost. But when the cost of shipping began to come close to the cost of the merchandise itself, you had to think about what you needed in advance more strategically, and I was never particularly good at that. It was easy to make mistakes in either direction — to be sure you'd sell hundreds of something that would wind up filling your shelves for the next year — or to run out of something you'd underestimated and be unable to get more.

To be fair, it was equally hard on manufacturers. They were in the same boat I was, just in a different part of the water. They didn't know whether something they made was going to be a smash hit, and now they couldn't afford to rush stock in by air from China or India or wherever their factories were. And more stores were hedging their bets and placing big holiday orders at the last minute when wholesaler's inventories, once they'd sold out, might be gone for months. Trying to keep your best sellers in stock was much more nerve wracking than it had been, for retailers and wholesalers both.

Commercial wholesalers were clearly not doing as well as in the past. I used to place orders slightly before I needed them, because I knew it would take a busy warehouse as long as two or three weeks to get to my order unless it was an emergency and I had begged for special treatment. Now I faxed in an order and within hours, would get a notice that it had shipped. This was nice in one way, but it made me feel uneasy too. No company with a decent amount of orders would ship that quickly. Retailers and wholesalers alike, we were all second guessing ourselves more now. And I found that with fewer customers and less to choose from at the shows, my confidence as a buyer changed. There were certainly things I instantly knew we must have, but I also second guessed myself and felt less confident in general.

We still had loyal customers who loved us, even if they didn't buy as much as they once had. But we had a lot of slow days. With fewer stores in the neighborhood, and many people feeling economic pressure, there were long quiet stretches. Looking back at our last logbooks in the process of writing this book was unsettling. The funny stories and complaints of years past had mostly been replaced with entries complaining about being BORED. Questioning *"are we still a store?"* In truth, it could be excruciating sitting there for hours with only a few people coming in, even if they were great people and fun to talk to.

I'll be the first to admit there were probably things I could have done that might have helped business. I probably should have put the store on Instagram, especially after my nieces and younger customers began to ask if we were. At the time, I felt, we're already doing Facebook, do we really need to do that too, but I think it may well have lost us business. We didn't have constant sales and discounts to promote. We also never made our website smartphone friendly, another mistake, as increasingly, that was the way people were accessing the internet. My reluctance to do some of these things made me feel like an anachronism. And I both regretted and took pride in that.

It took me several years — at least — to admit that things had really changed. We'd have a good day, and I'd be encouraged, or I'd have some great interactions with customers and remember just what I loved about sitting behind that front counter. But those logbook entries kept on coming too.

*"Trying not to complain, but it's BEYOND DEAD."*
*"This is pretty much a genuinely boring day so far."*
*"3 pm. Worst day in forever!!! White Flag? Red Flag?"*
*"Another deadly slow day."*
*"Terrible, awful, very bad day. So S L O W !!!"*

Sometimes these days would have a great big sale toward the end, which made them look passable on paper, but did little to alleviate the boredom and despair. But over time, those slow days gave me a lot of time to think about what I was doing. What exactly was my plan? Was I going to run the store into the ground and be forced out? Was I getting closer to making the big decision? I still loved what I did — when it was working. But having two, three or more terrible days in a row really affected my sense of self and self-worth. A bad day in the past? Easy to write off, they occasionally happened, but a series of bad days was frightening and energy sapping.

If no one came in, why was I there? I often compared it to being a musician, playing in a club — to three people. And those people might love and appreciate your music, but you have to make money to be able to keep doing it. I had no idea what I would do if I closed the store. I knew I would miss parts of it terribly. But it wasn't really working and I had my diminished bank account to prove it. I kept going back and forth. And back and forth. And writing in that logbook.

*"4 pm. Today is slower than yesterday — and yesterday was the big snow day. Maybe a dozen people in all day, not counting UPS and the mail. It's exactly like not being here at all. Every once in awhile the (talking) Monty Python wallet goes off and I go change its position. The phone doesn't ring and 90% of the email is solicitations. But I am not despondent. I am reading 'And the Pursuit of Happiness' by Maira Kalman. (a*

*wonderful book we were selling) And I notice I'm emulating her matter of fact yet — or and — slightly lyrical writing style. And I'm thinking about the pursuit of my own happiness. (sorry, that's what happens when no_one comes in!!)*

CHAPTER 41

# Two Questions

"Why don't you just keep the store going online?" Logical question, but I never even considered it. We did have a website, but I found the idea of everything happening only online deeply unappealing; it did not suit me at all. Maurice Sendak once said about e-books, "I hate them. It's like making believe there's another kind of sex. There isn't another kind of sex. There isn't "another kind of book! A book is a book is a book!" That was my feeling about having a "store" online. That would be something else entirely. Not a store. And not something I could imagine getting any personal satisfaction out of.

"Why not sell it?" I also heard this a lot. And why not? Why not take the money and run? It's not the American way to let an opportunity to wring some money out of something pass you by. The store was well loved, if I sold it, it would carry on in some way. But I didn't want to sell.

There were practical reasons. Anyone looking at my books would doubtless have said, ummm — no thanks. Joie didn't look so good on paper these days. I'd been okay with just getting by for awhile now, but someone new would doubtless expect, and need, more income. I knew I would feel I was taking advantage of the naivety of anyone who didn't know the gift business, and thought anyone who did know the business would probably rather start something of their own. My accounting methods were also quite old-fashioned. I had no spread sheets to show, no profit and loss statements, no computerized inventory, just the minimal records I was required to keep by law. We still wrote out sales slips by hand, and our antiquated register did nothing more than hold our cash. I couldn't really talk the talk that would help me sell a business. The most likely buyer would have been someone who already had a store and wanted a second location and the inventory.

But none of these explanations got at the most important reason. Joie de Vivre was my creation, my baby. I'd worked with a few people over the years I could have imagined taking on as a partner, and even discussed it with one or two, but the timing or the finances were never right. With those exceptions, I felt no one else would be able to keep the spirit of the store the same. I conceived it, opened it, worked early mornings and late nights in it, and had a very particular vision of what was right for it. Had it been doing really well, I probably would have given the staff a good raise, worked less myself, and kept it going for at least a while longer. But it wasn't doing well.

I lived nearby too. I didn't think I'd be able to watch it change, as it would inevitably do with someone else at the helm, without some pain. When my ex-husband moved to another state, and found a new girlfriend and life, at least I didn't have to see it. If I had planned to move to the other side of the country, I might have considered trying to sell. But I didn't want to walk by the store and see something I never would have ordered on display in the window. Joie de Vivre would close, not change hands.

CHAPTER 42

# Promise You'll Always be Here

"What would we do without you?" "You're an institution!" "You can never close!" "Promise you'll always be here." Customers were starting to ask for reassurance. I knew they were beginning to worry and I understood. I said the same kind of thing to my beloved dentist. Telling him I didn't want him to retire before I died was just my way of letting him know how much I loved him, though I knew perfectly well he would do what he needed to. I now felt I had to begin to let people know that the thought of closing was on my mind. But as I had made no definite decisions, I tried saying things like "I can't promise I'll be here forever. After all, it may not be too late to be a ballerina." And they'd laugh, and I would too.

My two full time employees had been there awhile, my sister for eighteen years, and Jenn for almost ten. They knew things weren't going that well. They sat there on Saturdays when not many people came in. They sat there many other days when no one did. They read the *New Yorker*, did crossword puzzles, checked their email and they too wrote in the log book of being bored. I knew they were both at least theoretically looking for "real jobs" though I wasn't sure how hard. Still, I particularly wanted them to have plenty of notice. And I felt I needed to tell my stalwart perennial Christmas staffers too.

In the fall of 2019, I threw a dinner for everyone. I didn't want my decision to come as a shock when I finally decided, and I wanted them all to know I was thinking December 2019 might well be Joie de Vivre's last holiday season. (And this was only partly a ploy to make sure they all wanted to work that year!) I was honest. I owed the bank money. I had credit card debt. The store was barely holding its own and it was hard to see how business would get better. No one there was happy to hear this. Most everyone at this dinner had worked at Joie on and off for at least twenty years. But no one was shocked. And everyone signed up to work at Christmas.

In January 2020, with the whirlwind of the holidays done, I knew that if I was going to close, I needed to start making plans. Instead, I began to rationalize maybe staying open one more year. I wanted to write this book, and I started telling myself that it might be better to write it while I was still in business. (Now that I've written it, I'm not sure how realistic that was — I strongly suspect not very.) The winter gift shows were starting up, and off I went. I'd been telling some of my suppliers for a while that I was thinking about closing, and I continued to do so, but I'm not sure they believed me. Many of us who had been in the retail for a long time were thinking about it. We all knew how difficult it was to give it up.

And so, against my better judgment, I started thinking I might stay in business one more year. It was the end of January when I boarded a train to New York to attend the Gift Show. By then there had been some discussion in the news of a new virus circulating in China. I hadn't been paying much attention; only medical professionals and scientists were, though we now know the virus had already begun to spread. The first known case here was announced on January 21st and when I left for the show on the 31st, there were seven. No one at the show was particularly concerned and talk was more along the usual lines of "How much longer are you going to do this?" The New York Show was once again smaller. Exhibitors who'd done it forever were starting to get serious about giving it up to concentrate on the newer and bigger venues of Atlanta and Las Vegas.

Three weeks later, February 22nd, I was on another train, heading back for the Toy Fair. There were now officially fifteen cases of Covid in the United States, though none in New York, where the first case was not formally identified until February 28th. At the show, Covid was very much on people's minds, but all thoughts were about China, and the potential effects of this virus on merchandise supply. So many toys, so much of everything came from China. Companies were reluctant to promise goods at a certain date, unsure if they would be able to deliver. No one seemed too worried about it spreading much here though now we know we should have been. We went out to dinner, rode the subway, did all the usual things. The last days of normalcy. Six weeks later, the Jacob Javits Center was a hospital for Covid patients. And Toy Fair 2020 turned out to be the last show I would ever attend, at least as a buyer for Joie de Vivre.

Back home, I waited for our new things to start arriving, writing *"I'm excited for the little red squeeze monsters to arrive!"* and *"Finally here: exploding corn dish towel!"* in the logbook, rearranging displays and thinking about an Easter/spring window. I always came back from shows eager to mess around in my little retail kingdom. Meanwhile, Massachusetts had reported its second case of Covid on March 2nd and there were another hundred more in the country now. Six people had died. Things started moving fast. On March 11, the WHO officially declared a global pandemic. The numbers were up: 100 cases in Massachusetts, and 2000 across the country. Nervous, we started using hand sanitizer, cleaning everything like crazy and trying to keep our distance from customers though there was no mask mandate in place, the CDC didn't officially recommend masking until April 3rd. But we were worried and our logbook started to fill with entries like *"Two more people in, one walked by the hand sanitizer, one stopped, looked at it, and didn't use it."*

The papers were full of exhortations to "flatten the curve." Shutting things down was the way to help do this, and I started to think about closing for awhile. Naively, I imagined we might close for two weeks. I sent an email to our neighborhood retail store owners group to see what others thought. No one wanted to close unless forced to. It was definitely a huge deal to lose two weeks of income, even at a relatively slow time of year. Times were already hard enough. But I couldn't get the idea that I should close for awhile out of my mind.

On Friday, March 13th, I had two friends to my house for dinner. They were a couple, so to use a phrase I came to dislike quite a bit, "out of an abundance of caution," I sat them at one end of the table, I sat at the other. We were beginning dessert when the phone rang. It was my neighbor Brian who worked at Mass General Hospital. We'd talked a few nights earlier and he knew I was trying to decide whether to close. He jumped right in. "I think you should do it," he told me. "Right away." He described the overload beginning at the hospital and his concern that this was going to get very bad quickly. "Okay," I said. "I'll close after tomorrow."

I was instantly flooded with both relief, and disbelief. But I was glad to have made the decision. The next morning I told Nancy and Jenn and they were relieved as well. We quickly made signs to explain, and that night locked the door feeling good about doing our part. We wanted to fight this, to help bring the pandemic to a close as quickly as possible. Two days later the Governor declared a state of emergency and closed everyone down anyway. We sent out a letter to our mailing list, updated our website info, wrote a Facebook post and made fancier signs for the door, saying we thought we'd be closed for two weeks. That turned out to be quite optimistic. A surreal time, strange, sad and terrible, was about to begin.

We remained closed for three months. I went in most days, and sat at my desk in the back of the store. We used Facebook and our newsletter to drum up a little business and keep the customers informed, and we shipped orders, delivered some locally, and started a curbside pickup service. Like everyone else in the business, we sold a lot of jigsaw puzzles. Some of our extremely generous customers bought gift certificates to use down the road, and some ordered care packages for their families, stuck at home across the country. We decided to completely update our website, which Nancy did from home. I stayed home weekends and Jenn came in for a few hours to answer the phone should it ring. It didn't ring often.

In March we had about 50% of our usual sales, but we'd been open for its first two weeks. Our April sales were down 85%. May was worse. There was a little money left over from Christmas sales, and I had some small savings, but we still had to pay rent, and I was paying two salaries, so that money disappeared quickly. I spent a lot of time applying for government grants. There were loans available too, but I couldn't see how I would be able to pay them back. The grant paperwork was tedious and frustrating and the rules and requirements changed more than once while I was applying, but we were lucky. On the second round of government grants, we received one, enough to pay our expenses for a month or two. We also received a grant from the City of Cambridge, which made me regret every little complaint I'd ever made about our local bureaucracy. The two made it possible for us to get through to mid-June when we were allowed to reopen — with a long list of rules and restrictions.

The biggest restriction was how many people allowed per square foot of space. I got our measuring tape and found we'd be allowed three or four in the store at a time at the most. Not very many! Of course shoppers would have to be masked and use hand sanitizer, and we would have to monitor that, a bit stressful as it turned out, though we had no serious confrontations. Some customers waltzed right by our hand sanitizer stand but our worst problems tended to be people who didn't seem to get how to wear a mask, that it had to cover their nose. Sometimes we'd have to remind a customer half a dozen times to pull theirs up. It was not fun being the mask and sanitizer police.

My lease was up August 1st. I'd spent a lot of time thinking about things in the three months I worked alone in the back of the store while we were closed. I read as much as I could about the different ways the pandemic might proceed. The one that seemed the most threatening was the possibility of a deadly fall surge, one that might combine with the regular flu season. Tellingly, although I saw that companies I ordered from were starting to make silly masks, the kind of thing that our customers would expect us to have, I didn't have the urge to order them. I tried to imagine our busiest season when typically, the store would be crammed with shoppers. It definitely didn't seem that Covid was going to just go away, so being open for Christmas seemed risky. Would people really wait in line to get in if it was freezing outside? Snowing? I would need to order a lot of merchandise to be prepared. What if the pandemic was still raging? How would I make enough money to pay for it all? What if I was left with a mountain of debt in January and the pandemic was still going on? All this uncertainty combined with the words of my brother-in-law still echoing in my head. You should close when you can choose to do it. Keep it under your control. Don't wait until you are forced.

By the time we were allowed to reopen in June, I'd pretty much decided I was going to close the store, and had a rough time table. I didn't want to go through Christmas but we'd need enough time to let everyone know and have a big sale, then clear the rest out, and most likely, leave the space as empty as I found it. All that would take awhile. I thought of a plan. Instead of renewing the lease, I'd see if I could get my landlady to let me be a tenant at will. If she agreed, I would then give my notice just two months later, on October 1st, leaving two months to tell customers, have a sale and wrap everything up.

The last few times I'd renewed, I'd been open about how business was going, in hopes of keeping the inevitable rent increase to a minimum. I'd sent her long letters spelling out the changes in the neighborhood and the problems of competing with the internet. And in my favor, the pandemic was a legitimate reason for asking to be a tenant at will. Under the circumstances, with people actually closing down, I thought she'd likely agree, and she did though she was among those who never wanted me to leave. I said I would give two months' notice, she asked for three. I agreed and on August first, I signed the new agreement with my secret plan firmly in place. I had finally made my decision. Only the staff, my family, and a few close friends knew this was about to happen. We would carry on as usual while I worked out exactly how I would tell everyone else.

CHAPTER 43

# Word is Out

When we reopened in June, our local customers were thrilled to see us back, at least the ones who felt comfortable coming inside. They told us how much we'd been missed, how happy and relieved they were that we'd made it through, that Joie de Vivre was still here. Of course this felt great. But I started trying to prepare them. "Well, we haven't made it yet," I'd say. "We really don't know what will happen come the fall." This was in no way a lie. We were not making close to enough money to stay afloat.

But I knew what I was really thinking and felt terrible guilt. And interestingly, a little unexpected sympathy for my ex-husband. Before our marriage ended, I knew we were struggling but he'd hadn't let me know he was thinking of leaving, actually considering a divorce, until a few months before the end, though he'd been thinking about it for more than a year. He still loved me, and part of him couldn't bear the thought of telling me. And he wasn't completely sure he was doing the right thing. Of course closing a business and leaving a marriage are not the same, but I suddenly understood more clearly how difficult it must have been for him. Here I was, accepting compliments and congratulations and love, while secretly figuring out a plan to close the doors forever. I wasn't completely sure I was doing the right thing either. And I definitely couldn't bear the thought of telling the customers Joie de Vivre would close.

I realized there were customers I wanted to tell before I made it public. Several had become genuine personal friends. And I knew others counted on us seriously for emotional support. They were quite direct about it, telling me again and again how they would come in when feeling down or depressed, and leave with their mood lightened. They said we were one of their life-savers, and I believed them. So I sat down to write a lot of letters to send individually in advance to specific people, so that they heard the news directly from me, before getting the newsletter announcement.

Although we had many people who claimed to be "our best customers," the ones who most often claimed to be, rarely were. But I did have two best customers, two very different women, both of whom I considered friends, and they were the two I was most afraid to tell. I started to feel awkward when they came in to shop or say hello. They had both been extremely supportive not just throughout the pandemic, but for years before as well. Except for wonderful surprises, I don't like keeping secrets unless there's a good reason, and I couldn't think of a good one now. I needed to woman up and tell the truth. I decided to start gradually, by saying I was seriously thinking about it.

This confession resulted in offers of help. Unsurprisingly, their minds went immediately to the pandemic, and how to get us through it, but I let them know that this was something I'd been thinking about for a while now. "I'm so glad you told me," said one. "I thought you'd been acting a bit distant, and was sure I had offended you in some way." Nothing could have been farther from the truth, but this person was always sure that she was somehow in the wrong. It was a relief to both of us, though a real blow to her, to have the truth come out, and she said we might not see her for a while; she didn't think she'd be able to come in without crying. The other person was less fragile so a little easier to tell, and once reassured that I wasn't making an impulsive decision based on the pandemic, though disappointed, she supported my decision. I sent short notes to about thirty or forty others, asking them not to spread the word yet as I wouldn't make the announcement until September 1.

Now I just had to write the newsletter. What to say, how to begin?

*There is no easy way to say this, so here goes. I have made the decision to close Joie de Vivre, and our final day will be sometime in the first weeks of November. It is, of course, a decision dictated by the losses we've incurred during the pandemic and the uncertainty about what will develop this fall, but to be honest, that is not the only reason, in fact, I've been considering doing this for several years at least, but have never been able to bring myself to actually make the decision.*

*It's certainly not because I no longer enjoy it. I have always loved, and still love, almost everything about running this store, from finding the unexpected things we sell (as I've said before, you never go looking for a Singing Hamster or a cat paw — you just find them) to the fun of showing off the products but most of all, all the relationships with you wonderful customers, the wonderful people who have worked here over the last 36 years, and all the wonderful people I've met because I buy things from them. When I think of my closest friends, I realize the great majority are in some way associated with the existence of Joie, and running it has brought me untold satisfaction, fun, and happiness.*

*So, why had I been thinking of closing for the last few years? The simple truth is, despite the business we get (& appreciate!!) from all of you, we really have not been making enough money.*

I continued for another page, explaining my reasons as well as how we would do it considering we couldn't have more than a few people in the store at a time. No party, no closing toasts, but we would have a big sale for the entire last month. I did put some of the blame on the pandemic. It was true enough, it had been devastating, but I also knew it would give people a concrete way to understand my decision. And I knew telling them I was about to turn seventy and loathe to take a big financial risk would make sense to them too. I worked on the letter on and off for a week, and finally, alone in the morning in the back of the store, pressed the button that sent it out. No going back now.

Within hours, the responses started coming, in person and by email. A week later, handwritten letters. One devoted customer came in as soon as she heard, her protective mask altered with a pinned on, handprinted, tragically sad expression, specifically created to show us just how she felt. It was uncannily effective and I could hardly bear to look at it. She wore it every time she came in until the last day, and it never lost its truly unsettling power. We pleaded with her to take it off but she resolutely refused.

Hearing and reading what people had to say about the store was by no means a surprise. Whenever we celebrated our anniversary, particularly as years passed and we got to twenty, twenty-five, thirty, we'd received many lovely accolades and tributes. And customers came right out and told us how much they liked the store all the time. I knew Joie was loved by many, what a part of individual and community life it had become. But that knowledge didn't lessen the impact of the letters and emails we were receiving now. They were heartwarming and poignant, a flood of memories, sorrow, love, and support.

"My partner and I are both crying right now. You're going to break so many hearts. I don't know how I'm going to tell my mother and brother."

"NOOOOOOOOOO!!!! This is the beginning of the apocalypse!!!!!! NOOOOOOOOO!!!"

"So sorry to hear the news. I also am seventy years old. For it seems like half my life my sisters and now my daughter, my nieces and my three granddaughters have loved to visit your store. Every year we purchased Christmas ornaments that have become keepsakes. When I retired two years ago the coworkers that knew me best bought their gifts for me from you. When I turned seventy the gifts and cards were from your shop."

"After living abroad for a year and a half, I had a choice in the 1980s to move anywhere in the US; your store in Cambridge was one of a few between Harvard Square and Porter Square that prompted me to move to your neighborhood. I'll miss conversations with you and your staff as much as I'll miss finding perfect cards and gifts from your shelves."

"As an old devoted customer I am so saddened by the news that you are closing. Your store brought me much joy over the years. I used to live just a couple of doors down and I think I came in the first or second day you opened. It was love at first sight. My home is filled with all the wonderful whimsy I found there. Just a small note — one of the first things I bought from you was a small wind-up Godzilla which trundles along spitting sparks. It still works! And it still makes me smile."

"A few years ago I moved to Germany, so I'm not able to stop by as much as I'd like, but every fall when I take my trip home I look forward to my outing in the store. Obviously this year won't be possible for a couple of reasons, but I'd like to thank you for sticking around for so long and infusing curiosity, imagination, and total hilarity into my life as I grew up."

"This poses a metaphysical conundrum: Can the earth even rotate on its axis without Joie?! I guess we're going to find out. I'm going with no..."

"I've been a customer of yours through three (!) marriages, countless presents shared with countless friends and families. Gifts esoteric, whacky, occasionally truly useful, always truly imaginative. I still pull out my rubber chicken handbag for special moments. Life will be distinctly grayer without Joie de Vivre."

"NOOOOOOOOOOO!!! Please! I can't take it! Godammit, that's the last straw! Life is just misery and suffering..."

"Your store has put a smile on many hearts and warmed many celebratory gatherings... your store has been the butterfly wings that flap and leave joie de vivre in places far away."

"Thank you for all the years of joy! No other place has offered delight, escape, laughter, and that special neighborhood vibe quite like JDV! We will miss it so much, and we feel grateful for all the years you shared your energy and this one-of-a-kind, unique happy place and with us all."

"Well damn, I'm crying. I guess I knew this might happen someday, but I was really hoping I'd be too far along into dementia by then to realize it. Ye gods, you will be missed. Joie has been a magical spot for me and for anyone else who was a regular."

There were so many more. And people came in to tell us in person as well. One came in to try to persuade me not to close. "You can't," he said, close to tears. Then he added, "I know billionaires. Just say the word and you won't have to close." I knew he was serious and I promised to consider it. But I also knew I wouldn't want to stay in business using someone else's cash. If I had won the lottery, maybe. But I didn't want to feel obligated to anyone.

People began doing some serious shopping. I had let everyone know we would have a sale before closing, but it wouldn't begin until the last month; two weeks at 25% off and our final two and a half weeks — 50%. Business had remained quite slow over the summer, even though in-store shopping was possible again, but there was a big change once that letter went out. The sale would not begin for another month and a half, but customers started shopping in earnest, saying they were buying their next years' worth of goods. And it was a strange feeling not to immediately reorder things we sold out of. This went against every retail bone in my body.

The reordering issue turned into a bit of a conundrum. A supplier would come out with something new I thought was really funny. Why resist? And I didn't want us to run out of our most popular items, our classics, but was it worth ordering enough to keep them in stock right up to the end, effectively selling them at cost when we began the sale? I decided there were a few items that I would just do that with, a parting gift to customers. And I was reordering cards. Cards were one of our big draws, and I didn't want to let people down by running out of our standards. They were the exception to our sale — cards remained full price until the very last days. There were also a few timely items I felt we needed to keep in stock.

By chance, our going out of business sale was going to coincide with the 2020 Presidential Election and in our liberal corner of the universe, hopes and tensions were high. I deliberately chose a last day that fell a week or so after the election, feeling community at that time would be needed — by me as much as anyone. We were selling Joe Biden and Kamala Harris action figures and I decided that they must be kept in stock, along with our "Trump for Ex-President" pins and a few other political items. And Ruth Bader Ginsburg had just died. We needed to keep our Dissent jewelry in stock to honor her extraordinary life and life's work.

Like many things about the store, our going out of business sale didn't make good business sense. At first I thought, if someone wants to special order something, I'll just explain that they have to pay full price. But in the end, I felt honor bound to make the last days as painless as possible for the customers, and if someone wanted rainbow makers and we were out of them, I just placed the order and sold them at cost. I figured I wasn't making any profit, but if I wasn't actually losing money, why not? I was hard wired to please people, to make them happy, and I didn't want additional disappointment to cloud our final days. We'd keep our rainbow makers and chicken bags and yodeling pickles, devil ducks, white mouse puppets and a few other classics in stock to the end.

CHAPTER 44

# That's All Folks!

"That's all Folks!" We needed one last window display, and my sister Nancy, our resident artist, made a Joie version of the famous Warner Brothers logo, the signature closing image for Looney Tunes which — seemed appropriate! It broke my heart when I first saw it, with devil duckie, the white mouse and our little French fairy tucked inside the rings, replacing the iconic cartoon characters. We made buttons of this image to give away, and blew it up to a large poster size to place on a wooden easel in the window. (Writing this, I suddenly thought we should have made t-shirts!) In any case, the secret was out, though I knew many customers would not find out before we closed for good. This made me feel awful.

Our mailing list and Facebook friends were only a small percent of the people who shopped at Joie. Many of them didn't use Facebook, or didn't want to be on a mailing list, or had never been asked, as we did a fairly lousy job of signing people up. And we had lots of customers who lived out of town and came only once or twice a year. Now they would show up and we wouldn't be there. I consoled myself that due to the pandemic there was at least a chance they'd call first or google to see if we were open for in-person shopping or had changed our hours. But I knew there was an unhappy surprise in store for many.

Those last three months were hard in expected and unexpected ways. I expected to feel sad when seeing customers for the last time and I did. There were so many of them I'd always enjoyed talking to. Our relationship had mostly been confined to their visits to the store, but after knowing them for years, they felt like friends and I felt a real sense of loss when we said a final goodbye. I knew that despite the best intentions, I probably wouldn't see most of them again. It's just not possible to keep up with that many people. The store had been a good third place for many, not home and not work. And yes, it had been a job for me, but I got a great deal of pleasure from the social aspects of standing behind that desk.

We were promising we'd have a big party if possible, when all pandemic restrictions had been lifted. I was hoping it might even be a book party. But I was well aware how easy it was to make promises, and hard it could be to make them come true a year or more down the road. I would have wanted a big open house for the entire last two weeks, with toasts and long talks, and laughter and tears. That's how I always imagined going out. Instead, we were masked and carefully monitoring how much time people spent in the store. That too went against all my instincts. Joie de Vivre had always been a place where people could browse as long as they liked and no one ever felt rushed. Now, just when everyone wanted to linger for the last time, to tell us stories about what they'd bought over the years, how they'd found us, how long they'd been coming, their children's favorite gifts, we had to hurry them along because there was a line outside, other customers waiting to come in and do the same thing.

I walked the line, reassuring people that if they'd arrived before our closing time, we would get them in no matter what. Some were there mostly for the sale. Some wanted their last Joie experience. A few came back almost every day for the last two weeks. We tried to keep the displays looking fresh and not picked over and mostly succeeded though the stockroom was noticeably emptier. Election Day came and went with no immediate results but soon we shared a shout of joy with the four customers in the store, and could hear the cheers erupt from the line outside. The election had officially been called for Biden. We had a new President. And then it was the last Saturday, the last Monday, the last Wednesday. And then, we

THE BOOK OF JOIE

came to the end, the last Thursday, a day I chose because a Thursday was our very first day.

Customers sent flowers and brought gifts. Plants, champagne, promises of drinks and dinner to come. It all felt a little surreal. I wondered if we'd have too many people in line at the end but the gods helped us out and we locked the door right at 5 pm, the same hour we had first opened back in 1984. We then retired to the backroom to have a glass of champagne. We looked at each other in disbelief. Joie de Vivre was closed. Forever.

I was right back in there the next morning. There was a lot to do in the next two and a half weeks. A few prospects had looked at the space, but no one had committed. I wasn't sure if the landlady wanted us to remove all the fixtures and neither was she, but I had to get rid of a lot of leftover merchandise, and I wanted to find the best home for as much of it as I could. The big sale had worked out well, so luckily I felt no pressure to sell the remaining stock. But who to give what to? And what to take home to deal with later? There were places we'd donated to over the years, a church up the street that had a yearly rummage sale, a local school that ran a "Kids Only" Christmas store so their students could buy things for their family and friends. Another place that ran bookstores staffed by disadvantaged teens. A home goods/bric-a-brac store run by the Aids Action Committee, and even the local Goodwill. They would all benefit from the end of Joie de Vivre.

Then there were more specialized things that would be harder to donate — no one would know what they were without explanation. For example, our lithophanes, porcelain nightlights that revealed their image only when plugged in. In their box, they didn't look like much at all. I called their maker on the west coast. "Who else around here sells your lights?" I asked him. "I have stock left, and I want to give them to someone." He gave me some names, and I picked the closest one, a few towns away. They were somewhat taken aback when I called — how often do people call galleries and donate goods? But the pandemic had made times hard for them too and they were thrilled. And in a funny twist, when they came to collect the lights, we found we not only had a friend in common but had been to the same party once or twice. "You… look familiar," they said. And they wound up buying some of our other crafts at wholesale.

Through sales rep friends, I hooked up with a few more places, and donated more of our harder to just give away stock. And I found a community art project in my own town in need of stickers and anything that could be used for collage. We gave away a lot. The rest I packed up and took home to deal with later. I also called everyone I knew who had worked for me and lived reasonably close by. "Please come and take whatever you want," I told them.

It was a little difficult to convince them I was serious but once they believed me, they took a fair amount, some things for themselves, some to give away. I had never been able to pay them what I thought they were really worth, so any opportunity to give back — pay it backwards? — made me a very happy ex-boss. They would come by late in the day and we'd share a glass or two of wine in the process. I think the closing was harder on them than me. To me the decision was sad, but a relief. I'd been thinking about it for a long time. To them it was a shock, removing a home of sorts, a place that held memories and important personal history.

Part of me hoped that my landlady would say just leave all your displays but word finally came down that she wanted the place "broom clean." Everything the way I found it — or should have found it — when I first unlocked the door. Even the shelves in the backroom would have to go. I wasn't really surprised. The fixtures were not in good shape. I never dreamed that the ones from our old woodworking business would last thirty-six years. They were clearly showing their age, and I'm sure their presence would have made it hard for someone new to re-imagine the space, and she thought she had a tenant. She did say we could leave a few signs on the window, directing those who'd be shocked to find us closed to our website and I was grateful for that.

I had volunteers signed up to help, and hired a friend's brother to do most of the actual dismantling. We had about two weeks and somehow, we got it done. The front desk had been built on a platform that had to be ripped out. It was solidly made, and took some serious work. As we removed shelves and counters, lots of interesting little Joie artifacts emerged from behind and underneath, some of which I hadn't seen for, in some cases, at least thirty years. Small plastic animals, coins, glittery pieces of star shaped confetti, a postcard or two, single earrings, unrecognizable bits of unremembered things and behind one shelf that we could never get flush to the wall, a bunch of magnets, notepads and several books.

I suddenly realized, wait, we can't fit all the debris in our tiny dumpster. I hadn't given enough thought to what would happen once we'd closed the door. But luckily, my neighbor's brother had a friend who hauled stuff away. It's always those connections that make things easier — the friend of a brother of a friend to the rescue. They took our old cash register too, solid metal and so heavy that two guys struggled to pick it up. "They don't make them like this anymore!" one said. I never thought the old warhorse that I'd paid $50 for in 1984 would still be there in 2020, but there it was.

My friend JoeD was helping and suggested we photograph the back shelves, break them down in sets and put them up on Freecycle, a website where you advertised things you wanted to give away. I feared that might take too much time, too much back and forth, but was amazed how quickly people both signed up and showed up to take it all away. It was a lot of good solid wood, and every single piece was taken. We took down the sign on the front. I didn't know where it would end up, but for the moment it would live in my basement. Lots of other things wound up down there too, though one of our display cases now lives in a workshop in Newcastle Maine, and some of our backroom shelves went to my sister's house in Somerville. They turned out to be just the right size for her space. For our last job, we swept and vacuumed and got it as clean as we could, certainly much cleaner than it had been when Mr. Fox turned in his key.

Dismantling everything was a lot of work but I wound up being glad we had to do it. It felt fitting. I walked in, June 1984, and there was nothing. I walked out, leaving the space the same way and the physical work of stripping everything away and cleaning really helped me believe the store was gone. Friends who stopped in to say hi were shocked and sad seeing the demolition in process, but being in the middle of it, it somehow bothered me less. I was just doing what I absolutely had to in order to clear out by December 1st. On our final day, the last person came to pick up their free shelves about twenty minutes before our deadline. We took a look around; there was really nothing left to do.

There wasn't quite "nothing" left behind. We left our remaining cleaning supplies, a key to the dumpster on a funny keychain, and I wrote a note wishing good luck to the new tenants, whoever they turned out to be. I said I hoped they would love running a business in that space as much as I had. And we left two little sticky sumo wrestlers on the ceiling out front. We'd thrown them up there one slow afternoon, curious to see how long they'd stick on. Four years later they were still there. I wondered what the new tenants would think when they finally noticed them.

We were done. Again, we sat on the floor and had a toast, the last of the many we'd had inside that space. Afterwards, I put the keys in the landlady's mailbox and went to have pizza with friends. I needed to tell the tale of the last day, to begin to process that we'd actually closed. I didn't want to do it alone, not just yet anyway. I knew there would be plenty of time for that.

I'd seen a therapist on and off for years, initially for relationship problems, but had kept up the connection. I thought back to maybe ten years earlier when I'd confessed to her that I was feeling like a failure. "My marriage didn't work, and my store is struggling," I lamented. "Your marriage is one thing," she replied. "But no matter what happens going forward, your business is a success. You've run it for over twenty-five years. It's a success, even if you close tomorrow." This brought me up short. She was right. People loved the store and we'd already had a good run. No matter what happened, I had not failed there.

Still, in some ways the store did become like a relationship that had once been great but wasn't really working anymore. You might still love a person and occasionally have a wonderful time with them — but want out because much of the time, the problems were just too much. That's always difficult and heartbreaking — much easier to hate someone, or something, and I still loved my store. Happily, unlike a romantic breakup, I was overwhelmed with positive feedback and love during the last three months we were open. It left me feeling sure that I'd done a good thing not only for myself, but for many others by opening and running the store for so long.

In the years leading up to the end, when people asked how long we'd been open, I would tell them and feel a strong sense of disbelief. How could twenty-five, thirty, thirty-five years have gone by so quickly? And yet it didn't seem like "only yesterday." Thirty-six years is a long time. I began something. It turned from an experiment into a life's work and it gave me more than I could have imagined — a mission, friends, a husband, a community, great satisfaction and some serious joy. I'm proud and grateful. Despite the difficulties, I loved running a physical store, a place where people came to have fun, bring their friends, their kids or spouses, linger to explore, discover, and play. Retail is really as much of a performance as a piece of music. It requires a receptive audience and Joie de Vivre was lucky to find ours in Cambridge, the Boston area, and beyond. I truly appreciate each and every person who helped us make it through thirty-six years. Also those who helped set me on my path. Thank you to my parents, Lore and Vern, the customers, the staff, the makers, my sister, my husband, his brother, the suppliers, my fellow shopkeepers, the post office, UPS, Fed-Ex, Santa Claus, everyone.

Canadian author Michael Ondaatje once wrote, "The right ending is an open door you can't see too far out of." When I closed the store I had no more idea what I wanted to do next than I had when I was young. I do know what was most important to me about running Joie de Vivre: feeling I was providing something of value to people and the community while also expressing myself creatively. And I loved interacting with all kinds and ages of people. In person. My main concern about life post Joie is that I won't easily find the things I liked so much about that experience doing anything else. I certainly will never do anything else for so long. But I'm ready to see what's next. The door is open.

CHAPTER 45

# Lessons Learned

To close, some of the many things I went into this career not knowing —
that are now things I absolutely know for sure.

Retail is very zen. You must be able to say the same thing over and over.
   With conviction and enthusiasm.

Young children do not do well with large gift certificates. They get
   overwhelmed.

No matter how hard you try, you can't convince certain men that yes,
   their wife really does want a piece by Thomas Mann Design,
   even if their wives have sent them in to buy just that.

Never say "I'll get you a nice new one." The one the customer is holding
   may be the last one, and after saying that, it will invariably seem less
   desirable.

Check the box before gift wrapping just in case… there's nothing in it.
Corollary: If a customer comes in and says they received a gift that was
   an empty box, they are probably telling the truth.

Put batteries in items that require immediate "show off," otherwise the
gift will be opened at a party and it won't do anything.

Keep batteries in all display clocks and don't sell them unless the time is
correct.
Corollary: Remove batteries before boxing clocks so the hands don't get
all messed up.

Really special expensive items will draw people into the store just to see
them. They will bring their friends and they will buy small things.
And you will almost certainly, at some point, sell the really special
expensive thing.

Cardboard boxes can last a surprisingly long time — a good twenty-five
years before they fall apart.

"Can I help you?" is not a good conversation starter unless a customer is
standing in front of you with their arms full of goods.

Related note: "Just looking" does not always mean just looking, it may
mean "Please don't try too hard to sell me something." Or, it may
mean just looking, which is a fine thing to be doing.

"My friend said my work would be perfect for your store" is highly
unlikely to be true but, you never know.

Sometimes companies screw things into the boxes and they are very hard
to remove if you are not aware of this. And if you get frustrated while
trying to remove something and you don't check for this, you *will*
destroy the box and possibly the item.

With exceptions, like MAJOR hurricanes and blizzards, the weather
doesn't really affect sales as much as you think it will. A very rainy
day can be "good," a beautiful day can be "bad."

Some people are really afraid of snakes, even wiggly wooden ones.

Assortments of things are often a problem. One design will be more
    popular and everyone will want that one. Or three of four colors are
    popular and every time you order you wind up with more yellow.
Corollary: Yellow is a good color for suns, stars, butterflies, and that's
    about it.

Children are fascinated — absolutely drawn to fake food and spills.
    (And a few adults as well.)

Children and adults are BIG fans of tiny tiny things. Tiny glass animals,
    doll-house sized Hostess cupcakes, tiny devil ducks, tiny automata.
Corollary: Giant things, with a few exceptions, not so much.

You will break far more things than the customers do.
Corollary One: Adults break pretty much as many things as children do.
Corollary Two: If a young child is in the store and you have no idea what
    adult is with that child, it is not a good sign.

Some people cannot be convinced that it is okay to buy a blank card and
    write "Happy Birthday" in it, no matter how much they like the card.
    Don't argue with them.

Having money does not make you a nicer person. But neither does not
    having it.

It always pays to be honest with people. I used to slink by booths where
    I had once ordered a lot, hoping they wouldn't see me, or saying "I'll
    be back" and not returning because I didn't want to disappoint them
    by not ordering. It's better to just to say: I'm sorry, I really like your
    work your products etc., but for some reason they have not sold well
    for us. People really appreciated knowing what was up.

If you really want something you're selling, take it home. There were things I didn't wind up with because I waited, and then we were down to the last one and someone bought it, and when I went to reorder, it was discontinued — I could never get more.

If someone returns a KitCat Clock and says that it doesn't work, test it yourself. There is a 99.9% chance that it works just fine. They are just a little trickier than most.

Never underestimate the allure, or success, of the small item. Customers would return after Christmas to say the flip book or the wind-up toy was the hit of Christmas or the party.
Corollary: You don't need to spend big bucks to give a much-appreciated gift.

The word "eclectic" is annoying but useful when trying to describe the store.

Never say Never. Items that were "permanently discontinued" have in fact sometimes returned.

There is a mind-blowing amount of wasteful packaging in the commercial world, and way too much of it is non-recyclable plastic.

Letting customers use the bathroom is a good idea, especially if their young child needs it.
Corollary: Leaving your wallet in the bathroom is not a good idea.

It is impossible for three individuals to agree on an appropriate temperature for any given space. Someone will always be freezing. Someone will always be roasting.

Pumpkins will rot if left in the front window too long.

If someone does not speak English, and you do not speak their language, talking louder will not help. Get out the paper and pencils and prepare to draw.

Nothing lasts forever. The star will fall off your expensive sign, the neon will stop working, the sign itself will start to buckle — ditto rugs, counters, etc. Maintenance required.

Things that you would never expect can bring controversy — our "Ring Bell, Win A Cat" doormat was objected to by PETA. ("Doormat sends the Wrong Message" said the sign taped on our door!) And we found "Offensive to women" stickers slapped on 50s style mermaid and cocktail picks.

Never underestimate the power of the classics — Bubbles, Slinkies, Etch-a-Sketch, Magic 8 Balls.

You will inevitably have to break your own rules. For example, "no refunds." Sometimes you will just have to give in. You must also communicate that rules can occasionally be broken to your employees.
Corollary: You are not obligated to even give store credit to someone who tries to return an item that has clearly been damaged by them, for example, a music box that looks like it was run over by a truck.

Customer's don't always get your jokes. Every year we would give away our remaining calendars in February. We'd display them with a sign saying "Calendars — 100% off! It's surprising how much confusion this can cause. People will think it's some kind of trick when really, it's just a cute, mathematical way of saying "free!" You'll get the question "What does that mean, 100% off?" (But once they realize you mean it, you'll get the next question, "How many can I take?" and soon, your calendars gone.)

# Epilogue

After we closed, I wound up with a lot of boxes in my basement to deal with "at some point." There hadn't been time to sell all the stock, or even give it all away. Amazingly, we had the foresight to label the contents, so I could grab something when I needed a gift, or let a friend "shop." I thought I would hold a garage sale in the spring, but the pandemic was still with us so it wasn't until a year later that "Joie de Garage" took place — in my actual garage.

It was fun to work physically again, building shelves, hanging lights and creating a makeshift but reasonable facsimile of Joie. The sale was a big success. The first morning, it felt like the Christmas rush, with a line of people clutching things and waiting to pay. Everyone was happy to see me and to be in "the store," and I was equally happy to see them. And I got another shot of much appreciated love and memories as people shared stories and told me how much they missed us. The little "store" stayed up for a couple of weeks.

After that I really did give everything away. Boxes to Goodwill, boxes to a woman's shelter, and a few other places. I was left with two tables full of small things: wind-up bugs, rainbow discs, dinosaur keychains, lenticular rulers, wish tokens and various other unpackaged items. These would be hard to donate, but I had my own stash and didn't want to keep them. Inspiration struck and I made up twenty Joie "Surprise Boxes" to give away. Many more than twenty people applied for one, so we held a raffle online. And as the winners came by to pick up their boxes I felt it was really the end of Joie de Vivre. I was wrong.

There's certainly no trace of us left in our former space, though our name is still on a small concrete paver in the little garden out front. The new tenant is a Taiwanese Bubble Tea shop, a chain advertising over thirty locations in the U.S. alone with "more coming." You place your order not from a person, but a screen set in the wall, and when I went in with a friend and we asked a question about the menu, the person working the counter did not even try to answer though we were the only customers. As unlike Joie as a place could possibly be.

But Joie de Vivre lives on. Everywhere I look in my house, full of things that came from it. In one of the shops I donated to that I visited and found Joie items on display. "Thank you so much, they're really selling well," gushed the owner when I said, "I brought you these a few weeks ago." It lives on in the homes, hearts, traditions and memories of family, friends and customers from all over the country, many of who have taken the time to write to me and tell me how much they cherish their Joie de Vivre treasures. Now it lives on in this book. Thank you for reading it.

This story could easily have been ten times as long. So many funny, touching and interesting things happened in the years I ran the shop. But I'm not sure I would have the same success if I opened it today and I hope the subtext on every page reads loud and clear — support small businesses wherever and whenever you find them. They know you, or want to, and they care. You may pay a little more, but the streets of your city or town will be lined with interesting, quirky places to shop, not chain stores, corporate banks that no one goes in, and empty storefronts. Where you spend your money makes a huge difference in this world in many important ways. Shop small, and shop local. And Vive la Joie!

1984 — 2020

Practicing for one of my early career choices: Princess.

The Village Gallery, Croton-On-Hudson, circa 1968.

Woodworker's girlfriend! Selling our wares at the WBAI Craft Fair in New York.

*before Joie de Vivre*

*playground in France... I chose the right name!*

*first sign and rather spare opening look*

*the store gets fuller*

*business cards*

*store signs (1984, 1989, 2016)*

Everything at Joie says yes to this!

New arrivals surveying the terrain.

Well behaved women rarely make history.

Who me?

This fooled SO many people…

Day at the Beach — Gumby and Pokey check it out.

*display vignettes*

A gnome, a genie, a bunny, a heart...
and that's all I need!

Pole pole animals listening to story.

Spilled coffee.

Prairie Dog finger puppet visits
the Bavarian pewter.

Yoga Joe poses for the kitties.

*more vignettes*

Teddy Bears' breakfast

the Christmas cathedral

Happy Halloween!

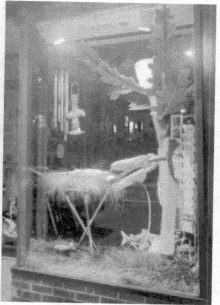

Grilling the wind-up toys…

*window displays*

Trick or Treat!

Smells good!

Peace on Earth

Let's go skating!

*window displays*

Valentine's Day 2020

Happy Birthday 1994!

2004!!

2014!!!

*and more window displays*

*the Unholy Trinity*

dancing ballerina

finger monster

stardust
(Reinhold Marxhausen)

Pipe Dreams
(Woodstock Percussion)

penguin race

yodeling pickle

windup mouse

Thomas Mann earrings

pinscreen

spilled coffee

fork mobile

kaleidoscopes

*Joie icons*

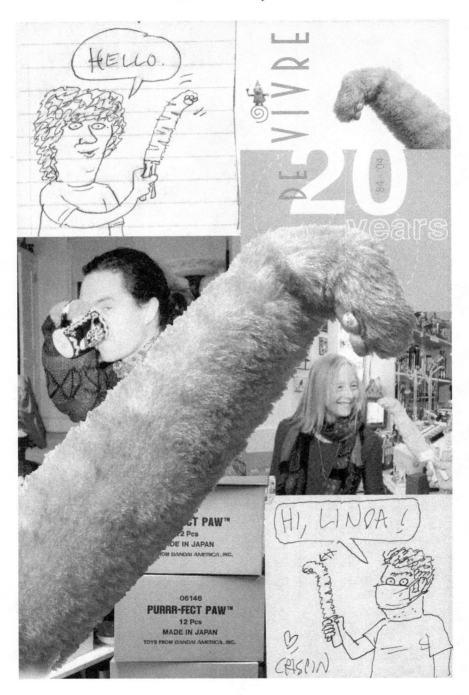

*It's a cat paw!*

The much lamented
discontinued Tiki Time

Paris Bottman porcelain
rabbits

Chicken in a Blanket!

Singing Hamsters: the two
first, and the two best

Backroom items! Surprise
Bride and Surprise Chicken

The special bring-your-
friend-to-see-it Teacup Fairy

The forever requested
Toilet Paper Man

Woodland Diorama

Fish Music Box

*too briefly here*

*Christmas!*

*other holidays*

Alex and Josie visit!

Kitty, Ali and Lucas sporting their Squirelzilla tees.

Pam sporting our fabulous chicken purse.

Daisy modeling our Christmas specs.

What happens at Joie... stays at Joie.

Julia and Jody, ready to assist.

Visiting niece Zoey on a break from the circus!

Front desk fun.

Emily with Santa Squirrel.

*Joie staff and fans*

Found some great walking dinosaurs!

Big but very friendly…

If my ten year old self could see me now!

Sadly, did not win this duck.

Jacob K. Javits Convention Center

True!

*At the Javits Center*

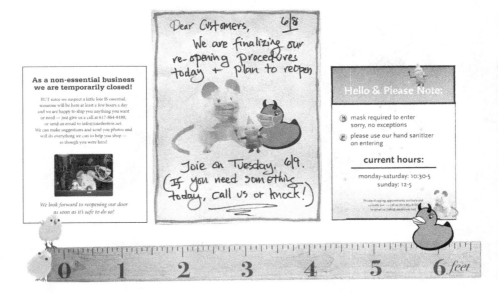

*with masks and hand sanitizer*

She wore this in every time
after our closing announcement.

Waiting in (socially distanced) line
to say goodbye.

Letters from customers letting us know how they felt about our closing.

Toast to all on our last day of business.

*closing time*

*getting leaner*

The wrestlers we left on the ceiling.

It's a smile of relief — job done on time!

*and leaner*

*Goodbye!*

# Appendix

It would be impossible to list all the things you could have bought at Joie de Vivre from our first day in 1984, to our last day in 2020, but we will attempt to list some of them!

*Little Things*
Finger monsters, wind-up toys, magic flowers, squirrel coffee cups, panic buttons, "any" keys, party poppers, mini slinkies, Department 56 pencils with things on top, tiny fezzes, tiny Santa hats, high bounce balls, Koosh balls, squish balls, stress balls, glitter balls, fortune telling fish, million dollar bills, Boinks, bubbles, hedgehog nailbrushes, double dice, round dice, palm puppets, magic capsules, wish tokens, panic buttons, tiny seeds with little elephants inside, tin bird and butterfly pins, buttons, stickers, tiny hands, Nunzilla, Blue Q gum, bull dog guns, dazers, plastic fish, tiny rubber animals, tiny devil ducks and ninjas, donut seeds, chocolate globes, chocolate baseballs, cars and bugs, color changing rubber ducks, flipbooks, alligator clickers, temporary tattoos, bug guns, finger tentacles, chinese yo-yos, water marbles, sticky wrestlers, fairy dust...

*Jewelry*
Cracker Jill, Missing Men, Beadweaver, snowglobe rings, fruit rings, flashing rings, pinwheel rings, sushi earrings, grape and cherry earrings, level earrings, compass necklaces, Designs From the Deep, Everyday Artifacts, Barb-wire, Bijou Graphique, Theresa LaGuardia, Hotcakes, Eric Silva, Peggy Johnson, Tom Mann, Kit Carson, Edward Gorey, Mullanium, Detail, Loeber-Look real fish pins, Scrabble earrings, Prozac earrings, Zarah, William Spear, dollhouse food earrings, Clay Art Xmas bulb necklace, Xmas bulb earrings, mood rings...

*Animals, Animals, Animals*
Wooden snakes, plastic frogs, alligators and turtles, rubber ducks, animal noses, iron bear bookends and small iron animals from Japan, puppets, snoozy lambs, cat paws, Warm Whiskers heating pads, Pole Pole, Linda the squirrel puppet, animal heads from Elope, fish pillows, fish purses, fish neckties, butterfly bowties, butterfly mobiles, duck mirror, duck in a ball, tiny glass animals, sloth puppets, sloth pillows, dog and pony purses, otter tape dispenser, beaver pencil sharpener, monster nightlights, Sigikid Beasts, nervous hamsters, inflatable Godzillas, walking rubber animals and dinosaurs, egg laying clucking tin hen, duck on bike, plastic fish pencil cases, snake balance toy, nodding penguins, seals and more. Chicken Purse, Penguin Race, and — Singing Hamsters!

*Completely Silly*
Winston, the repeating gnome, Dancing Coke Bottles, Besame Mucho singing cow, walking oinking pig, motion activated framed Mona Lisa that stuck out her tongue, coke bottle encased in lucite, Feisty Pets, rolling, laughing animals, squeaky Venus de Milo and David bath toys, marabou feather phones, Let Me Out of Here box, Billy Bass, fish phones, "Who Cares?" calculator, Actual Bead of Elvis' Sweat, Instant Irish Accent breath spray, Emergency Clown Nose, talking llama, Boxing Nun, voodoo doll, vegetable goddess, AquaPets, Jabber Balls, and — Singing Hamsters!

*Is This a Cat Store?*
Maybe! Cat doorstops, Flat Cats, Cat-a-Pults, Cat Paws, glass cats, cat socks, cat playing cards, yoga cats, blind box cats, cat jokes, Kit Kat Clocks, cat alarm clocks, Emergency Cat sound machine, cat potholders, cat kitchen timers, "Ring Bell, Win a Cat" doormat, Apocalypse Meow! t-shirt...

*Science*
Hoberman Spheres, holograms, laser cubes, dazers, The Mind Altering Goldfish, Bucky Balls, Magneto Toys, Romp!, singing magnets, Strobotops, Handboilers, hanging Fresnel Lens, Powers of Ten flipbook, Levitrons, Mova Globes, Hydrodynamic Building Set, moiré books, Newton's Cradles, Jim Clift Compasses, Wonder Wires, Ball of Whacks, solar lamps, Cinespinners, Lollipopters, Phi Tops...

*American Crafts*
Jax jack-in-the-boxes: Dracula, Shakespeare, Fairy Godmother, White Rabbit, Einstein, Creatures by Aviva Schneider, Pat Probst Gilman porcelain dragons and dragon mugs, Sarah Spaceman mugs, Polly Frizzell clocks and cat on couch salt peppers, Susie Ketchum, Dennis and Joanne Delomba, Solveig Cox, Dona Dalton wooden animals, Josh Simpson glass planets, Fecher-Gramstead Lips on stick and "Time Flies" winged clock, Michel Harvey paper bag vases, Milton Townsend glass mermaids, Chris Roberts-Antieau, Tomas Savrda, Peter Chapman animal puzzles, and many more...

*Books*
Andy Goldsworthy, *CDB, CDC, 101 Unuseless Japanese Inventions, Lost Balls, Why Cats Paint, French for Cats, Porn for Women,* (we would hear people laughing hysterically over those photos of men vacuuming, cleaning, making dinner), *Schottenfreude, Growing Old is not for Sissies, Old Age is Not Important Unless You're a Cheese,* Pigeon books, everything by Roz Chast, Paris books, *Little Prince, The Encyclopedia of Bad Taste,*

*The Encyclopedia of Immaturity*, *The Pretty Good Joke Book*, and in the end, many funny books that started as websites: *Cakewrecks*, *Awkward Family Photos*, *Chinglish*, *Stuff White People Like*, *I Can Haz Cheezburger…*

## Lights and Lamps

Woogie Lights, Lava Lights, Jellyfish Light, Illume Light, Carlisle revolving dolphin lamps, MOMA Block Light, Mathmos glowing balls, Gladys Goose, flamingo lights, Egmont hedgehogs, chickens, rabbits and gators, StarLights, Artecnica/Tord Boontje paper flower lights, chili pepper lights, Primal Lights, Kurt Adler christmas lights, Kikkerland small garlands, Dream Lights, Bella Luz nightlights, Lamp-in-a-Box, Statue of Liberty nightlights, Porcelain Garden Lithophanes, Monster nightlight, Blowfish nightlights, Magic Ball lights, fiberoptic flashlights…

## What time is it?

Elvis clock, neon Moon clock, Designs from Deep clocks, Chalkboard, Dali, Boss/Brown, Diane Markin Silverware clock, Backwards clock, Fantazein, first Canetti wall clocks, Italianissimo, Feldstein musical alarm clocks, Homer Simpson clock, Audubon bird clocks, Math "Pop Quiz" clock, Elephant Coo-Coo clock, Whatever clock, plates with cake or veggies for numbers clocks, Kit Cat Clocks, the little robot clock that kept getting stolen, VW watches, Pascale Judet, ring watches, color wheel watches, M and Co. blurry clock, airplane clock, Mickey Mouse in Space alarm clock, sundials, Tokyo Bay mini clocks, singing pink worm clock, crowing rooster clock, Kikkerland "Sliced" grandfather clock, Purple Cow clock…

## Music/Sound

Reuge waltzing couples, Italian inlaid jewelry boxes, Steiff musical bears, Koji Murai dancing clown boxes, dancing penguins, Dr. Seuss fish in bowl box, Little Prince with pull down moon, Mr. Christmas, the three early ones from Fitz and Floyd, airplane, fish and ocean liner, that hung on the wall, Stockhausen zodiac boxes AND — music boxes where the songs were wildly inappropriate — "Hey Jude" on the dancing bunny, "Old MacDonald" — with two elephants, etc. — the rabbit that played "Oh Danny Boy," Woodstock Chimes, Obsidian Chimes, harmonicas, Temple Bells, Takara bug and butterfly boxes, accordions, xylophones, maracas, rainsticks, slide whistles, nose flutes, make your own music box, Indian bells, and of course singing animals, especially — Singing Hamsters!

*Snow globes*

Plastic classics: bride and groom, flamingos, people skiing, palm trees, Statue of Liberty, Elvis, the wonderful California and Florida snowmen (a hat and carrot floating in water,) the big musical Wizard of Oz globes, the classic Austrian snowmen, Christmas trees and Santas, The Eiffel Tower, skiers, ballerinas, penguins, polar bears, and Coolsnowglobes Buddhas, cairns, blue trees in twilight, the very zen nothing but snow, and several varieties of "make your own" by inserting a photo…

*Very Very Special*

Stardust, kaleidoscopes, Tomas Savrda sculptures, Grace Gunning, Paris Bottman, St. Leger miniature automata, Austrian bronzes, Petites Choses, Daniel Essig books, Tracy Gallup dolls, Georgia Landau dolls, Wood and Lucker, teacup fairies, Coral and Tusk pillows and linens, Kata Golda, Kikkerland Woodland diorama with disappearing animals, Wee Forest Folk, Kristiana Parn, Mincing Mockingbird, Christina Goodman jewelry, and — Singing Hamsters!

*Does This Thing Have an Off Button?*

Sound machines: original, horror, cartoon, space, sports, diva, music, pirate, Talking Keychains: Mr. T, Austin Powers, Mr. Rogers, Get Off the Phone Fast sound machine, Atomic Doorbell, Monty Python talking key chain, Screaming Goat, No! Yes! Maybe! Sorry! buttons, crashing hammer, screaming, whistling, laughing mirrors, train alarm clock, tiki drummer, Breezy Singers, yodeling pickles, Jabber Balls,

Emergency Affirmation button, ("You are Awesome!") Thunder tubes, and — Singing Hamsters!

*Christmas*
Glass ornaments, snowflake decals, Santa string lights, Italian angels, candy canes, stockings, singing animals, (no Christmas hamsters, alas), flipbooks, Swedish Angel Chimes, ornament earrings, mini Xmas light necklaces, Mr. Christmas music boxes, glass icicles, advent calendars, reindeer candleholders, winter tree votive lights, gumdrop trees, bottle brush trees, tiny light up trees, snow globes, felt birds, Magic Yule Logs, Speak and Repeat Dancing Gingerbread Man, felt animals, felt mice in sweaters, coal, boxed cards, single cards, Santa hats, elf hats, reindeer antlers, feathery angel halos, instant snow, star garlands, solar Santas, Christmas crackers, Austrian pewter angels, Santa and snowman matroushkas, sequin neckties, and lots and lots and lots of 3D magic spectacles...

*Banks*
Venus Flytrap, Bandit Box, Bathtub bank, Mailbox banks, King Kong, Classic Piggy, Karl Marx "Das Capital," Blue Q tin banks, Guinea Piggy bank, Vortex bank, Sneaky Kitty and Gobbling Dog banks...

*Paris*
(When I named the store, I don't think I was quite aware of how very much people love Paris, but I began to see how true that was. Any French related items I ordered sold out quickly, and gradually, we developed a small French section. Once, a woman rushed into the store just before closing. "I was just in Paris and I didn't have time to buy gifts for people!" she told me, and she piled up a bunch of "souvenirs" to give as gifts.) Eiffel Tower models, Paris jigsaw puzzles, Paris snowglobes, Eiffel Tower keychains, Tintin and Babar figurines, "I'd Rather Be in Paris" pillows, "Take me to Paris!" magnets, Barbapapa figurines, rhinestone Eiffel Tower pins, black beret shower caps...

*Dress up*

Birthday Cake hat, Spring Chicken hat, Propeller Beanies, Christmas hats, wooden neckties, plastic neckties filled with confetti, Escher ties, highway ties with car tie tacks, candy leis, baseball caps, zydeco washboard ties, Blue Q socks, rubber ties, jeweled plastic crowns, inflatable crowns, and t-shirts: "Sorry About Our President," Shakespeare Comedy/Tragedy, "Sleeps with Dogs," "It's All Fun and Games Until Someone Winds Up in a Cone," Squirrelzilla, "Round Earth Society (established 590 b.c.)," "Dance Like Russia Isn't Watching..."

*Food and Drink*

Frozen Moments, coffee spills, ice-cream spills, wine spills, tiny ceramic fruit and vegetable tea sets, Writer's Block cutting boards, potholders, Extend-a-Fork, salt and pepper shakers, moiré coasters, marble coasters, Three Blind Mice cheeseboard set, cupcake pillows, pizza pillows, taco pillows, dishtowels, lunchboxes, elephant corkscrews, swan ladles, Tea Duckie infuser, flasks, cookie tins, bacon wallets, bacon bandaids, bacon gummy strips, astronaut ice-cream, freeze dried cheese, chocolate roses, slant glasses, tipsy wine glasses, giant wine glass (held one bottle,) squid whisks, cold cut coasters, maraca cocktail shaker, Potato Clips, Star Chart wineglasses, Silly Straws...

*And That's Not All !*

Umbrellas, rubberstamps, jeweled calculators, license plate bags and photo albums, little car crumb sweeper, Car Art car magnets, Ego Boosters, Fish Frame, sand paintings, Ocean in a Bottle, floating penguin toy, cloud umbrellas, exploding golf balls, Magnetic Poetry, Dress Me David, Laini's Ladies, shower curtains, Yip-Yaps, Surprise Balls, sparklers, Bougie Magique, Pino-Pinos, inflatable globes, slang flashcards, hourglasses, Colorforms, Magic Gardens, Etch-a-Sketches, Critters, Ruby Slippers doorstop, hot air balloons, Godzilla cigarette lighter, fish phones, Chicken-in-a-Blanket, Forkmobiles, candy kaleidoscopes, wooden tops, blank journals, cards, postcards, Inflatable Scream, movie viewer "key chains," The Little Fridge, picture frames, bumper stickers, Tavern Puzzles, jigsaw puzzles, brainteasers, Rudi aka Easter Island tissue box, Mysterio baby onesies, librarian action figures, Shakespeare Insult mugs, Bend-a-Family, Pylones toasters, graters, fish lighters, bicycle bells, birds on wheels, blank books, photo albums, Audubon birdcalls, RBG finger puppets, Fifteen Puzzles, Tangles, James Baldwin prayer candles, Log pillows, Toilet Paper Man, Microcopters, Pop-up New York Story, Cubies, Dancing Flowers, Blue Q bags, marbles, jacks, pick-up sticks, 18 carat Gold Slinkies, Photoing on Car, and always, always, always, the Penguin Race! Buddha Boards, Rainbow Makers, art prints, Magic 8 Balls, Space Tubes, Matrouskas, Acrobats/Quili, Solar Queens, Popes, Einsteins, and Corgis, Finnish Snowballs, monster slippers, globe pillows, tiny kites, art glass marbles, Demeter Scent Library, and, did we mention — Singing Hamsters?

*And, that's still not all, but that's all for here!*

# Acknowledgments

There are many people I want to thank. I'll start with my mother and father, who though they had their doubts, agreed to lend me the money I needed to get the Joie adventure started. I wish my Dad had lived to see it finished, and thank you Mom, for your love and support along the way. A special thank you to the late Lore and Vernon Stromberg, my first employers, also Ed and Barbara Morrow of the Northshire Bookstore, for generously sharing their retail know-how with me. Thank you to my Harvard writing professors, in particular Chris Walsh, who was supportive of this project before it really even was one. And thank you Jane Forsyth, for writing and general encouragement.

Thank you Gerard Nadeau for all the amazing window displays and for so much more. Thanks to Bill Patrick, Joe Denatale and Bill Barash for essentially donating their labor to build out the store. (And thanks for the woodworking displays Bill, and for changing the outdoor light bulbs for thirty-six years, JoeD!) Thank you Trisha Copeland, Emily Winston, Danielle Nekimken and Linda Jorgenson for ongoing friendship and moral support. Thank you Barbara Dollar for your very good advice and even better friendship.

As I hope I've managed to express in this book, I could not have made the store work without my employees. I thank them all, especially my long time "I'll always come back and work at Christmas" gang: Emily Winston, Julia Willwerth, Barb MacEachern, Kate Sanders-Fleming, Camilla Elvis, Joe Denatale and Peter Nadeau. Big thanks to my sister Nancy Given and to Jenn Cummings-Saxton who were the stalwart year-round staff for Joie's last ten years. Also Danielle Nekimken, Deb Cantrell, Crispin Wood, Ashling Barr, Sarah Boggan Dodd, Kana Matsumoto, Jeannie Serwich, Danielle Bailey, Leah Nickel, Emily Raine, Katie Brittingham, Ian Gibson, Jodi Varasso and everyone else who worked at Joie, whether for a year, more, or just a Christmas season. And there are four others I wish could read this thanks: the late Ronnie Lebensbaum, Patricia McMillan, Aine Farrell and Rusty Glicksman, all gone before their time.

I really enjoyed writing this book and reliving my life in retail. Thank you Nancy Given, Tom Phillips and Steve Netsky for proofing and editing assistance and suggestions, you made it better. Thank you Nancy Given and Danielle Nekimken for the beautiful design and the perfect illustrations, and for your dedication, patience, time and help putting it together. And finally, thank you again to all our wonderful customers and everyone who understood and loved Joie de Vivre. (And to everyone who's reading these very last words in the book — thank you very much for reading it!)

# About the Author

Linda Given grew up in New York's Hudson Valley, never suspecting she would spend thirty-six years of her life running a store. She enjoyed writing from a young age and after filling her first few diaries with stories of horses, friends and complaints about family, filled journal after journal with her thoughts, observations and laments about life and love. Along the way, she worked in retail, was a bilingual waitress in Montreal, a violinist in a chamber music ensemble, an administrative assistant, managed an American Craft gallery and later, living in Vermont, a woodworker's girlfriend, making and selling rolling pins and cutting boards.

When she opened Joie de Vivre in Cambridge MA in 1984, it was an experiment, and happily, one that surprisingly quickly succeeded, bringing "joie" and fun to the local community and beyond. After being in business for many years, she decided to finish her college education, earning a degree in writing and psychology from the Harvard Extension School, while continuing to run the store full time. Joie de Vivre made her happy in countless ways and in 2020, after closing what had become a Cambridge institution, she decided to write its story. If she ever wins the lottery she just might open another store. For now, she continues to live and write in the Boston area.

CPSIA information can be obtained
at www.ICGtesting.com
Printed in the USA
LVHW090514110723
752027LV00003B/225

9 798218 190064